AUSTRALIAN INTERNATIONAL PICTURES
(1946–75)

Traditions in World Cinema

General Editors
Linda Badley (Middle Tennessee State University)
R. Barton Palmer (Clemson University)
Founding Editor
Steven Jay Schneider (New York University)

Titles in the series include:

Traditions in World Cinema
Linda Badley, R. Barton Palmer and Steven Jay Schneider (eds)

Post-beur Cinema: North African Émigré and Maghrebi-French Filmmaking in France since 2000
Will Higbee

New Taiwanese Cinema in Focus: Moving Within and Beyond the Frame
Flannery Wilson

International Noir
Homer B. Pettey and R. Barton Palmer (eds)

Films on Ice: Cinemas of the Arctic
Scott MacKenzie and Anna Westerståhl Stenport (eds)

Nordic Genre Film: Small Nation Film Cultures in the Global Marketplace
Tommy Gustafsson and Pietari Kääpä (eds)

Contemporary Japanese Cinema Since Hana-Bi
Adam Bingham

Chinese Martial Arts Cinema: The Wuxia Tradition (2nd edition)
Stephen Teo

Slow Cinema
Tiago de Luca and Nuno Barradas Jorge

Expressionism in the Cinema
Olaf Brill and Gary D. Rhodes (eds)

French-language Road Cinema: Borders, Diasporas, Migration and 'New Europe'
Michael Gott

Transnational Film Remakes
Iain Robert Smith and Constantine Verevis

Coming-of-Age Cinema in New Zealand
Alistair Fox

New Transnationalisms in Contemporary Latin American Cinemas
Dolores Tierney

Celluloid Singapore: Cinema, Performance and the National
Edna Lim

Short Films from a Small Nation: Danish Informational Cinema 1935–1965
C. Claire Thomson

B-Movie Gothic: International Perspectives
Justin D. Edwards and Johan Höglund (eds)

Francophone Belgian Cinema
Jamie Steele

The New Romanian Cinema
Christina Stojanova (ed.) with the participation of Dana Duma

French Blockbusters: Cultural Politics of a Transnational Cinema
Charlie Michael

Nordic Film Cultures and Cinemas of Elsewhere
Anna Westerståhl Stenport and Arne Lunde (eds)

New Realism: Contemporary British Cinema
David Forrest

Contemporary Balkan Cinema: Transnational Exchanges and Global Circuits
Lydia Papadimitriou and Ana Grgić (eds)

Mapping the Rockumentary: Images of Sound and Fury
Gunnar Iversen and Scott MacKenzie (eds)

Images of Apartheid: Filmmaking on the Fringe in the Old South Africa
Calum Waddell

Greek Film Noir
Anna Poupou, Nikitas Fessas, and Maria Chalkou (eds)

Norwegian Nightmares: The Horror Cinema of a Nordic Country
Christer Bakke Andresen

Late-colonial French Cinema: Filming the Algerian War of Independence
Mani Sharpe

Australian International Pictures (1946–75)
Adrian Danks and Constantine Verevis

Please see our website for a complete list of titles in the series
www.edinburghuniversitypress.com/series/TIWC

AUSTRALIAN INTERNATIONAL PICTURES (1946–75)

Adrian Danks and Constantine Verevis

EDINBURGH
University Press

Edinburgh University Press is one of the leading university presses in the UK. We publish academic books and journals in our selected subject areas across the humanities and social sciences, combining cutting-edge scholarship with high editorial and production values to produce academic works of lasting importance. For more information visit our website: edinburghuniversitypress.com

© Adrian Danks and Constantine Verevis 2023, 2024

Adrian Danks (2016), 'South of Ealing: Recasting a British Studio's Antipodean Escapade', *Studies in Australasian Cinema*, 10: 2, 223–36. Revised here as Chapter 2 *The Overlanders* (1946) and Ealing Down Under

Adrian Danks (2018), '"Something short of fascinating": Re-examining Fred Zinnemann's *The Sundowners* (1960)', *Screening the Past*, 43, April, http://www.screeningthepast.com/issue-43-dossier/something-short-of-fascinating-re-examining-fred-zinnemanns-the-sundowners-1960/. Revised here as Chapter 5 *The Sundowners* (1960)

Constantine Verevis (2010), 'Dead on Arrival: The Fate of Australian Film Noir', *Studies in Australasian Cinema*, 4: 3, 243–53. Revised here as Chapter 8 *Color Me Dead* (1970)

Constantine Verevis (2014), '*The Man from Hong Kong*', *Metro*, 180, March, 105–13. Revised here as Chapter 12 *The Man from Hong Kong* (1975)

Constantine Verevis (2017), '*Kangaroo*: The Australian Story', *Critical Arts*, 31: 5, 171–85. Revised here as Chapter 3 *Kangaroo* (1952)

Edinburgh University Press Ltd
13 Infirmary Street
Edinburgh EH1 1LT

First published in hardback by Edinburgh University Press 2023

Typeset in 10/12.5 pt Sabon by
Cheshire Typesetting Ltd, Cuddington, Cheshire

A CIP record for this book is available from the British Library

ISBN 978 0 7486 9306 1 (hardback)
ISBN 978 1 3995 4112 1 (paperback)
ISBN 978 0 7486 9307 8 (webready PDF)
ISBN 978 0 7486 9308 5 (epub)

The right of Adrian Danks and Constantine Verevis to be identified as the authors of this work has been asserted in accordance with the Copyright, Designs and Patents Act 1988, and the Copyright and Related Rights Regulations 2003 (SI No. 2498).

CONTENTS

Acknowledgements   vi
Traditions in World Cinema   vii

1. Australian International Pictures (1946–75)   1
2. *The Overlanders* (1946) and Ealing Down Under   14
3. *Kangaroo* (1952)   32
4. *On the Beach* (1959)   48
5. *The Sundowners* (1960)   64
6. *The Drifting Avenger* (1968)   80
7. *Age of Consent* (1969)   95
8. *Color Me Dead* (1970)   112
9. *Ned Kelly* (1970)   127
10. *Walkabout* (1971)   144
11. *Wake in Fright* (1971)   160
12. *The Man from Hong Kong* (1975)   176

References   192
Index   205

ACKNOWLEDGEMENTS

We would like to thank, in particular, Gillian Leslie, Richard Strachan and Sam Johnson at Edinburgh University Press; Linda Badley and R. Barton Palmer, editors of Traditions in World Cinema; Alex Gionfriddo, Olympia Barron, Simon Strong and the AFI Research Collection at RMIT University; the editors of the various publications in which earlier versions of some of these chapters appeared. Thanks also to Ross Gibson and Deane Williams. Adrian would also like to acknowledge the wonderful support of his immediate family, Karli, Amelia, Selene and Glamour Puss, and dedicates this book to the loving memory of his father, David John Danks, who passed away in the latter stages of its completion.

Material contributing to this book appeared in earlier versions in the following publications and is reprinted here with the kind permission of the editors and publishers: Adrian Danks (2016), 'South of Ealing: Recasting a British Studio's Antipodean Escapade', *Studies in Australasian Cinema*, 10: 2, 223–36; Adrian Danks (2018), '"Something short of fascinating": Re-examining Fred Zinnemann's *The Sundowners* (1960)', *Screening the Past*, 43, April, http://www.screeningthepast.com/issue-43-dossier/something-short-of-fascinating-re-examining-fred-zinnemanns-the-sundowners-1960/; Constantine Verevis (2010), 'Dead on Arrival: The Fate of Australian Film Noir', *Studies in Australasian Cinema*, 4: 3, 243–53; Constantine Verevis (2014), '*The Man from Hong Kong*', *Metro*, 180, March, 105–13; Constantine Verevis (2017), '*Kangaroo*: The Australian Story', *Critical Arts*, 31: 5, 171–85.

TRADITIONS IN WORLD CINEMA

General editors: **Linda Badley and R. Barton Palmer**
Founding editor: **Steven Jay Schneider**

Traditions in World Cinema is a series of textbooks and monographs devoted to the analysis of currently popular and previously underexamined or undervalued film movements from around the globe. Also intended for general interest readers, the textbooks in this series offer undergraduate- and graduate-level film students accessible and comprehensive introductions to diverse traditions in world cinema. The monographs open up for advanced academic study more specialised groups of films, including those that require theoretically-oriented approaches. Both textbooks and monographs provide thorough examinations of the industrial, cultural and socio-historical conditions of production and reception.

The flagship textbook for the series includes chapters by noted scholars on traditions of acknowledged importance (the French New Wave, German Expressionism), recent and emergent traditions (New Iranian, post-Cinema Novo) and those whose rightful claim to recognition has yet to be established (the Israeli persecution film, global found footage cinema). Other volumes concentrate on individual national, regional or global cinema traditions. As the introductory chapter to each volume makes clear, the films under discussion form a coherent group on the basis of substantive and relatively transparent, if not always obvious, commonalities. These commonalities may be formal, stylistic or thematic, and the groupings may, although they need not, be popularly identified as genres, cycles or movements (Japanese horror, Chinese martial arts cinema, Italian Neorealism). Indeed, in cases in which a group of films is not already commonly identified as a tradition, one purpose of the volume is to establish its claim to importance and make it visible (East Central European Magical Realist cinema, Palestinian cinema).

Textbooks and monographs include:

- an introduction that clarifies the rationale for the grouping of films under examination
- a concise history of the regional, national or transnational cinema in question
- a summary of previous published work on the tradition
- contextual analysis of industrial, cultural and socio-historical conditions of production and reception
- textual analysis of specific and notable films, with clear and judicious application of relevant film theoretical approaches
- bibliograph(ies)/filmograph(ies).

Monographs may additionally include:

- discussion of the dynamics of cross-cultural exchange in light of current research and thinking about cultural imperialism and globalisation, as well as issues of regional/national cinema or political/aesthetic movements (such as new waves, postmodernism or identity politics)
- interview(s) with key filmmakers working within the tradition.

1. AUSTRALIAN INTERNATIONAL PICTURES (1946–75)

Populating the Void

The quarter of a century stretching from the end of World War II to the early 1970s is often characterised as a period of virtually no activity in the Australian film industry. This perception can be best understood as part of an argument considered necessary to help facilitate and evaluate the Australian film 'revival' or New Wave of the 1970s. However, such an understanding is only true if discussion is limited to wholly Australian-financed and '-created' feature-film productions and avoids more dynamic and diverse areas such as screen culture, amateur or non-theatrical film, government-funded documentary production, and global trends in co-production and location-based filming. Additionally, it ignores the fact that some of the most enduring and formative images of Australian cinema were fashioned during this seemingly 'fallow' period, representing 'Australia' to the world on a level unmatched until the early to mid-1980s with the global phenomena of films such as *Mad Max* (George Miller, 1979), *The Man from Snowy River* (George T. Miller, 1982) and *Crocodile Dundee* (Peter Faiman, 1986). Of particular interest in these earlier, post-World War II films are the views of urban and outback landscapes and the Australian 'character' created by significant, sometimes visionary, overseas-based filmmakers such as Harry Watt (*The Overlanders*, 1946; *Eureka Stockade*, 1949; *The Siege of Pinchgut*, 1959), Lewis Milestone (*Kangaroo*, 1952), Stanley Kramer (*On the Beach*, 1959), Fred Zinnemann

(*The Sundowners*, 1960), Michael Powell (*They're a Weird Mob*, 1966; *Age of Consent*, 1969), Junya Sato (*Koya no toseinin, The Drifting Avenger*, 1968), Tony Richardson (*Ned Kelly*, 1970), Nicolas Roeg (*Walkabout*, 1971) and Ted Kotcheff (*Wake in Fright*, 1971).

The 'imagination' of Australia – the work of identity formation – characterised by these films, and other international features made during this 'interval', is one of the key areas investigated in *Australian International Pictures (1946–75)*. The value of this study resides not only in its production of new historical, textual and institutional knowledge, but also in the ways it illuminates and reframes the films and filmmakers of the 'revival' themselves, questions essentialist approaches to Australian cinema, and suggests important links between this earlier diverse grouping of films and many developments in the 'national' cinema since the mid-1970s, including the current era of local-global film production.

This book focuses on these 'Australian international pictures' to redress the surprising critical neglect of an important, often highly visible group of films that, nevertheless, frames many accounts of Australian cinema, in particular those approaches that are principally concerned with questions of nationalism, national identity, colonialism and the production and projection of a national culture. Some of the best academic studies of Australian film – such as Susan Dermody and Elizabeth Jacka's two-volume *The Screening of Australia* (1987 and 1988) – focus on the Australian film 'revival' of the 1970s and its aftermath despite the broader historical implications of their findings. Others – such as Albert Moran and Tom O'Regan's seminal edited collections, *An Australian Film Reader* (1985) and *The Australian Screen* (1989) – take a wider view, but their discussion of the international co-productions examined in this book is still very limited, often parochial and situates these films as largely antithetical to the national cinema project. Even O'Regan's wonderfully expansive, highly influential and productively revisionist *Australian National Cinema* (1996) – which argues for a 'relational' approach to Australian cinema that always implicates the international and transnational – makes only brief and passing reference to many of the films considered herein. Andrew Pike and Ross Cooper's ground-breaking and highly influential study, *Australian Film 1900–1977: A Guide to Feature Film Production* ([1980] 1998), does include formative analyses of many of these internationally oriented productions but is limited by its imperative to systematically cover each of the hundreds of features made across a seventy-seven-year period. More recent books – such as Olivia Khoo, Belinda Smaill and Audrey Yue's *Transnational Australian Cinema: Ethics in the Asian Diasporas* (2013), Adrian Danks, Stephen Gaunson and Peter C. Kunze's *American-Australian Cinema: Transnational Connections* (2018), and Felicity Collins, Jane Landman and Susan Bye's massive *A Companion to Australian Cinema* (2019) – include extensive work on contemporary transnational filmmaking but provide only limited accounts of the histories that inform this mode of production.[1] This shift to an increased focus on the twenty-first century is also characteristic of two further recent edited collections that provide surveys of Australian cinema: Mark David Ryan and Ben Goldsmith's *Australian Screen in the 2000s* (2017) and Kelly McWilliam and Mark David Ryan's *Australian Genre Film* (2021). Many of the chapters included in these edited collections highlight the importance of transnational and international flows of creative talent, genre, finance, content and modes of production, but few of the writers connect the films and television programmes they discuss to the earlier 'moment' analysed and described in *Australian International Pictures*. According to Pike and Cooper (1998), only seventy-seven feature films were made in Australia between 1946 and 1971, with a number of these years marked by no Australian related feature-film releases whatsoever.

SAME AS IT EVER WAS:
THE INTERNATIONALISATION OF AUSTRALIAN CINEMA

Nevertheless, as we will discuss, most of the key films made during this period were international productions, either financed and crewed solely from overseas or in collaboration with local interests. These films and the models of filmmaking they suggest prepare the way for the 'international turn' in the Australian cinema of the post-'revival' era (see Goldsmith 2010: 199–214). Aside from *The Man from Hong Kong* (Brian Trenchard-Smith, 1975) – which represents a then unique co-production between Australia and Hong Kong – the films covered in this book were made between 1946 and 1971. This 'tailing off' of international production after 1971 is the result of a number of factors, including the introduction of direct government subsidy under the auspices of the Experimental Film and Television Fund and the Australian Film Development Corporation (both established in 1970). The first films supported by both organisations appeared in 1971 and helped shift the momentum towards homegrown modes of production and financing. The significant local commercial success of Tim Burstall's *Stork* (1971) in early 1972 was another important ingredient along with the election of a highly sympathetic Labor government under Gough Whitlam towards the end of the year.

The few writers who have more directly addressed this earlier period of production of what we are calling 'Australian international pictures' emphasise the scarcity of feature filmmaking to claim that a 'void' (Shirley and Adams 1989) or 'interval' (Molloy 1990) occurs during this era, but again mostly fail to analyse, in any detail, the small – though significant – number of 'location[ist] films' (O'Regan 1987) made during these so-called 'decades of survival' (Cunningham 1989).[2] Aside from discussion of the postwar work of Charles Chauvel, *Sons of Matthew* (1949) and *Jedda* (1955), many of these accounts also give short shrift to the very small number of truly local features made during this era such as Cecil Holmes' *Captain Thunderbolt* (1953) and *Three in One* (1956). But even these films closely reflect specific international trends and influences in filmmaking across these decades. From the early 1950s until the mid-to-late 1960s, feature filmmaking in Australia is defined by these international practices of location-based shooting and co-production. For example, only two of the twelve features made in Australia between 1956 and 1960 – *Three in One* and *Dust in the Sun* (Lee Robinson, 1958) – did not rely upon significant international involvement (and even *Dust in the Sun* featured a British lead actress and was initially scripted by a British writer). In order to gain a proper understanding of this important and formative era of Australian cinema it is essential to look beyond those films that fit a narrow definition of 'Australianness'.

Focusing on many of the international productions and co-productions filmed in Australia between 1945 and 1975 – the first of these, *The Overlanders*, was shot over five months from April 1945 but released in Australia and internationally in 1946 – this book provides not only a contextual account of the industrial, cultural and political conditions of the period but also a close analysis of how these feature films – their genre conventions, narrative devices, audiovisual aesthetics, spatial representations, promotion, mode of production, reception and interactions with local communities – helped shape the public imagination of the Australian environment and its peoples in the decades following World War II. This book examines carefully selected films of this period from a variety of perspectives – production history, cultural formations, economic implications and reception contexts – and also attends to each film's 'borderlessness'; that is, its relationship to global trends and flows in international cinema and film culture. The group of films investigated in *Australian International Pictures* range from the relatively familiar to the unheralded, covers the output of major international studios and independent entrepreneur-producers, describes films that are variously made by celebrated author-creators and journeyman Hollywood directors, and covers work which ranges in style or genre from the documentary realism of Ealing Studios' *The Overlanders* and *Bitter Springs* and the location-based 'super-productions' exemplified by *On the Beach* and *The Sundowners* to the outback samurai swordplay and western gunfighting of Toei Company's *The Drifting Avenger* and 'chop-socky' antics of the Golden Harvest co-produced, *The Man from Hong Kong*. It provides a particular focus on the late 1960s and early 1970s as this is an increasingly productive moment for the 'international' filmmaking in Australia that precedes the 'revival'.

WHAT PRICE HOLLYWOOD? AUSTRALIA AS LOCATION AND INTERNATIONAL PRODUCTION HUB

The films of these 'decades of survival' are also important because of their connection to the wide-scale resurgence of 'locationist' filmmaking in the 1990s and early 2000s. This was the era of 'Hollywood Downunder' (as described by *Australian Vogue*) characterised by films such as *Dark City* (Alex Proyas, 1998), *Babe: Pig in the City* (George Miller, 1998), *The Matrix* (Lana and Lilly Wachowski, 1999) and *Mission: Impossible II* (John Woo, 2000). The films produced at Fox Studios Australia in Sydney (opened 1998), Docklands Studios Melbourne (opened 2004) and the Gold Coast Studios complex (initially opened in 1986) have important connections to the major international studio and genre-based productions of the immediate post-World War II decades.

As a result of these developments, Australia has, over the past two decades or more, become a significant site for globally themed, often 'borderless' or 'local Hollywood' productions (O'Regan, Goldsmith and Ward 2010) made by a variety of countries, including India, the United States, Japan and Hong Kong. In addition to anticipating these forms of globalisation, the international films made in Australia during these 'decades of survival' connect to a large number of contemporaneous international productions – the hundreds of so-called 'runaway films' made during the post-World War II period (see Lev 2003) – that relocated Hollywood stars and genres to other places, using local topographies, co-stars and extras to add colour to familiar ingredients for US domestic and international audiences. The Australian examples discussed in this book could be matched, for instance, by Italian, German, Spanish and Japanese made or located films and so connect to broader trends in international filmmaking in the postwar decades. This book thus reveals and examines the porous nature of Australian and international filmmaking dating back to before World War II – see, for example, late silent-era films such as *For the Term of His Natural Life* (Norman Dawn, 1927) – and the cross-cultural formations and hybridisations created by these globally targeted but locally focused productions of the postwar era. Significantly, this book's analysis of filmmaking in Australia in the immediate post-World War II period through to the 1970s 'revival' – its practitioners, texts, production modes, institutions and cultural contexts – can tell us much about the ongoing complexities, benefits and dangers of global film culture, and the difficulties of and possibilities for effectively local film production – relating to government policy, production procedures and international practices – in this context.

In dealing with these issues, *Australian International Pictures* provides an important insight into the formative moments of global film culture in Australia. Specifically, the aims of this book are to: provide an understanding and evaluation of the 'decades of survival' through an investigation of a significant but selective body of films made in and representing Australia, and produced (or co-produced) by international companies deploying non-Australian major production personnel and/or actors; understand and assess this 'minor' period of Australian film history, the production practices it promotes and establishes, and the images of Australia it generates in relation to a more deliberate attempt to project an Australian cultural identity to a national and international audience during the core decade of the 'revival' (1975–85); comprehend the alignment and flows of 'Australian international' film production with respect to specific intellectual communities (geographic), institutions (production houses and studios) and personnel (production cast and crew), and the commercial, aesthetic and regulatory relationship between these films and their international counterparts of the same period; examine the porous nature of Australian and international filmmaking, the cross-cultural formations and hybridisations created by globally targeted but locally focused genre films, and the ways these productions prefigure the heightened globalisation of the current moment; and interrogate the often poor critical reputation – or perception of such – earned by many of these films and the ways in which each operated – to varying degrees – in an international cultural marketplace in which (predominantly) US perceptions and representations of other cultures circulated as a persistent and significant ingredient of international popular cinema. In order to achieve these various aims, this book provides a detailed investigation of specific 'Australian international pictures' of the period, most evidently through a close analysis of the aesthetic, industrial and generic characteristics of the films themselves (and adjacent and connected productions of relevant studios and individual filmmakers), but also through their production histories and reception contexts.

The assertion that many of the most enduring and formative images of Australian cinema were fashioned in the quarter-century following World War II makes a case for the fundamental significance of many of the international films made in Australia during this era and the lessons these works can provide in the current era of widespread transnational co-production. This book not only provides a unique account of the nation's film (and other cultural) productions of the period but also tracks the specificity of Australian cinema and situates it within a broader international field. *Australian International Pictures* moves into a space created by the ongoing critical neglect of the feature-film productions made in the lean years that precede the mid-1970s 'revival'. It also redirects an analytical framework that insisted upon a perceived 'void' or 'interval' in Australian film production in the 1950s and 1960s in order to successfully argue for a government or public-centred approach to the revival of the industry in the 1970s and beyond.

Decades of Survival?

As briefly mentioned earlier, Cunningham adopts the phrase 'decades of survival' to describe the four-decade-long period – 'from the end of the silent film period to the beginnings of the [new] Australian cinema' – during which feature filmmaking *'persisted* in the face of at times severe constraints' (1989: 54) and with little in the way of consistent or substantial government assistance or guidance.[3] Cunningham divides these forty-odd years into three periods and sets of issues: the 1930s and the British 'Empire connection'; the mid-1940s to the mid-1950s as a moment of 'Australian innovation'; and the mid-1950s to around the mid-1960s as a period of 'international co-production'. The first of these lies outside the scope of this book, but as Cunningham writes, the 'Empire connection' did not disappear in the decades following the 1930s but found expression in the British documentary movement led by figures like John Grierson that informed the era of 'Australian innovation' in such works as: Watt's first two features made for Ealing Studios in Australia, *The Overlanders* and *Eureka Stockade*; Ralph Smart's *Bitter Springs* (1950), also for Ealing; and John Heyer's widely-seen feature documentary, *The Back of Beyond* (1954), made for the Shell Film Unit. Even more pertinent to this book is the third period – 'usually regarded as the lowest point the Australian cinema reached' (Cunningham 1989: 67) – of international co-production. In Cunningham's account, this period includes not only the co-productions entered into by Southern International and Australian Television Enterprises (both led by writer-director Lee Robinson and actor-producer Chips Rafferty) – *Walk into Paradise* (Lee Robinson and Marcello Pagliero, 1956), *The Stowaway* (Lee Robinson and Ralph Habib, 1958) and *The Restless and the Damned* (Yves Allégret, 1959) – but also the 'locationist' films that are central to the arguments of this book: the British features *The Overlanders* and *Bitter Springs*, and US films such as *Kangaroo*, *On the Beach* and *The Sundowners*.

In the debut issue of Australian journal *Continuum* devoted to 'Australian Film in the 1950s', Tom O'Regan writes that 'location films' of the 'interval' are 'generally seen to be either under-capitalised or culturally inauthentic', and typically derive their meaning from 'negative' comparisons with the period that immediately preceded them, or (more often) the 'revival' that followed (1987: 1). In this context, the location film of this era is most often understood to refer to 'Hollywood in Australia' in the wake of 1950s runaway American productions like *Kangaroo*, *On the Beach* and *Summer of the Seventeenth Doll* (Leslie Norman, 1959), and with respect to the 'vitriolic attacks' on these films by national cinema campaigners of the 1960s and early 1970s (see O'Regan 1987: 6; see also O'Regan 1983: 33).[4] O'Regan, though, characteristically seeks to open up a discussion of locationist films of the period, arguing that the practice is more varied than typically believed. Accordingly, he makes a case for at least five categories of location-based film: (1) the documentarist and docu-drama 'location film' central to Ealing's and the government Film Division's Australian practice, and exemplified (in O'Regan's essay) by *The Overlanders* and *The Back of Beyond*; (2) location shooting which draws upon stylistic ensembles familiar from European art cinema, and is typified by the works of Cecil Holmes (*Captain Thunderbolt* and *Three in One*); (3) the 'landscape exploitationism' of Lee Robinson and Chips Rafferty that utilises 'exotic' locations such as the Australian inland (*The Phantom Stockman*, Lee Robinson, 1953), Thursday Island (*King of the Coral Sea*, Lee Robinson, 1954) and New Guinea (*Walk into Paradise*); (4) the television output of Charles and Elsa Chauvel with its singular ideology of location, exemplified by *Australian Walkabout* (BBC, 1958); and (5) the 'actual Hollywood location filmmaking' of directors like Lewis Milestone (*Kangaroo*), Stanley Kramer (*On the Beach*) and Leslie Norman (*Summer of the Seventeenth Doll*) (1987: 6–7).

Continuous Production: Transnational Australian Cinema in the Postwar Era

Like O'Regan's formative essay, this book seeks to interrogate and expand upon the notion of the locationist or 'location film', taking as its case studies eleven of the feature films produced, directed and/or financed (in whole or part) by British, US, Japanese, Canadian and Hong Kong production companies and/or studios in the quarter of a century following World War II. It opens with a discussion of the five films made by Ealing Studios in Australia between 1945 and 1959. Focusing on the first of these, the ground-breaking *The Overlanders*, it uses the fate of Ealing in Australia to explore the complex processes of adaptation, innovation, financing and technological change that mark all of the films discussed in this book. Ealing was the most prolific, long-term and, arguably, successful of the various international companies and studios that ventured to Australia during this era, providing an important frame of reference and even impetus for other organisations like Twentieth Century-Fox (*Kangaroo*), Warner Bros. Productions (*The Sundowners*) and Rank Organisation (*Bush Christmas*, Ralph Smart, 1947; and *Robbery Under Arms*, Jack Lee, 1957). The first three films Ealing made 'down under' – *The Overlanders*, *Eureka Stockade* and *Bitter Springs* – not only represent the period of 'Australian innovation' and the 'documentarist location film' (as described above) but also pave the way for much that followed. The final two films made by the studio – *The Shiralee* and *The Siege of Pinchgut* – reflect an increasingly composite mode of production that reveals the growing influence of transnational forms of filmmaking involving the movement of cast and crew between locations and studios across several continents. Ealing's relatively piecemeal tenure in Australia – the five films produced in two spurts in the second half of the 1940s and at the end of the 1950s – also highlights the difficulties of maintaining continuous production in Australia, with *The Siege of Pinchgut* representing the last feature completed by this iteration of the company anywhere in the world. Continuity of production has remained a key problem for the Australian film industry well into the twenty-first century.

In a discussion of Ealing's plan for continuous postwar production in Australia, Peter Limbrick writes that 'of the five Australian productions, all except *Pinchgut* used a mise-en-scène and story material familiar from westerns' (2007: 68–9). Although it can be argued that *The Overlanders* and *Bitter Springs* are demonstrably *not* westerns – or are, at least, significant variations on the form – Limbrick's interrogation of these films' reception '*as* westerns . . . suggests the malleability of that term and . . . reveals a surprisingly consistent discourse about the western as a *transnational*, colonial, generic form' (2007: 71, emphasis added). Understood in this way, several more films included in this book – *Kangaroo*, *The Sundowners*, *The Drifting Avenger* and *Ned Kelly* – can be characterised as 'bush' or 'kangaroo' or 'meat pie' westerns and provide an important framework for understanding other 'Australian international westerns' of this period and beyond. These include: *The Kangaroo Kid* (Lesley Selander, 1950), a B-western 'made in Australia but directed by an American . . . [which] uses familiar Western material' ('*The Kangaroo Kid*' 1952: 21); *Shadow of the Boomerang* (Dick Ross, 1960), a 'Christian western', filmed in Australia by the motion picture division of the Billy Graham Evangelistic Association, that tells the story of siblings who come to Australia to manage their father's cattle station (Pike and Cooper 1998: 229); and *Adam's Woman* (Philip Leacock, 1970), a 'convict western' starring Beau Bridges that was billed as 'Australia's first multi-million dollar co-production' (Pike and Cooper 1998: 249).

Runaway: Auteurs, Children and Television Content

The Australian 'westerns' directed by Milestone, Zinnemann and Richardson – *Kangaroo*, *The Sundowners* and *Ned Kelly*, respectively – are representative, too, of the work undertaken in Australia by established (auteur) filmmakers from the US and the UK. Other examples of work by significant directors examined in this book include Nicolas Roeg's ground-breaking if sometimes troubling exploration of Aboriginal culture and character, combined with a reworking of the Australian folkloric tradition of lost children, in *Walkabout* (1971); Stanley Kramer's adaptation of Nevil Shute's widely discussed nuclear holocaust novel, *On the Beach* (1959); and *Age of Consent* (1969), Michael Powell's second adaptation of a significant Australian novel after the enormously successful *They're a Weird Mob* (1966). Further examples of film adaptations by overseas (albeit by lesser-known) filmmakers working in

Australia include: Jack Lee's version of Rolf Boldrewood's novel *Robbery Under Arms* filmed near the Flinders Ranges and the back of Bourke; Leslie Norman's adaptation of Ray Lawler's widely-staged play *Summer of the Seventeenth Doll*; and Byron Haskin's *Long John Silver* (1954), a follow-up to his Disney adaptation of Robert Louis Stevenson's *Treasure Island* (1950). The latter example is significant in that it draws attention away from the more prestigious US runaway productions that featured A-list stars – notably, Peter Lawford and Maureen O'Hara in *Kangaroo*, Ava Gardner, Gregory Peck and Fred Astaire in *On the Beach*, Robert Mitchum and Deborah Kerr in *The Sundowners* – towards more modestly scaled productions. However, this is not to say that the production company, Treasure Island Pictures, formed to produce *Long John Silver* was without ambition. The full-length feature film was but one part of a larger initiative that also included radio plays and a twenty-six-episode television series, *The Adventures of Long John Silver* (1955), filmed in Australia over a two-year period for reasons of 'reduced economy' and the advantages of a location with an 'English-speaking background' (King, Verevis and Williams 2014: 40). It is also an illustration of the ambition of many of these international productions in Australia, and their attempts to forge a production slate beyond an initial, territory-staking film.

The example of *Long John Silver* opens up two further aspects of these 'Australian international pictures': television content and children's entertainment. Although only briefly covered in this book, the first of these – the made-for-television movie – is represented by *Color Me Dead* (1970), one of three films (including *It Takes All Kinds*, 1969, and *That Lady from Peking*, 1970) written and directed by Eddie Davis. Low-budget 'quickies' featuring US television actors, the three films were produced by local entrepreneur Reginald Goldsworthy in collaboration with American company Commonwealth United Corporation, primarily for the US colour television market. Although greater in number, children's entertainment films sadly have not found a place in this book. Perhaps most notable of this group is one of the earliest films from the period under consideration: Smart's *Bush Christmas* tells of a group of children who become lost in the Blue Mountains. Made by the British Children's Entertainment Films (the Children's Film Foundation from 1951) for the Rank Organisation and enthusiastically received by both children and critics, the success of *Bush Christmas* was matched by London Films' *Smiley* (Anthony Kimmins, 1956) a decade later, a story (derived from the novel by Moore Raymond) of an adventurous young boy in the small bush town of Murrumbilla who seeks to earn enough to buy himself a bicycle. Described as 'the most refreshing film with an Australian background since *Bush Christmas*' ('*Smiley*' 1956: 100), *Smiley* was almost immediately followed by *Smiley Gets a Gun* (Anthony Kimmins, 1958). Other children's films included the Children's Film Foundation's second feature, *Bungala Boys* (Jim Jeffrey, 1961), *They*

Found a Cave (Andrew Steane, 1962), one of the few fully local features of the first half of the 1960s made by Visatone Island Pictures in Tasmania, and two films produced primarily for the colour television market in the US by American Mass-Brown Corporation in association with the Australian television studio, Artransa Park: *Strange Holiday* (Mende Brown, 1970) and *Little Jungle Boy* (Mende Brown, 1970).

Looking Elsewhere: Regional and Demographic Shifts in Australian International Pictures

While the overwhelming majority of 'Australian international pictures' produced during the period under consideration represented British and US interests, there are some exceptions. *Wake in Fright* was the second film (following *Squeeze a Flower*, Marc Daniels, 1970) produced by Sydney-based NLT Productions television company in association with Group W Films, a division of American company Westinghouse. The difference in this case was that director Ted Kotcheff, though based in the UK, was a Canadian and brought to his adaptation of Kenneth Cook's novel a unique understanding of the likeness between the former British settler colonies of Canada and Australia. A more striking example is the case of *The Drifting Avenger* which, along with *Moeru tairiku* (*Blazing Continent*, Shogoro Nishimura, 1968) and some scenes included in *Nyu jirando no wakadaisho* (*Young Guy on Mt. Cook*, Jun Fukuda, 1969), was filmed in Australia by a major Japanese film studio, Toei Company, with the other two films being made by Nikkatsu Corporation and Toho Co., respectively. Made with minimal, though variable levels of direct Australian input – *The Drifting Avenger* features a mostly Australian cast and engaged significantly with local communities and film supply companies – each film invests in the wide-open spaces of its Australian locations while registering the increasing regional importance of Asia as an economic and cultural influence. *Blazing Continent* also provides an unusually contemporary view of Sydney as a modern(ist) metropolis. The final case study (discussed in this book) is *The Man from Hong Kong*. This film is unique for being the first ever Australian-Hong Kong co-production, and the only film in this survey that extends its reach beyond the twenty-five-year period following World War II. Other examples of non-Anglo-American productions made during this era include: *Funny Things Happen Down Under* (Joe McCormick, 1965), a spin-off from the television series, *The Adventures of the Terrible Ten* (1959–60) created by New Zealand's Pacific Films; and *Bello onesto emigrato Australia sposerebbe compaesana illibata* (*A Girl in Australia*, Luigi Zampa, 1971), a wholly Italian production which – like *They're a Weird Mob* – deals with the challenges faced by 'new Australians' of southern European backgrounds in the 1960s and early 1970s.

A Girl in Australia was distributed (in Australia) by Columbia Pictures and screened – with English subtitles – mostly in Italian cinemas in capital cities (Pike and Cooper 1998: 263). By contrast, *They're a Weird Mob* played widely and was an 'extraordinary success' (McLachlan 1968: 507) in Australia and New Zealand. Sylvia Lawson wrote that the 'overstrained, manufactured Australianism' of its companion piece, *Age of Consent*, demonstrated 'the total inadequacy, so far as Australian self-interpretation is concerned, of [any] British- or American-based film project which uses Australia as a location', but added the proviso that the film was also doing 'roaring business . . . suggest[ing] the extent of audience-hunger to see Australian backgrounds, Australian life and performers on the screen' (1969: 22). Harnessed to a campaign for the support of 'fully indigenous and fully professional Australian feature-films' (1969: 19), Lawson's comments provide a further critical and cultural context for the period of international filmmaking surveyed in this book, but these arguments and calls for action have, for too long, displaced a sustained analysis of the films themselves. This book therefore puts forward the twenty-five-year period of Australian filmmaking following World War II as a site for renewed consideration, drawing attention not only to its strategies, production histories and discourses but also to its textual production. In doing so, this book has critical importance not only for the analytical conclusions it offers in relation to the films of this period, but also for the foundation and pathways it establishes for the future of scholarship in the area.

Australian International Pictures advances the knowledge base of Australian (film) studies, and its public engagement will hopefully provide a wider and deeper understanding of Australian international film culture and its histories. Most significantly, this book benefits an understanding of the significance of social and cultural representations of Australia in the current period of heightened transnational film production. The following chapter on Ealing's five films in Australia provides a framework for much of the discussion that will follow. The initial films made by Ealing are probably the exception in terms of sustained critical discussion as well as their incorporation into the mainstream of Australian cinema history. As this book goes on to argue, they are merely the first stage in a fascinating history of transnational film production in postwar Australia.

Notes

1. Khoo, Smaill and Yue (2013) include a revised version of an essay on *The Drifting Avenger* from 'Australian International Pictures', a special issue of *Studies in Australasian Cinema* (2010) edited by Adrian Danks and Constantine Verevis.
2. Molloy (1990) does provide detailed thematic readings of the films that Ealing Studios made in Australia in terms of their portrayal of landscape, bush life, gender

and class, but has little to say about the other international features released between 1945 and 1960.
3. Cunningham notes the 'recurring metaphors' employed to characterise the period: 'failure and emptiness', 'the long stagnation' (Lawson 1982), 'interval' (Molloy 1990), 'into the void' (Shirley and Adams 1989) and 'bust' (Pike 1980).
4. For accounts of how some of the failures and successes of the 'interval' are harnessed to arguments for a revived, government-supported film culture and industry see: Holmes (1954), Weir (1958), Lawson (1965, 1969), McLachlan (1968) and O'Brien (1970b).

2. *THE OVERLANDERS* (1946) AND EALING DOWN UNDER

TOUCHING AND GOING

[They] should be primarily outdoor stories. They should ... be on a large enough canvas to appeal to world-wide audiences. And they should compensate with action what they will lose through lack of polish in the actors.[1] (Kemp 1999: 151)

In 1955, Ealing made its last films at its studios in West London prior to commencing short allegiances with production facilities owned by larger, often monopolistic corporations Rank Organisation and British MGM, before ceasing operations in 1959. The final two films made by Ealing at its famed, boutique studios, the generally forgotten *Touch and Go* (Michael Truman) and the widely celebrated *The Ladykillers* (Alexander Mackendrick), bear striking similarities in their rendering of highly restrictive and patently artificial physical environments. This sense of artifice and of an antiquated, patently unreal world plays into the insularity of the former film and the heightened, disarmingly murderous fantasy of the latter. Each is largely isolated to a single London street or neighbourhood and relies extensively on the control afforded by such contained and highly regulated studio production.

The first of these, *Touch and Go*, is an oddly desiccated and largely uneventful film focusing on the failure of an upper-middle-class English family to emigrate to Australia. As Charles Barr has ironically argued, one of the most striking things about this film is its disinterest in presenting Australia as anything other than a 'card played' or an 'abstraction' (1977: 175), a vision that helps stage these characters' frustration and dissatisfaction with their place in a bland, conservative and cosy postwar Britain: 'It has never been revived, which is not surprising ... [It is] an example of late, mainstream Ealing at its most suffocating' (1977: 174). In *Touch and Go*, the momentous decision to emigrate to Australia is taken by the father alone (played by a stalwart but blustery and constantly irritated Jack Hawkins), and is little more than a tantrum aimed at the staidness of the design company he works for which won't embrace his plans for Scandinavian 'innovation'. Revealingly, his firm continues to favour the comfiness and ugliness of overstuffed, chunky British furniture, a style that perhaps resonates with Hawkins' stiff-upper-lip star image and common accounts of the personal predilections of Ealing's production head, Michael Balcon.

Touch and Go stages a series of encounters with spaces (the old English pub across the street, the unrealistically benign banks of the River Thames, the neatly cramped interior of the home), technologies (a 1932 model car) and familiars (the old cat which proves to be the biggest obstacle of all and appears to go on a hunger strike). These encounters provide a windy pastiche of now common, if often inaccurate ideas or clichés of the prototypical Ealing concoction and its concern with English eccentricity, tradition, inbred (though elsewhere often more multinational) community and quietly triumphant failure. Though its output appears markedly varied when looked at more closely, Ealing Studios has emerged, along with Hammer Films, as one of the most easily identified and caricatured production entities in the history of British, if not global cinema. As Mark Duguid has argued:

> 'Ealing', as an adjective, is at least as likely to be used by politicians or political journalists as by film historians. The meaning is imprecise but it embraces both modestly progressive values and a respect for tradition; both a decent, cheery public spiritedness and a resistance to stern authority and bureaucracy; both an embodiment of community and an endearing eccentricity; and, above all, a profoundly British sensibility. (2012: 54)

But as Sue Harper and Vincent Porter (2003) have claimed, and Duguid goes on to confirm, this view of the studio is largely dependent on a small number of celebrated comedies produced in the late 1940s and very early 1950s such as *Hue and Cry* (Charles Crichton, 1947), *Kind Hearts and Coronets* (Robert Hamer, 1949), *The Man in the White Suit* (Alexander Mackendrick, 1951) and *The Lavender Hill Mob* (Charles Crichton, 1951). In the 1950s, '[t]he coherence of Ealing's output became compromised, and Balcon made many expensive mistakes' (Harper and Porter 2003: 57). Although this suggests a greater coherency and consistency in the films of the 1940s and very early 1950s than is actually the case, it can definitely be argued that many of the Ealing films made in the latter decade betray and portray an increasingly conservative, generic and insular set of values, while the studio's diminishing slate of productions managed to stretch across a more disparate and less engaging set of genres and tones.

As set out above, Barr (1977) has rightly singled out *Touch and Go* as symptomatic of the stagnation and even general critical and commercial failure of Ealing production in this period after 1951. But he doesn't address or even mention its curiosity in relation to the five fiction features made by Ealing in Australia between 1944 and 1959: *The Overlanders* (Harry Watt) released in 1946, *Eureka Stockade* (Harry Watt) in 1949, *Bitter Springs* (Ralph Smart) in 1950, before the long gap and initial abandonment of Australian production prior to returning, at a very different stage in the company's history and fortunes, for the more integrated, picaresque and genuinely transnational *The Shiralee* (Leslie Norman) in 1957, and the last film produced under the company's banner, the Sydney Harbour-set crime film *The Siege of Pinchgut* (Harry Watt) in 1959. It also fails to take account of the two feature-length travel films the studio produced around the time of *Touch and Go*'s creation: *Armand and Michaela Denis Under the Southern Cross* (1954) and *Armand and Michaela Denis on the Barrier Reef* (1955). Nevertheless, as we will argue throughout this chapter, these shifts in Ealing's output, approach and identity are reflected in the differences between the two groups of films made by the studio on each of its sojourns to Australia.

Transnational Ealing

Touch and Go is the kind of film that might emerge from a studio that had no direct experience of Australia. But it is a surprising and revealing artefact for a studio that had undertaken a thwarted, heroic and deeply paradoxical filmmaking venture throughout the second half of the 1940s. This is significant as we need to remember that Ealing was a highly collaborative, communal and relatively small production concern, and these films represented around 10–15 per cent of its output during their core period of operations between 1942 and 1959; the era fully overseen by studio head Balcon and widely considered to be the period of 'classic' Ealing. There is also no hint in *Touch and Go* of a possible, even imminent, return to Australia. The insularity and sense of retreat it represents, as well as the lack of any concrete vision or idea of Australia itself other than in terms of the briefly glimpsed exterior of Australia House in London and a muddled version of 'Waltzing Matilda' on the soundtrack, almost suggests the repression of those earlier, more 'optimistic' experiences as problematically representative of a less defined, homogeneous and distinctly 'British' entity. But as we will argue, Ealing's often transnational, if partly imperial, mode of production had a significant impact on the film industries and national cinemas of several countries, Australia most profoundly. It would also provide a model or example for many of the international films shot in Australia between 1945 and 1975.

A film like *Touch and Go*, despite its patent lack of cinematic interest, is closer in spirit and in its overriding cultural and social values to the famously chauvinistic and nationalistic statement Balcon had inscribed on a plaque to mark the studio's long occupancy of its West London home in 1955: 'Here during a quarter of a century many films were made projecting Britain and the British character.' Balcon's neat summation does not recognise the more schizophrenic and ambitious dimensions of the company's activities or its diverse filmic output. Ealing tried out various new modes of production and genre in the second half of the 1940s, but this truly exploratory approach had largely ceased by the mid-1950s. Nevertheless, the sense of quietly patrician and profoundly British Ealing presented and demonstrated by this unremarkable film, and even Balcon's much-noted claim of 'projecting Britain', fails to sketch an accurate picture of the small company's wider (even imperial or colonial) ambitions and output. It also doesn't account for its constant and genuine struggle to maintain a place within a largely monopolistic and transnational film production, distribution and exhibition environment in Britain and elsewhere in the world, including Australia. For instance, in the mid-1940s the Rank Organisation owned 56 per cent of all studio space in Britain as well as the major British film distributor (General Film Distributors) and one of its key cinema chains (Odeon) (see Brown 1984: 32–3). These figures alone speak to the difficulties faced by a smaller studio like Ealing which was hoping to expand its international and even transnational production base as well as the scale of the projects it planned to undertake. For example, the slate of films made in the late 1940s includes such large-scale historical narratives as *Saraband for Dead Lovers* (Basil Dearden, 1948) and *Scott of the Antarctic* (Charles Frend, 1948). Ealing was also dependent on Rank for many of its British and international distribution and exhibition deals, again including Australia.

The films made by Ealing in Australia and shot in other parts of the Commonwealth and the British Isles paint a more complex picture that suggests the studio fitfully embraced the possibilities of transnational film production, the opportunities of climate, space and economics offered by the Dominions, and entertained ambitions that its various privations of distribution, exhibition and studio real estate severely hampered and curtailed. A closer look at the films themselves reveal and frame many of these ambitions, tensions, compromises and hardships, ranging from the embrace of documentary realism to take advantage of locations and deflect attention from the limited reserves of local experience, expertise and production infrastructure, to the use of both local and international (compromisingly so, in some cases) actors, and the combination of landscapes and interiors, wide-open and enclosed spaces, location shooting and studio production, English proximity and foreign exoticism.

The five films Ealing Studios made in Australia have largely been analysed and 'reclaimed' by figures such as Bruce Molloy (1990), in his seminal work *Before the Interval: Australian Mythology and Feature Films, 1930–1960*, as key works of Australian national cinema, locally oriented movies that populate a period of meagre feature-film production in Australia while largely reworking popular genres such as the western and the crime film. Until very recently these movies have also had very little traction in the voluminous accounts of the 'little studio that could': 'Given these films have always existed on the geographic periphery of Ealing production, so they have been marginalised within historical studies of Ealing Studios' (Morgan 2012: 173). The key formative works on Ealing by John Ellis (1975), Charles Barr (1977) and George Perry (1981) find it difficult to incorporate these films into their particular, constraining visions of Ealing and its place in the bordered histories of British cinema. This is despite the British and broader Commonwealth concerns of these 'foreign' films as well as the continuing relevance of pan-British values and identities to a country like Australia during this time.

Nevertheless, in the last twenty or so years, writers such as Philip Kemp (1999), Elizabeth Webby (2004), Deb Verhoeven (2006), Peter Limbrick (2010) and Stephen Morgan (2012) have offered a more complex and incorporative account of these films – particularly the first three, *The Shiralee* and *The Siege of Pinchgut* are widely, if incorrectly, considered 'afterthoughts' – and how they might fit into broader patterns of international production at the time. Limbrick and Verhoeven also explicitly analyse these works within the framework of imperial and settler-colonial cinema. Although these films can and should be read symptomatically in terms of their 'localised' renderings of landscape, character and narrative, they have seldom been substantively discussed in regards to the broader patterns and practices of Ealing film production itself, the studio's common preoccupation with interiorised communities, work, Englishness (or a pan-Britishness, perhaps) and small-scale settlements on the geographic fringes of Britain and the Commonwealth (or Britain and its Dominions in the language of Ealing's corporate documents). They have also not been analysed in relation to the various other films – such as the Kenya-, Uganda-, Tanganyika-, Zanzibar-shot and -set *Where No Vultures Fly* (1951) and *West of Zanzibar* (1954), filmed more exotically in Technicolor and both also directed by Harry Watt – that light upon far-flung locations and settlements, at least in geographic relation to the cosy, teatime perspective of Little England Ealing is most commonly associated with. Although these Africa-shot productions are the only truly comparative films made by Ealing elsewhere in the Commonwealth, they betray a less committed, integrated and more exotic mode of production that is fully evident onscreen.

Placing Ealing

This chapter offers some observations on the place of these Australia-made films within broader patterns and practices of Ealing film production, specifically its approach to location, geography, shifting international film production methods and the construction of filmic space. Analysing these five films as a group allows us to better establish the broader context for international film production in Australia in the 1940s and 1950s and set out some of the key paradigms, questions and approaches taken by the diverse slate of films made 'down under' by overseas producers and companies from the end of World War II to the 1970s 'revival'. It will also help establish the key relationships and connections between Australian cinema and wider patterns of international and transnational production in the postwar era.

Ealing's initial venture in Australia – lasting from 1944 until 1950 or 1951 (it sold its interests in Sydney's Pagewood Studios in 1952 to completely sever local connections and investments) – needs to be placed alongside broader developments within British cinema in this period. It also needs to be examined in relation to patterns of boom and bust triggered by changes in government policy, such as the imposition and relaxation of import quotas and taxes, and the opportunistic international expansion of significant players like J. Arthur Rank and Alexander Korda, both of whom also dabbled in Australian production. Rank, in particular, was central to Ealing's ambitions and mixed fortunes due to its financing and distribution agreements with the smaller studio and was also directly behind the making of two other Australian productions, *Bush Christmas* (Ralph Smart, 1947) and *Robbery Under Arms* (Jack Lee, 1957).

As Perry (1981) has argued, it is not productive to think about Ealing's Antipodean adventure in terms of an overall missed opportunity or an arrangement that may have led to a much larger slate of production. Even though initial plans and reports suggest that up to ten films might have been produced in Australia in the five years following the unprecedented success of *The Overlanders*, Ealing's precarious finances, tight margins and weak distribution deals meant that it was highly unlikely that this ambitious slate would come to fruition. Ealing's experiences in Australia were reminiscent of its fate as a small to medium-scale studio in Britain – making four to six films per year on average – which struggled to wrest favourable distribution deals, production financing agreements and spatial arrangements from its larger partners. Its failure to develop an agreement with the notoriously production-shy exhibitor Greater Union showed things were very similar in Australia as well as controlled by many of the same entities and interests. In this regard, and despite its larger economies of scale and significant successes, Ealing was not so far removed from the fate suffered and difficulties encountered by Australian film producers during the same period. As we will discuss, the success of its first feature, *The Overlanders*, also helped create a false sense of possibility, a utopian vision of what could have been, that has dogged proper understanding of Ealing's production in Australia and its legacy until the present day. The peculiar conditions which led to the making of this first film, and the degree of commitment and long-term engagement expressed and demonstrated by its director Harry Watt, could not be replicated in a postwar environment of increased international production and co-production, a mode of practice that only ever achieved peripatetic traction in Australia.

Ealing's Antipodean adventure – or nightmare if some accounts of the making of the subsequent *Eureka Stockade*, *Bitter Springs* and *The Siege of Pinchgut* are taken into consideration – also needs to be examined through a transnational lens. This helps focus attention on the widely unacknowledged thematic, generic, spatial and production parallels between such Ealing films as *Eureka Stockade* and *Passport to Pimlico* (Henry Cornelius, 1949), *The Siege of Pinchgut* and *Nowhere to Go* (Seth Holt, 1958), *The Overlanders* and various movies set on the outskirts of the British Isles – *Whisky Galore!* (Alexander Mackendrick, 1949), *Another Shore* (Charles Crichton, 1949), and so on – or with a significant European focus such as the Belgian resistance film, *Against the Wind* (Charles Crichton, 1948). We don't have the space here to explore these revealing connections in any detail but will demonstrate these correspondences through a discussion of some of the parallels between *Eureka Stockade* and the contemporaneously made *Passport to Pimlico*, one of Ealing's most celebrated and fondly remembered films.

Watt envisaged *Eureka Stockade* as the first of a series examining the 'birth' of democracy in different Commonwealth countries. He felt that the stand taken by Victorian miners of various nationalities was 'an episode that I have always felt was a turning point in the history of the British Empire' (Watt 1958: 107). Although none of the subsequent entries in this series was ever made, *Eureka Stockade* resonates closely with many other Ealing films of this period. A significant number of these films rely upon the drawing together of loosely related individuals from various national and ethnic backgrounds to form a community. These films also question and poke fun at authority while expressing an ultimate respect for law and order and the bonds of a broader commonwealth of individuals and communities. This community is often situated within, in relation to or on the periphery of a broader society. It is then the role of the film's narrative to mend this rift. For example, *Passport to Pimlico* comically documents the formation of a breakaway republic within the suburbs of London. Although playfully questioning commonly held stereotypes of nationality, ethnicity, identity and place – for example, the sun stops shining when the newly formed municipality is reincorporated back into London and England – it is still the job of the narrative to stitch back together the parts of community, and its daily rituals, severed by this newer formation. Similarly, in *Eureka Stockade* the trauma of armed conflict and the establishment of a 'republic' within the Victorian colony ultimately act to unify the population and legitimise those figures – such as Peter Lalor (Chips Rafferty; an iconic common presence in the first three Ealing films made in Australia) – who strike out for democratic representation and basic human rights. In both films, the concepts of nationhood and a unified community are only strengthened by secession and rebellion.

Notions of place and space are central to many of these Ealing films and how they illustrate the concepts of belonging and connectivity. Although Ealing films are routinely associated with an interiorised, cosy and often intimate notion of Britishness, they are also remarkable for the ways in which they represent particular far-flung geographies and places, even within Britain itself. Part of the reason why Ealing's Australian films have lasted in the popular and critical imagination, at least in Australia, is their general attentiveness to the specificities of place. Whereas equivalent Hollywood films shot in Australia at this time such as *Kangaroo* (Lewis Milestone, 1952) have only circumspect relationships to a particular place or geography, works like *The Overlanders*, *Bitter Springs* and *The Shiralee* demonstrate an attentiveness to place betraying a genuine attempt to capture the specificity of particular environments not widely represented elsewhere: the north of Australia in *The Overlanders* or the Flinders Ranges in *Bitter Springs*, for instance. Even the major exception to this approach to environment and geography, *Eureka Stockade*, is preoccupied with the material detail of the Ballarat goldfields in the 1850s and drew upon many accounts of the events and actual figures involved in the Eureka conflict. The decision to film 150 miles outside of Sydney near Singleton rather than around Ballarat was determined more by the transformation of the original landscape *during* the gold rush than the greater proximity it afforded to the country's filmmaking centre.

These first three Ealing films all bear the marks of extensive location shooting that was in keeping with Watt's pointed though somewhat inaccurate comments on the filmmaking environment he encountered in Australia in the mid-1940s:

> Studying these films [the roughly contemporaneous features of Charles Chauvel and Ken G. Hall specifically] convinced me of one thing – that studio facilities and equipment were so poor that indoor films were useless to attempt in Australia and that that had been the basic mistake of Australian film-makers. Their huge, exciting, hard country had never been used by them at all. (Watt 1949: 11)

The shift to interiors, cities, studios and genuinely transnational film production in the final two Ealing films made in the late 1950s suggests that these two small groups of movies were indeed conceived in vastly different corporate, economic and even technological environments and reflected changing modes of international and transnational filmmaking practice.

The Overlanders: Ealing's First Journey Down Under

Various writers such as Deane Williams have done significant work placing Ealing's first Australian production within specific patterns and movements of international cinema, particularly developments in postwar documentary realism (2007: 79–89). The film details an 1,800-mile cattle drive from Wyndham in northern Western Australia to Brisbane, its narrative following an actual journey undertaken in 1942. The cast features a number of professional actors, such as Chips Rafferty in the iconic role of Don McAlpine, alongside those appearing onscreen for the first time such as Daphne Campbell (then a corporal in the Australian Army Medical Women's Service). Shooting took five months from April 1945 and the 500 cattle bought for the production were sold at a small profit at the conclusion of filming.

As is clear from even a cursory examination of its production and the finished film's opening moments, *The Overlanders* is a hybrid that draws together particular forms of documentary and location-based narrative cinema that were significant in the mid-1940s. The film's director, Scot Harry Watt, has often been configured as a 'sympathetic outsider' who contributed significantly to the development of cinema in Australia during this period and was careful to draw upon and nurture the contributions and careers of various nascent film workers such as celebrated documentarian John Heyer, who was second unit director on *The Overlanders*. Watt also proclaimed the necessity of Australia developing its own film industry, seeing *The Overlanders* as an important step in this process: 'We have started to put Australian films on the screens of the world. We've raised the pay of both technicians and actors in Australia by about 100 per cent. And we've given creative work to a lot of people who otherwise were smothering with frustration' (Watt 1949: 16). He even openly protested his socialist allegiances in testy correspondences with Balcon (see Kemp 1999: 154). Watt's famous claim that 'You start from scratch in Australia' (Watt 1949: 10) has routinely been interpreted as a reflection on the barren state of Australian feature-film production during this period. But Watt's various accounts of his experience – and its favouring of a particular mode of dramatised documentary shot on location and using predominantly non-professional actors – does not give full credit to the ambitions of Ealing in Australia at this point in time.

Watt was plainly something of a maverick who was not easily contained by the restrictiveness of British-based studio filmmaking, and most of the films (seven out of nine) that Ealing made in Australia and Africa were instigated and directed by him. Even his first feature for Ealing, *Nine Men*, produced in 1942 in the middle of World War II, features significant filming undertaken on beaches in North Wales and utilises a mix of professional and non-professional actors (actual soldiers in the latter case). From various accounts, Watt was a combative figure who gained a reputation for making films in 'exotic' locations far from direct studio interference. As he himself admitted, 'My films became known at Ealing as Watt's Tropical Tours' (Watt 1974: 194).

Watt's background as a documentary filmmaker, working for the GPO Film Unit and collaborating with celebrated figures like Humphrey Jennings, is also a significant influence on *The Overlanders*. Ealing's initial venture to Australia was at the behest of the British Ministry of Information in response to a request by the Australian government to boost and improve British propaganda efforts in its Dominion. It attained significant cooperation from federal and state governments and departments (as did all the later films) and was a genuinely transnational production, largely crewed by Australians and shot almost exclusively on location with few marks of the studio. Despite the uniqueness of this production environment and the surprising wide-scale success of the film, a broader plan quickly emerged to shift a percentage of the studio's production to Australia. Although Watt was correct in identifying the 'exploitative' potential of the Australian landscape and its wealth of possible subjects, the even greater attraction for Ealing was the possibility of setting up a studio, with near exclusive access and control, in another country – even if on the other side of the world. This runs counter to the common critical view, supported by Watt in his various articles, interviews and book, that Ealing had little interest in replicating the kinds of films and production conditions found in Britain: 'this location shooting can also be seen as a desire by Ealing not to duplicate its British studio operations: Ealing and Watt would not have been looking to the Australian production of something that could be easily produced within British studios' (O'Regan 1987: 8–9). Although Tom O'Regan is correct in identifying Ealing's desire to produce more locationist films in Australia, movies that exploited the natural conditions and advantages of the country's climate and geography and worked within such familiar genres as the western, his argument underestimates the attraction of lucrative financial enticements and clear access to underutilised studio facilities.

This combination of overseas locations and readily available studio facilities is a harbinger of the development of large studios on Australia's eastern seaboard in the 1980s and 1990s and demonstrative of the increasingly composite nature of a wider international filmmaking in the late 1940s and 1950s. Although the attraction of wide-open spaces was a significant factor in this venture, so was the possibility of controlling proximate studio space. Hostile meteorological conditions encountered on Ealing's second and third features would further highlight this need for greater climatic control and largely led to the scuppering of plans to produce more films in Australia. This intention to work globally in a range of different formats is made clear in the comments made by production head Balcon to Australian director and impresario Ken G. Hall prior to the release of *Eureka Stockade*:

> *As you know, Ealing has always had the imperial plan.* I think the ideal would be 4/5 films a year here [Britain], 1/2 in Australia, 1 in South Africa and 1 in Canada. This, however, is a very long-term plan and one which is beyond our capitalization for the time being. The only way to get it going would be to have capital support from the Dominions. (Balcon in Limbrick 2010: 115)

Head of Ealing Studios, Major Reginald Baker, saw this move to Australia more pragmatically in terms of the lack of available studio space in Britain, and the need to therefore strike ahead with production in other Commonwealth countries (a policy that only led to piecemeal production in Australia and East Africa for Ealing). Ealing plainly saw Australia as a location to make films but also as a potential imperialistic studio base that could incorporate and centre the emerging studio-locationist practices of modern filmmaking across other places such as New Zealand and elsewhere in the Southern Pacific. In this respect, working in Australia sat in contradistinction to a largely monopolistic and tight studio environment in England.

The Overlanders has also rightly been characterised as a particular type of realist production that combines fictionalised narrative with many of the components of dramatised documentary – antecedents include Watt's own *Target for Tonight* (1941), Humphrey Jennings' *Fires Were Started* (1943) and an earlier Ealing feature, *San Demetrio London* (Charles Frend, 1943). Watt himself suggested that this kind of film was ideal for the production-poor conditions in Australia; the problematic 'terra nullius' suggested by his dismissal of the work of existing Australian-born filmmakers like Hall and Chauvel, his damnation of the existing production facilities, as well as the symbolic 'scorched earth and space' detailed in the film's opening voiceover. But this form of realist drama was quickly and more generally being normalised and integrated into Ealing's more systemised modes of production as well as that of other British and even Hollywood studios working in Australia (where a kind of realism was indicated by the choice of specific locations and situations rather than in terms of the holistic, collaborative, responsive type of filmmaking Watt favoured). To place this in a corporate context, after *The Overlanders* the only fully sustained location film made by Ealing anywhere was *Whisky Galore!* in 1949. All its other films bear the clear and, for the studio, necessary marks of the integration of location shooting with controlled studio conditions. The much later *The Shiralee* provides a clear illustration and refinement of this practice. Although it is plainly obvious that specific actors such as Tessie O'Shea and Sid James never left Britain – or at least did not need to film their scenes there – expert matching of footage and mise-en-scène, use of doubles and rear-projection, and the constant shifting between exterior and interior locations carefully sutures these figures into the film. This is far from the almost dreamlike disjunctions in geography and topography staged in Hall's attempts to match standards of international film practice in his Bondi Junction studios in the late 1930s in works such as the exotic hybrid *Lovers and Luggers* (1937), but there are some interesting correspondences (see Danks 2018: 19–39).

The opening of *The Overlanders* also highlights notions of openness and ownership through its combination of starkly composed images, flat or 'arid' geographies, symphonic music by prestige composer John Ireland, paternalistic voiceover and proprietary titlecards. The latter trumpets the film's production in Australia, the cooperation of Commonwealth and state governments, the inappropriately verdant seal of 'Ealing Studios' (when stamped on such low and minimally vegetated horizons, dusty landscapes and sparsely populated frames) and other markers that highlight Ealing's carefully articulated presence in Australia. This meticulously constructed credit sequence of eight shots, joined together with quick dissolves, and featuring bold white type over moving images, has an almost symphonic introductory quality that then gives way to the film's most overly constructed and 'artificial' section: narrating and visualising the garish spectre of Japanese imperialism framed in terms of a cartoonish soldier inexpertly manhandling several moving aerial perspectives of 'the largest undeveloped region in the world'. This brief sequence, also framed by the threat of 'He's coming south' emblazoned at the top of the garish 'poster' we are shown, pits the artifice of confected, animated filmmaking against more appropriate and palatable forms of documentary practice. It is this latter mode that dominates the rest of the film. The failure of the Japanese occupation and invasion of Australia – and by the 1946 release this was definitely part of history – is largely communicated through the stasis, compositeness and out-of-placeness of this initial image. This type of overly composed and condensed filmmaking is countered elsewhere by *The Overlanders*' denial of then common techniques like rear-projection, its clear placement of actors on location, its de-dramatised narrative, and its focus on the detail and cyclical nature of work. But this dominant mode of contemporary, arguably transnational film practice is then inevitably and increasingly incorporated into Ealing's subsequent Australian films.

After *The Overlanders*

Almost despite its long gestation – Watt spent close to two years travelling across northern Australia, finding a subject and undertaking pre-production – episodic structure and ground-breaking combination of documentary and fiction, *The Overlanders* was a significant financial and critical success, particularly in Australia and Britain. It was the first Ealing film to open widely in Europe and has been an important touchstone for Australian cinema ever since. For example, it was partially and self-consciously remade by Baz Luhrmann as *Australia* in 2008. Largely shot around Alice Springs, Roper River, Elsey Station (also the setting for Jeannie Gunn's landmark novel, *We of the Never Never*) and the Quarantine Station on Sydney's North Head (often standing in for Wyndham in the opening sequences), it opened at Sydney's Lyceum Theatre on 27 September 1946, breaking box-office records, before a mid-October premiere in London and early December New York release. It was the subject of significant pre-publicity in newspapers and magazines such as the *Australian Women's Weekly*. Articles in the latter ranged from reports on director of photography Osmond Borradaile's penchant for collecting pets to proclamations that star Chips Rafferty was 'Australia's Gary Cooper' (see 'Worth Reporting' 1945: 15; 'Australia's Gary Cooper' 1946: 29). Local and international critics were uniform in their acclaim, with the former often arguing for the film's significance to the nation's cinema: 'On its reception largely depends the future of the Australian film industry, and let there be no doubt that it will be successful, probably immensely successful, in Britain' ('London Views *The Overlanders* as Truly Epic Film' 1946: 8). The reviewer for *The Sydney Morning Herald* found that the film was in no way 'an anti-climax to the publicity superlatives' while claiming it 'as fine a piece of work as present-day cinema has produced, and the finest that has come from Australia' ('New Films Reviewed' 1946: 10). Many of these reviews highlighted the film's Australianness – '*It's Australian every inch of the way*' (Te Pana 1946: 1) – the production's epic scale and the way in which it placed the landscape and character front and centre: 'Rarely has the camera caught so magnificently the brilliant light of the outback. Cameraman Osmond Borrodaile [sic] has taken many unforgettable shots which have the details of a fine etching. Watching, you almost feel the stifling heat and sense the sweaty smell of cattle' ('Film Reviews' 1946: 36). In keeping with this, *The Overlanders* received an uncommonly lavish release, including an accompanying programme that claimed the film echoed 'the heartbeat of Australia's greatness' and a bestselling novelisation by Dora Birtles (1987 [1946]), a researcher on the production. None of the subsequent films made by Ealing in Australia received anything like its level of exposure or commercial and critical success, and the next completed project, *Eureka Stockade*, was a significant financial failure (it also cost a large amount at around £125,000) that severely dented the studio's plans for expanded film production, and soured Watt's ambitions to make further films in Australia.

Eureka Stockade is a fascinatingly flawed film that draws on the conventions of the 'gold rush' western while emphasising notions of identity, ordered democracy and nation building. The latter is made explicit in the opening moments as a voice announces, 'The story of the world is the story of Man's fight for freedom. In that fight England has its Magna Carta . . . and Australia, Eureka Stockade.' It then quickly rushes to the urgent foundational claim that 'Australia had to face the problem that she'd become a nation' (even though 'she' hadn't). The complex interweaving of national, British and Commonwealth interests present in *The Overlanders*' opening moments, as well as elsewhere in the film – such as the campfire scene critiquing British 'migrant' Corky's prospectus to exploit the Northern Territory – is more explicitly outlined and narrativised in *Eureka Stockade* and positioned more directly in relation to England (the state of Victoria was still a British colony at the time the film is set).

Although *The Overlanders* contains explicit commentary on the exploitation of national resources, the necessary banding together of Australian and Commonwealth interests and, albeit briefly, the disinheritance of Aboriginal ownership of the land, it presents these ideas and themes in a laconic and largely unemphatic fashion. *Eureka Stockade* is a much more strident and schematic work that contains various scenes, characters and motifs designed to force the ideas of nation formation and national identity. For example, it features a female schoolteacher who speaks against the greed and excesses of the gold rush and the need for the miners to abandon their self-interest and parochial ethnic origins to help build a nation. This prim, cipher-like character also gets caught up in the design and creation of the Southern Cross flag, which pointedly transforms into the Australian flag in the final moments. The relative failure of *Eureka Stockade*, a film that relies upon national and ethnic stereotypes throughout, such as the militaristic German and the overly emotional Italian, Raffaello Carboni, partly emerges from its necessarily confusing promotion of rebellion *and* the need for law and order. In the role of Peter Lalor, the ubiquitous Chips Rafferty is denuded of any outward indication of his character's Irish heritage and is painstakingly hesitant in resorting to violence and armed resistance until after all other channels for achieving his modest and reasonable aims have been exhausted.

Ealing's subsequent and final film in its initial Australian venture, the almost equally vexed *Bitter Springs*, is, in many ways, an attempt to draw together the key elements of the two films that preceded it. By the time of its production, Ealing had largely decided to discontinue its grand Australian plans, and the film's shift in scale as well as its emphasis upon the relationship between invasive settlers and the land's First Nations inhabitants and traditional owners help frame this sense of disquiet. The elements that draw the film closer to *The Overlanders* are relatively perfunctory, with the long journey of the settlers little more than a precursor to the film's real, largely unresolvable conflict around notions of ownership and rightful occupation of the land. *Bitter Springs* is an important work of Australian cinema due to its willingness to confront and reflect upon race relations and, less overtly, the ruinous policies of assimilation then taking hold in government and broader settler-colonial society. This is reinforced by the film's overall reliance on location shooting, use of 'local' First Nations actors, and its attentiveness to environment and landscape. Nevertheless, *Bitter Springs'* reputation was seriously undermined by the scandal that erupted around the mishandled and inadequate transport of Indigenous actors to the film's locations and a revised ending that suggested a harmonious joining together of white settlers and Aboriginal inhabitants in the practice and business of sheep shearing (the originally planned and more forceful ending involved a massacre of many of the Indigenous characters).[2] These issues of inadequate and inappropriate transportation were compounded by underpayment, poor accommodation and disputes about who held responsibility for the Aboriginal actors between Ealing and the government of South Australia which had agreed to various conditions and concessions in order to lure the production to its state. The final, abrupt and largely 'unintegrated' image of assimilation that ends the film – and it is indeed just one shot showing a white shearer and an Aboriginal figure working together in the same frame – contrasts with the less forced, more organic and de-dramatised qualities of *The Overlanders*. Although one of the most remarkable aspects of *Bitter Springs* is the space it 'gives' to its Aboriginal characters and their daily rituals and tasks – such as the widely excerpted scene of the kangaroo hunt – these elements are circumscribed by the settler-colonial imperatives of the overriding narrative. The film's documentary-like qualities are also more clearly subsumed here than they are in *The Overlanders*. This favouring of narrative over documentary fidelity is an approach from which the Ealing films will never subsequently retreat.

'It won't last forever': Ealing's Return to Australia

It is somewhat unclear why Ealing returned to Australia to make two of its last seven films, *The Shiralee* in 1957 and *The Siege of Pinchgut* in 1959, while completing its co-production relationships with MGM and the Associated British Picture Corporation. Nevertheless, the increased size of production and studio access enabled by MGM – also demonstrated by the large-scale *Dunkirk* (Leslie Norman) completed in 1958 and which constituted the studio's last true commercial success – is certainly one factor. These last two Australian films are plainly less concerned with the local filmmaking environment and are more commonly described as British films shot on location.

In many respects, the decision to make *The Shiralee*, which was one of only two relative financial successes during Ealing's last phase and is, alongside *The Overlanders*, probably the best of the Australian Ealing films, is a result of a range of factors. These include: the international success of D'Arcy Niland's 1955 source novel; the favourable box-office response to several other British-produced locationist films made, at least in part, in Australia the previous year, *Smiley* (Anthony Kimmins, 1956) and *A Town Like Alice* (Jack Lee, 1956); the rising stardom of Australian actor Peter Finch; and the transnational studio practice that allowed *The Shiralee* to be made effectively and efficiently between Australia and England. *The Shiralee* is a relatively small-scale, episodic and often sparsely populated work that is both sympathetic to the Australian landscape and character and a plainly 'locationist' film that expertly utilises the production regimes of medium-sized international filmmaking of the period. Although saturated with small-scale observations on the Australian character, language and life – including the explanation of the film's title, and the knockabout antics of Finch's lead character – it is also populated by actors and interior locations whose provenance is more questionable, as outlined earlier.

The Siege of Pinchgut provides a more perplexing last gasp and a symbolic spatial retreat from the relentless movement across vast spaces captured in *The Overlanders* thirteen years earlier to the 14-foot-thick munitions bunker of the fortress-like island in Sydney Harbour. Watt's return to make *The Siege of Pinchgut* after ten years is also surprising considering the combative relationship he developed with Balcon and the latter's increased antipathy towards working with him (see Kemp 1999: 163). Thematically and spatially, the film sits comfortably within the mainstream of Ealing's output. Much of it is contained within a small space and community isolated from a larger, more imposing entity: Fort Denison, with its intimations of earlier convict incarceration in the mid-nineteenth century. The group of criminals is also characteristically differentiated in terms of nationality, character type and accent, oddly so in many respects. For reasons that are never fully explained, the gang appears to consist of an Englishman, an Italian, a Canadian and an American played by an imported star, Aldo Ray. It also has close correspondences with another late Ealing work – Seth Holt's darker crime entry, *Nowhere to Go* – as well as the contemporaneous *On the Beach* (Stanley Kramer, 1959). Both *The Siege of Pinchgut* and *On the Beach* waggishly feature the deserted streetscapes of Australia's two largest cities, indirectly referencing commonly held views on the uneventfulness of Antipodean city life during this era. As screenwriter Jon Cleary wrote to Balcon: 'The evacuation scenes had nothing, I thought – one man ... commented aloud that it looked like nothing more than the usual

Sydney on a Sunday morning: empty, but with no feeling of foreboding or impending doom' (Kemp 1999: 163).³

With its predominantly and noticeably non-Australian cast and crew, clear exploitation of the topography of Sydney, generic trappings and foregrounding of the rise of mass media, *The Siege of Pinchgut* represents the presence of a less engaged and more internationalist form of filmmaking within Australia. The film's relation to a specific genre is far more direct and less playful than the first three Ealing films. *The Overlanders*, for example, is notably self-conscious in its quotation and mischievous reworking of the conventions and motifs of the cattle-drive western; although the onlooking Aboriginal characters appear to communicate by smoke signals, and are shown to occupy the high ground of the landscape through which the cattle and drovers must travel, they wave benignly as the 'overlanders' pass below. The final moments of *The Siege of Pinchgut*, showing the surviving and most reluctant member of the criminal gang being taken away from the shores of Fort Denison, provide a neat analogue and appropriate endpoint to Ealing's Australian venture as well as the brief blossoming of international production in Australia at the very end of the 1950s. The gentle bobbing of the boat as it motors away is a long way from the low horizon lines and vast, stark, depopulated landscapes of the majestic opening images of *The Overlanders*. There is a sense of deflation and diminishment as the characters, and Ealing itself, beat the retreat. The relatively open-ended narrative, documentary impulses and potential of *The Overlanders* – at the end the characters venture out once again to begin another cattle drive – have ultimately led to this tightly controlled and spatially enclosed exercise in international genre filmmaking.

Going and Touching

As we argued at the start of this chapter, 1955's *Touch and Go* highlights some of the dominant ways of characterising and caricaturing Ealing's cinema. It also acts to obscure a much more complex and emblematic history, corporate memory and set of production practices. Obviously, Ealing was attracted to Australia due to its spatial possibilities (in terms of the studio, locations and even distance from the privations of postwar Britain), the financial prospects it offered (to make films with significant government support and potential Australian business investment) and the opportunities it allowed for the kind of international studio-location filmmaking that fully emerged in the late 1940s and 1950s. However, as we have claimed throughout this opening chapter, the company's exploits in Australia also need to be examined and explained in relation to the broader fate of Ealing Studios and how this waxed and waned across the 1940s and 1950s. Ealing largely limped through the 1950s before ceasing operations *during* its final Australian production. By then Ealing was hardly a going concern and had little control over the means of production and distribution, elements of the company's purview that were always compromised.

As is plainly evident when looking closely at the five films in question, as well as reading *Touch and Go* symptomatically, Ealing's, at times, intense and spluttering commitment to filmmaking in Australia cannot be understood through this inattentive, somewhat anomalous 1955 feature about not emigrating to Australia. It would therefore be wrong to characterise this sometimes-peripatetic production history in the terms suggested by the film's title, a question of 'touching' and then 'going'. Ealing's demise or fizzling out is inseparable from broader developments in international filmmaking – the decline of then established British cinema from the early 1950s – and the broader difficulties experienced by both Australian and British film production in terms of being crowded out by Hollywood interests and the ongoing problems of attaining distribution and exhibition. In these respects, the chances of long-term success for Ealing were never really 'touch and go' at all. Nevertheless, the five films made by Ealing Studios in Australia continue to make a significant contribution to historical understandings of Australian national cinema as well as contributing to a more complex image of the celebrated British studio. They also help to set the patterns of international and transnational film production in Australia across the postwar era.

Notes

1. Taken from an unsigned 1945 Report, 'Australian Production Scheme', from Ealing Studios to the Rank Organisation.
2. For an account of many of these issues and complaints see Verhoeven (2006: 240–54).
3. Cleary was a highly successful novelist, most famous for *The Sundowners* (1952). He was also an uncredited screenwriter on Fred Zinnemann's subsequent 1960 adaptation, as discussed later in this book.

3. KANGAROO (1952)

'THE AUSTRALIAN STORY': HOLLYWOOD ARRIVES DOWN UNDER

Observing that 'all national cinemas are implicated internationally' (1996: 56), Tom O'Regan makes note of the 'contribution' that Australian-made and shot films – in particular bushranger and drover films – have made to the western genre over a long period of time, starting with *The Story of the Kelly Gang* (Charles Tait, 1906) (1996: 168), often claimed to be the first feature film made anywhere in the world. Focusing on the former, William D. Routt attends specifically to the similarities between early US westerns and Australian bushranger films – the historical frontier settings, use of landscape and early twentieth-century period of production – but resists the label 'bush westerns', preferring to characterise a group of early bushranger films – several Kelly Gang films and up to fifteen others such as *Robbery Under Arms* (Charles MacMahon, 1907), *Thunderbolt* (John Gavin, 1910) and *Captain Starlight, or Gentleman of the Road* (Alfred Rolfe, 1911) – as belonging to a 'western-like genre' that grew out of local conditions (Routt 2001). Making a related argument, Peter Limbrick refers to the western as 'a settler colonial mode of cinema', describing all but the last of five films made by Ealing Studios in Australia in the 1940s and 1950s – *The Overlanders* (Harry Watt, 1946), *Eureka Stockade* (Harry Watt, 1949), *Bitter Springs* (Ralph Smart, 1950), *The Shiralee* (Leslie Norman, 1957) and *The Siege of Pinchgut* (Harry Watt, 1959) – as works that use the iconography and narrative situations familiar from the genre (2007: 68–9). While seeking to acknowledge the western's significant place, production and popularity outside of America, Limbrick cautions against ignoring the wider record of US interests in Australia, pointing out that Ealing's plan to establish an ongoing presence in the country was disrupted by a more general national turn away from Britain to the US in the postwar era, as well as the making of large-scale American 'runaway' productions such as *Kangaroo* (Lewis Milestone, 1952), *On the Beach* (Stanley Kramer, 1959) and *The Sundowners* (Fred Zinnemann, 1960) (Limbrick 2007: 83).

Attending to the specific context of the first of these Hollywood studio films made 'down under' – the so-called 'super-western', *Kangaroo* – in this chapter we analyse and explore a range of Australian-produced materials and local contexts, including trade papers and the popular press, to consider some of the benefits and dangers of an increasingly globalised film culture, and the difficulties of – and possibilities for – Australian (international) pictures in the immediate postwar years (and beyond). *Kangaroo* is particularly significant as it was the first Hollywood production made in Australia during the postwar era. An account of its production, and the many twists and turns encountered by the filmmakers on location and in negotiating competing demands, provides an important case study for researchers as well as a cautionary tale for the many international and transnational productions that followed. The sheer volume of newspaper and magazine articles published before, during and after production speaks to the high expectations held by the Australian press, public and film industry. The mistakes, difficulties, compromises *and* successes met and encountered by *Kangaroo* furnished a significant lesson for the more carefully grounded productions that followed like *On the Beach* and *The Sundowners*.

'The most unique thing ever put on the screen':
Bringing *Kangaroo* to Australia

Towards the end of October 1950, the *Advertiser* (Adelaide) ran an article with the heading: 'Hollywood Insists on Kangaroos' (Jones 1950b: 7). The story begins: 'If you've got – or know of – any kangaroos who would like to become movie actors, send them to Director Lewis Milestone, Port Augusta, South Australia. He needs them to play themselves in the 20th Century-Fox production *Kangaroo*, which is now getting ready to face the cameras' (Jones 1950b: 7). The article continues, explaining that Hollywood producer Robert Bassler was looking to secure at least 300 kangaroos for the picture's 'most thrilling scene', one without which the film would lose much of its international appeal. Specifically, the script called for hundreds of thirst-crazed kangaroos to descend upon a last remaining waterhole and put up a terrific battle for its contents – engage in 'hand-to-hand' combat – with the station hands guarding the waterhole. Bassler admitted that he didn't exactly know how the scene would be accomplished, but fancifully said: 'the sequence ... will be the most unique thing ever put on the screen. It could become the most talked-about scene in the history of movies.' Moreover, in a comment indicative of increased US economic and cultural dominance in the postwar years, Bassler insisted that it would be to Australia's distinct advantage to see that he got his kangaroos: 'This scene, if we get to shoot it ... will bring Australia to the attention of every American ... Everyone will want to visit the country to see the kangaroos in their natural state' (quoted in Jones 1950b: 7).

The story of the Twentieth Century-Fox production *Kangaroo* goes back to (at least) December 1949 when associate producer Robert Snody and art director Mark-Lee Kirk travelled to Australia to identify possible locations for a film – with the working title 'The Australian Story' – that Twentieth Century-Fox's head of production Darryl F. Zanuck was keen to produce (*Kangaroo* Special Report 1952a: 18). The pair made enthusiastic recommendations and early in the following year reports that Twentieth Century-Fox had plans for a 'runaway production' (or 'American-interest' picture) – the first full-length Technicolor film to be shot in Australia – began to appear in the local press ('February Start on *Kangaroo Kid*' 1950: 5). Defined as films financed in part or whole by an American company, but shot in another country and with foreign labour except for key crew and cast, hundreds of runaway productions were made by Hollywood companies between 1949 and 1956, mostly in Europe (see Lev 2003: 149–55). Over this period, runway productions were a solution to legislation introduced by some countries (including the UK and Australia) to 'block' portions of funds earned through film distribution leaving the home country. For the Hollywood studios, production abroad allowed them to make use of these otherwise unavailable funds, take advantage of often cheaper local labour, and exploit subsidies and protectionist rules developed to support local filmmakers (Lev 2003: 148–9). In the case of *Kangaroo*, the production was likely motivated by a need to access Twentieth Century-Fox funds frozen in Australia (S. S. 1950: 5) and was further incentivised by a devalued Australian pound ('US Films May Be Made Here' 1950: 7).

Later in 1950, it was announced that veteran Hollywood filmmaker Lewis Milestone, probably best known for his work on *All Quiet on the Western Front* (1930), *The Front Page* (1931) and *Of Mice and Men* (1939), had been signed to direct the film for a budget of around £900,000 (S. S. 1950: 5; '*Kangaroo* May Aid Film-making Here' 1950: 5). By this time known as 'The Bushranger' (and soon after, '*Kangaroo*'), the first draft of the scenario – set in the 1880s and concerned with a group of people living on a cattle station about 300 miles northwest of Sydney – promised to bring together two of the key character types of the Australian-produced western: the bushranger and the drover. As in the case of other runaway films, there would be roles for

Australian actors (notably Chips Rafferty, Charles 'Bud' Tingwell, John Fegan and Letty Craydon) and technicians, but Milestone said the principal crew and four lead roles – those of a gentleman-outlaw known as 'Kangaroo', his partner in crime, Jack Gamble, the station owner Michael McGuire, and the station owner's daughter, Dell – would all come from Hollywood. Milestone added that he wanted *Kangaroo* to be a 'true dramatic portrait of life in Australia in the 1880s', and if necessary the script would be rewritten to fit Australian conditions and peculiarities, and to assure the production's authenticity ('Plans for Film Here' 1950: 4).

In August 1950, an advance party from Hollywood – consisting of Milestone, Snody, Kirk, Charles G. Clarke (director of photography) and others – arrived in Sydney, where they began putting in place arrangements for the production (*Kangaroo* Special Report 1952a). The initial film script had called for drought conditions, but as the eastern part of Australia was experiencing better than average rainfall, the party was forced to look elsewhere for principal locations. Finding strong encouragement in discussions with South Australian Premier Tom Playford (who had recently played an active role in facilitating the production of Ealing's *Bitter Springs*) and other state government and municipal authorities, Snody decided upon an area near Port Augusta for location filming of outdoor scenes ('Playford Wins in Film Race' 1950: 6). That same month, Adelaide newspapers reported that the Mayor of Port Augusta, Lindsay Riches, had presided over a public meeting to enlist the cooperation of townspeople, including the speedy construction of a nineteenth-century cattle station homestead – a replica of one dated from 1892 – on the Woolundunga Station property 12 miles outside of Port Augusta at the foot of the scenic Flinders Ranges ('Port Augusta Plans to Help in *Kangaroo*' 1950: 3; 'Site for Film Homestead "Pin-pointed!"' 1950: 3). Moreover, in a move that may have contributed to the UK industry's 'imperial failure' and helped cruel its programme for sustained filmmaking in Australia in the postwar years (Limbrick 2007: 83–4), Twentieth Century-Fox additionally leased Ealing's Pagewood Studios in Sydney (opened in 1935, Pagewood was taken over and refurbished by Ealing at the start of the 1950s) – its equipment, its wardrobe of Australian period costumes and its permanent technical staff of forty – as production headquarters for the duration of filming ('Studio for Indoor Filming of *Kangaroo*' 1950: 4). Although there were many factors that inhibited local, international and transnational production in Australia during this period, a lack of adequate and technologically up-to-date studio facilities was an overriding and continuing problem. This also limited the ability of local crews to gain experience working on modern studio productions. Pagewood was seen as a major opportunity to help build capacity for local production, but had limited effect beyond the completion of a smattering of international and transnational films, even shutting its doors temporarily after *Kangaroo* finished filming.

Speculation around the casting of lead players for *Kangaroo* – including a suggestion that Errol Flynn would be perfect in the title role of the bushranger – came to an end when it was confirmed that Irish-American film star Maureen O'Hara was coming to Australia to play opposite male leads Peter Lawford, Richard Boone and Finlay Currie, with shooting scheduled to commence near Port Augusta as early as September 1950 ('Maureen O'Hara to Star in Australian Film' 1950: 2). However, filming would be delayed, first of all by the later than expected arrival of Currie (who would play the part of station owner McGuire), but also due to problems with accommodation for the international cast and crew, cinematographer Clarke ascribing blame to a 'hotel system . . . reportedly owned and controlled by the brewery interests throughout the land [and a] socialised government and a thirty-five hour working week [which meant] everything was in short supply' (Clarke 1952: 293). The housing problem was in fact so acute that Snody argued it would have been impossible to operate were it not for the extent of Premier Playford's cooperation, which included bringing forward construction of twenty-four houses (being provided for work on a state power project) for use by the film unit's 90–120 personnel. Accommodation was no less an issue in Sydney, where Twentieth Century-Fox was advised that it would be impossible to house its thirty-four staff members across the end of year holiday season ('*Kangaroo* Plans Altered' 1950: n.p.).

The costly delays not only impacted the film's schedule (with shooting by this time mooted to commence in November in South Australia) but also contributed to important changes to the screenplay. Bassler advised of a rewrite that not only altered the period setting – from the 1880s to the early 1900s – but also meant significant changes to *Kangaroo*'s opening sequences. Originally the story had faded in on a gentleman outlaw – the bushranger 'Kangaroo' (Lawford) – and his accomplice, Gamble (Boone), holding up a stagecoach on a lonely bush track. This was to have been Kangaroo's first meeting with Dell McGuire (O'Hara), a passenger on the coach. In this scenario, Kangaroo was to later pose, in an impersonation swindle, as a long-lost brother to Dell, only to fall in love with her instead. In the rewrite, the opening scene was switched to a flop-house in Sydney, where the Lawford character, now a petty-criminal named Connor, and his more sinister acquaintance, Gamble, become involved in a different type of crime – assault and robbery. To evade the law they are forced to follow Dell's father, the station owner McGuire, back to his property in South Australia. As in the earlier draft, the gentlemen of fortune scheme to steal McGuire's daughter and property, but drought and danger intervene and provoke a change of heart (Jones 1950a: 7). The alterations were significant not only in terms of location, but also for effecting a generic shift, with Bassler claiming that although there was 'action in it' *Kangaroo* was neither a bushranger film nor a bush western, but rather an outdoor melodrama, or a 'story of a man and his conscience' (Griffen-Foley 1950a: 19). Moreover (like

Milestone before him), Bassler insisted that in going abroad to make pictures, Twentieth Century-Fox was, in the first instance, 'out to achieve *authenticity* and capture the *true* local atmosphere' (quoted in Griffen-Foley 1950b: 3, emphasis added) of these peoples, places and locations.

'ALL THE GLAMOUR OF HOLLYWOOD': SHOOTING *KANGAROO*

After several false starts, Lawford and Boone flew into Sydney at the beginning of November 1950, and the first of the Sydney scenes (moved, in a further reschedule, to the head of the production) were shot at the foot of the Windmill Steps at Millers Point on the afternoon of 11 November, the Sydney *Sunday Herald* reporting that 'All the glamour of Hollywood [had] suddenly descended... on The Rocks district' ('The Hollywood Touch is Here' 1950: 6; see also 'First *Kangaroo* Scenes Filmed in Sydney' 1950: 3; 'Sydney Sees How Hollywood Makes a Movie' 1950: 5). The novelty of a Hollywood movie production attracted crowds of 'several hundred people ... [who] waited around for hours to see only a few minutes of actual shooting' ('First *Kangaroo* Scenes' 1950: 3). The attention attracted by the filming at the south end of the Sydney Harbour Bridge (and two days later at Sydney's historic Elizabeth Bay House), was soon eclipsed by the arrival of the film's biggest star – Maureen O'Hara – at the end of November. Welcomed at Mascot (airport) by press interviewers and photographers, a Movietone News crew and a waiting crowd of 250 people, the Hollywood star 'confessed' that all she knew about Australia was what she had read in the *Encyclopaedia Britannica* before she left the US: she was quoted as saying, 'I knew that people in Australia were not all black, because there are so many Irish out here.' And when asked if she had ever seen a kangaroo she answered: 'I think I saw one once in the London Zoo, but I'm not sure' ('Film Star Had Looked Us Up' 1950: 4). These opening remarks aside, O'Hara managed to 'captivate everybody' in a hectic five-day round of welcomes undertaken in Sydney before leaving the following week for Adelaide. Reporting on the carefully staged schedule of events – which included a Sunday morning mass at St Mary's Cathedral, a visit to Taronga Zoo and a Lord Mayor's reception at Sydney Town Hall – *Film Weekly* wrote that O'Hara 'handled them all with the tact and dignity of a career diplomat – plus [with] far more charm' ('Maureen O'Hara's Big Sydney Welcome' 1950: 5).

The week's rush of events in Sydney gave some indication of what was likely to happen in Adelaide and Port Augusta when the stars made their way to South Australia for location shooting on Thursday, 30 November. In a busy two days in Adelaide, O'Hara – along with Lawford, Boone and Currie, each of whom had assumed 'minor diplomatic status for the United States' due to their extended stays in Australia (*Kangaroo* Special Report 1952a: 22) – attended an afternoon garden party at Government House. This was followed by a reception given by Twentieth Century-Fox at the South Australian Hotel where the actors met state and industry representatives, including Premier Playford who welcomed *Kangaroo* as the 'best propaganda' for the country and an opportunity for 'South Australia to play its part in building up this great continent' (Meares 1950a: 3; see also '*Kangaroo* Stars Arrive' 1950: 3; '*Kangaroo* Stars to Have Short Stay Here' 1950: 3). More functions – including a civic welcome at the Town Hall and a luncheon at Parliament House – followed on the Friday (1 December), *Film Weekly* reporting that 'conservative Adelaide [had gone] wild' during the reception-packed visit: 'autograph hunters popped up even at the Government House garden party . . . Nothing like this has been seen . . . in its 100 years or more' ('20th-Fox Team Stirs Adelaide' 1950: 5).

Moving on to Port Augusta, the Hollywood cast was joined by Sydney Albright, managing director of Twentieth Century-Fox Film (Australia), and publicity director H. Stuart-Codde for the unveiling of the *Kangaroo* unit's Port Augusta accommodation of twenty-four prefabricated houses ('Albright Home' 1950: 1). Opening the facility – which had been named 'Zanuckville' in 'honor of the magnificently courageous enterprise of [Twentieth Century-Fox Head] Mr. Darryl Zanuck' – Playford (addressing several hundred guests) not only welcomed the economic boost the production would give to the local community but also predicted that *Kangaroo* would 'attract the attention of the [whole] world . . . and attract still more migrants to settle in Australia' ('*Kangaroo* Big Boost for Australia' 1950: 12). In a further, magnanimous statement, Playford – propped between American and Australian flags – recalled the 'providential help given us by our American cousins during the dark days of the last world war' and welcomed the production of *Kangaroo* as a 'gesture of practical friendliness and faith', one to be celebrated as another example of bilateral friendship and cooperation (*Kangaroo* Special Report 1952a: 23).

Further delays – including a longer than expected road trip of crew and equipment by convoy from Sydney (Meares 1950b: 3) – saw the start of regional filming held over to late December, the first interior scenes at Woolundunga Station shot on 21 December and outdoor location shooting following on 30 December ('First Scenes Shot for *Kangaroo*' 1950: 3; 'Outdoor Shooting for *Kangaroo* Begins' 1950: 3). Still further delays – including the filming of shipboard scenes on the Moonta (the vessel that brings the principal characters from Sydney to South Australia) which included many extras from Port Augusta – required a sixth revision to the shooting schedule (Meares 1950c: 4). Nonetheless, at least up until mid-December, Milestone was still hoping to get together a large enough number of kangaroos in order to show a thirst-crazed mob rushing to the only waterhole left moist during the drought. The *Advertiser* (Adelaide) reported that the production team was trying to get hold of anyone with 'expert knowledge of 'roos in South Australia' and was offering a bounty of £5 a head for kangaroos received (Meares 1950b: 3). Milestone eventually gave up on the idea of dramatically presenting the hostile mob, settling (in the film's title sequence) for two establishing shots of the local fauna and a couple of domesticated kangaroos on the homestead verandah.

Milestone's want for a dramatic encounter with 'hostiles' was met by replacing the marsupials with 'a tribe of warlike Aborigines' whose arrival at the station's water troughs taxes the very limited water supply. The Aborigines are the only thing keeping the herd of cattle from the water, but (as the film's situation has it) 'humanity demands' that McGuire let them drink, a disturbingly racist lap dissolve matching a tracking shot of the tribe drinking water at the long concrete trough with one of the cattle. In exchange, the Aborigines – recruited, as had been the case for *Bitter Springs*, from Ooldea Mission – promise a sacred rainmaking corroboree, which the homesteaders (improbably) watch from the comfort of their porch while taking afternoon tea (see 'Rain-making Ritual Shown in *Kangaroo*' 1951: 61; Millard 2019). Commenting upon but somehow failing to see the troubling nature of these representations of First Nations Australians, cinematographer Clarke (who provided the most comprehensive report of the location filming in South Australia) wrote:

> While kangaroos have very little to do with the [film's] story, no film about Australia is complete without one. They are Australia. We did have some amusing experiences in getting the scenes with them . . . I found the many strange animals of this exotic country the highlight of the trip. The lovable koala bears and childlike wombats . . . The unbelievable platypus and spiny ant eater are so fantastic they challenge one's credulity . . . We did manage to work in some of the aborigines – those strange human relics of the stone age. What an odd race! . . . We found them loveable, and when treated like children, responsive to our requirements. (Clarke 1952: 316–17)

A 'FULL AND COMPLETE ANSWER TO ANY EXHIBITOR'S PRAYER': RELEASING *KANGAROO*

Once underway, filming of *Kangaroo* continued through Christmas 1950 and into the New Year, to finally wrap up, following some additional work at Pagewood Studios, in the last week of February 1951, with the entire unit (including all technicians) leaving Australia by mid-March ('*Kangaroo* Going Well' 1951: 1; '*Kangaroo* Shooting Ending' 1951: 1). In the middle of the year, one report from Hollywood stated that Zanuck had seen the first cut of *Kangaroo* and had described it as 'the full and complete answer to any exhibitor's prayer' ('Praise for *Kangaroo*' 1951: 8). In a telegram to the Australian office, Zanuck was quoted as saying: 'it is a huge, spectacular, and thrilling adventure story that capitalises on the Australian bush country . . . It is spectacular in every sense of the word and loaded with showmanship from start to finish. I can frankly say that it exceeds my highest expectations' ('Praise for *Kangaroo*' 1951: 8). In Australia, interest in the film was maintained in mass-circulation publications such as the *Australian Women's Weekly*, which published (in the manner of Hollywood fan magazines) a brief, illustrated (image and text) breakdown of *Kangaroo*'s 'Australian adventure story' ('Australian Adventure Story' 1951: 43) and featured a full-page colour endorsement for Lux by O'Hara: '*Kangaroo* was filmed in the hot, dry areas of South Australia, yet in every scene lovely Maureen O'Hara kept her complexion fresh and radiantly beautiful [with] Lux Toilet Soap' ('I'm a Lux Girl' 1951: 26).

However, it took until the middle of the following year for the announcement of plans for the film's release to appear, with a New York City premiere scheduled for Friday, 16 May 1952 at the Roxy Theatre (off Times Square). Large advertisements in New York's Sunday papers (11 May 1952) described *Kangaroo* as 'The Australian Story', and Australia (in terms consistent with Clarke's assessment) as 'the continent that Time Forgot'. The posters promised the 'cry of mighty adventure' and featured a sensational sketch of O'Hara (in ripped dress) and Lawford (bare-chested, with stockwhip in hand) together on horseback, a giant kangaroo leaping towards them from a backdrop of stampeding cattle and raging bushfire. The ads impelled the public to 'SEE! Wild Aborigines of Australia dance the blood-tingling Corroboree! SEE! Giant lizards, wombats, dingoes and bull-ants – extinct everywhere else for 6,000,000 years!' Other advertisements said that *Kangaroo* had been filmed in a 'prehistoric wonderland' and that 'cameras had recorded the sight and sound of Aborigines in the exciting dance of the Corroboree – the sinister chant of spear-throwing Abos. They caught the thunder of thirst-crazed herds, the scream of the boomerang and a bull-whip fight never before seen on the screen' ('*Kangaroo* Film, N. York Premiere' 1952: 21).

Despite the strong publicity and 'a fairly nice $65,000 expected to be registered by *Kangaroo* in its first week at the Roxy' ('$65,000 for *Kangaroo*' 1952: 3), news arrived within a week from London saying that the Australian High Commissioner, Thomas White, was considering a proposal that Twentieth Century-Fox should be asked to make adjustments to the film. These suggestions were made in response to both its content and the particular slant of much of the publicity. The object of this would be to have it made clear that *Kangaroo* did *not* – in its presentation of a primitive, bleak and barren land, ravaged by drought and bushfire – 'portray present day Australia and that it [was] not officially sponsored' ('Officials Fear Film on Australia Misleading' 1952: 3). An advance print of *Kangaroo* had been shown at a private preview for South Australia's acting Agent-General, Alfred Greenham, and Australia House (London) officials, who thought that the film – with its depiction of human-centred violence and natural disasters – would present an unfavourable picture of Australian life, and (contra Premier Playford's earlier prediction) most likely be detrimental to immigration. Specifically, Greenham had suggested that White (who had not seen the film) make a presentation to Twentieth Century-Fox asking that the phrase 'The Australian Story' – which was being used as a subtitle after the name *Kangaroo* – no longer be employed in advertising ('Officials Fear Film' 1952: 3; see also 'Film Seen as Bad Publicity for Australia' 1952: 5).

Eighteen months earlier, at the reception at South Australia's Government House, O'Hara had expressed her hope that 'we wind up with a picture which Australia will be proud of as well as us' ('*Kangaroo* Stars Arrive' 1950: 3). In making these comments, O'Hara did not anticipate that those aspects of the film most recognisable in terms of the representation of the Australian environment and conventions of the western genre – in particular, the droving sequences across the drought-stricken terrain, during which many of the weakened cattle die, and the raging brush fire and maddened stampede that follows and threatens all – would meet with criticism. Although lauded by most reviewers for their 'authenticity', these harsh images of the Australian outback presented a problem for officials in London who were seeking to boost Australia's capacity for postwar agricultural and industrial growth through its proactive immigration policy. Already battling British authorities who were undertaking their own postwar reconstruction and were relatively unenthusiastic about encouraging emigration, the Australian government had introduced a £10 assisted passage migration scheme in the years following the war in the hope of attracting (white) British or selected European settlers (Sherington 1980: 129–31). The concerns from London that this type of incentive might be undermined by the film underscored the 'responsibility' implicitly assumed by overseas filmmakers in representing Australia to the world. In the absence of equivalent local feature films on the world stage – the only related work that reached a large audience around this time was the Shell-financed documentary, *The Back of Beyond* (John Heyer, 1954) – productions like *Kangaroo* and the films of Ealing came to illustrate both the possibilities and problems of overseas producers making films in Australia. These objections would find further voice and clearer shape in the arguments put forward for the 'revival' of the feature-film industry in the 1960s and early 1970s.

The objections reported from London did not, however, dampen enthusiasm for the film's Australian release. Indeed, in late May it was announced that Hoyts Theatres, Capital Canberra Picture Theatres Limited and Austin & Sibly Theatres (Port Augusta) had made 'key situations' available for simultaneous Red Cross benefit shows in Sydney, Canberra, Melbourne, Adelaide, Brisbane and Port Augusta ('Plans Set for *Kangaroo* Charity Shows' 1952: 1).[1] Arrangements for the premieres had been concluded after months of careful planning and 'fist-in-glove cooperation' between Hoyts and Twentieth Century-Fox. Each capital city preview, it was reported, would be under Vice-Regal patronage, and would be attended by high-ranking political and civic officials, together with top brass of the three armed services. Moreover, 'Hollywood glamour and glitter [would] be given [to] the four Hoyts Regent shows, with Army searchlights playing on the theatre fronts and bands stationed in the streets outside' ('Plans Set for *Kangaroo*' 1952: 1). In a further fillip, the Walt Disney Company (through RKO Pictures) had made available, free of charge, its Academy Award-winning short, *Nature's Half Acre* (James Algar, 1951) to Hoyts for the Red Cross premieres in Melbourne, Brisbane and Adelaide ('Disney Gesture to Red Cross' 1952: 1).

Predictably, the advertising campaign for the openings turned out to be among the most intense in the annals of Hoyts-Twentieth Century-Fox cooperation and the previews were expected to generate wide word-of-mouth publicity ('Plans Set for *Kangaroo*' 1952: 1). In one example, the *Advertiser* (Adelaide), in advance of the South Australian premiere on 4 June ran a full two-page spread, titled 'First S. A. Color Drama will Help Red Cross', which included not only several pieces about the film production, its cast and the work of the Red Cross, but also endorsements from, amongst others, TAA (Trans Australia Airlines), Coca-Cola, R. M. Williams and the iconographic Hills Hoist, the latter of which proclaimed, 'whenever she can, Maureen O'Hara attends to all the usual domestic chores. She was trained to be practical and like many thousands of Australian Housewives selected the Hills Rotary Clothes Hoist for convenience and efficiency' ('First S. A. Color Drama' 1952: 8). In addition, the local trade journal, *Film Weekly*, went so far as to predict that 'the event of June 4 undoubtedly will be the biggest of its kind in the history of the Australian motion picture industry' ('Plans Set for *Kangaroo*' 1952: 1).

A 'THIRST-CRAZED MOB': *KANGAROO*'S AUSTRALIAN PREMIERE

The press reaction to the premiere events – 'the culmination of an epic 18-months [production] period with an unprecedented goodwill gesture' – was effusive, if (in some cases) tempered by modest reactions to the film itself (see, for example, 'Gala Atmosphere for *Kangaroo* Preview' 1952: 2; '*Kangaroo*' 1952b: 10). From the Australian Capital Territory, *Film Weekly* managing director, Eric Solomon, wrote that the 'simultaneous six-theatre premiere of *Kangaroo* . . . rate[d] among the greatest national contributions to motion picture industry public relations in the history of the screen in Australia' (Solomon 1952: 36). It's only equivalent amongst the varied films discussed in this book, was the seventeen-city 'simultaneous' worldwide premiere marking the release of *On the Beach* in December 1959. Solomon's prediction for

Kangaroo – reflecting other opinions that 'authenticity keynotes the production throughout' (*Kangaroo* Special Report 1952a: 20) – was that

> *Kangaroo* should prove a box office certainty, as it contains very many of the ingredients that film patrons want. It is not an Australian documentary, nor an award-winning production, but it has big star value ... terrific action and the right degree of suspense, surprise, drama and romance. In wonderful Technicolor, it *truthfully* portrays the spirit of our great inland and the early pioneers who established our important cattle industry. Its producers backed *Kangaroo* with terrific capital investment and have made a grand outdoor spectacle. (Solomon 1952: 36, emphasis added)

Each of the state premieres attracted large crowds. In South Australia, the opening night at the Hoyts Regent – 'a brilliant piece of exploitation on every count ... singularly geared to the taste of Adelaide' (Armitage 1952: 40) – was held under the patronage of the Governor, Sir Willoughby Norrie, and Lady Norrie, the latter captured 'in powder blue and diamonds, smiling unconcernedly into a blaze of arc lights while she held a souvenir toy kangaroo' ('Lady Norrie Given Toy Kangaroo at Red Cross Film' 1952: 10; see also 'Brilliant Scene at Opening of *Kangaroo*' 1952: 1). Likewise, reporting from the 2,236-seat Hoyts Regent Theatre in Sydney, *Film Weekly* editor Peter Morrison described the Hollywood-style premiere as 'one of the most significant events in its [the theatre's] long history', and predicted, that 'as a box-office proposition, *Kangaroo*, with its star names, slick treatment and Australian background, cannot fail' (Morrison 1952: 37). Making note that 'the view has been voiced here as well as in America, that *Kangaroo* depicts a dry, fire-ravaged Australia, seething with primitive animal life, and that the total impression is misleading', Morrison went on to defend the film, stating: 'such a view is unbalanced. *Kangaroo* shows with greater attention to *authenticity* and with broader *truth* than we could have expected from an overseas unit, a page or two in the story of our development' (Morrison 1952: 37, emphasis added).

Notable among the attendees at the Sydney premiere, which included the guest of honour, His Excellency the Governor of NSW, Sir John Northcott, was 'Miss Kangaroo' – Loretta North – the young Australian model who, along with kangaroos Joey and Matilda, had done a gruelling three-week, thirty-two-city tour of the US earlier in the year (January 1952) to publicise the film. While certainly raising the profile of *Kangaroo* – touted as 'the first American picture made in Australia' – in other respects the promotional tour did not go terribly well: Matilda died in a wintery New York City, and a seemingly unsympathetic Loretta – evidently tired of chaperoning, and sharing quarters with, two non-house-trained kangaroos – complained (in terms that recalled the rumoured killing of New Zealand-bred racehorse Phar Lap by gangsters in the US): 'The Sydney papers made a big fuss about it . . . You'd think the Americans had poisoned her or something' (Mosby 1952: 9; see also '"Miss Kangaroo" Visits Washingon' 1952: 1; 'Miss Kangaroo Here with Pal Joey' 1952: 2).

In Melbourne, Hoyts management spared no effort or expense for the charity premiere, floodlights playing on the Regent Theatre from the opposite side of Collins Street. In the theatre, a handsome front of house display included Australian and American flags covering the side walls of the front entrance and – holding pride of place at the top of the front steps – a large stuffed kangaroo (borrowed from the Museum of Applied Science of Victoria) was a focal point for celebrity pictures. A 'social editress' on one of Melbourne's dailies described the occasion as 'a glamour parade in the best Hollywood tradition . . . True glamour shone from the superb frocks . . . [and a] fortune in jewels and furs drifting around the foyer' (quoted in Manzie 1952: 38; see also 'Vice-Regal Guests at Film Premiere' 1952: 5). Covering the event, *Film Weekly* correspondent and *Argus* film reviewer, Keith Manzie, wrote that *Kangaroo* was 'undoubtedly the best-handled production that has yet been made in Australia' (1952: 38). Like others, he conceded that 'the film reveals Australia in its worst possible aspect. In drought and dust-storm and bush fire; in arid desert country where dangerous snakes lurk; with the emphasis always on "hard" conditions and the lack of water', but hastily added that 'it is made quite clear that this is not the Australia of today or that conditions shown are typical of the entire continent' (1952: 38). More significantly, in Manzie's estimation – and in contrast to the 'boredom [of] so many pedestrian and loosely-knitted Australian-made movies' – *Kangaroo* amounted to 'an adequate film of average entertainment . . . [one which] should awaken other filmmakers in Hollywood and England to the infinite possibilities of film production in this country' (1952: 38).

Twentieth Century-Fox and Hoyts Theatres immediately capitalised upon the success of the precedent-setting, six-theatre *Kangaroo* charity premieres with the announcement of plans for a staggered, nationwide general release ('*Kangaroo* Release Set on Giant Scale' 1952: 1). Initial screenings included simultaneous seasons at three Sydney and three Melbourne theatres, and dates for Queensland, the Australian Capital Territory, Tasmania and Adelaide theatres. Within the month, the film would be rolled out at further east coast cinemas, from Cairns to Hobart. Announcing these release dates, Twentieth Century-Fox managing director Albright said, 'plans surrounding the general release of *Kangaroo* [would] create a dynamic approach, ensuring the maximum number of Australian audiences to see the picture at the earliest possible time, having regard to the number of Technicolor prints available in this country' (quoted in '*Kangaroo* Release Set' 1952: 1). Print ads for the local release declared:

> Never before has any film created such intense national interest!
> Adventure as far as the eye can see! ACTION. THRILLS and ROMANCE on Australia's sun-scorched plains as the man who came to rob – stayed to love! (*Kangaroo* Print Advertisement 1952: 12)

At the end of the month, *Film Weekly* ran a second (in this case, sixteen-page) special section devoted to the film, headlined with '*Kangaroo* is impressively Australian and All Box-Office' (*Kangaroo* Special Report 1952b). A self-congratulatory piece (no doubt underwritten by Twentieth Century-Fox and its partners) to laud its 'meritorious achievement', the lead article of the supplement declared:

> Well, the wiseacres have had their say – and the summation of their concerted wail is *Kangaroo* doesn't present Australia in the most favourable light ... Phooey to all that! ... No one can fault *Kangaroo* for truth in idiom; truth in background or truth in action! ... [W]hen writing the truth (and some honest ones do) they admit *Kangaroo* to be excellent mass entertainment ... The action moves right along, it is typically Australian and believable ... [*Kangaroo*] tell[s] the Australian Story, believably and well. (*Kangaroo* Special Report 1952b: 15)

'Kangaroo tripe' or 'super-western'

Upon closer inspection, *Kangaroo* plainly betrays – especially in its generic story and dialogue – some of the compromises and difficulties of its production (and in its inattentiveness to local elements), but reviews, internationally, were in the main positive (or at least tolerant). It was typically characterised as a western or, at least, as operating within the form's generic frame: *Variety* advised that 'Australia's wide-open spaces, not unlike the states' own west, get the Technicolor treatment ... The locale provides a fresh background for the runoff of what is a standard western feature plot' (Brog 1952: 6); *Newsweek* described the film as 'a regulation horse opera with a geographical difference ... [one that] gets [its] best effects from the Australian scene and from a heart-breaking cattle drive across a landscape that is suffocated in dust' ('*Kangaroo*' 1952a: 87); and the *Hollywood Reporter* headlined it as an 'Australian Sagebrusher': '*Kangaroo* is a *super-western* with an intriguing Australian background ... containing enough climatic action to satisfy blood-and-thunder fans. Although it is handicapped by a completely meaningless title this off-beat Down-Under oater should prove a healthy box office tonic' ('*Kangaroo:* An Intriguing Australian Sagebrusher' 1952: 3, emphasis added).²

The term 'super-western' had been coined by André Bazin to describe large-scale, innovative westerns of the late 1940s such as John Ford's *Fort Apache* (1948) which in some way – for example, size and place of production, subject matter, dramatic focus – extended the genre (1971: 151), but for all this *Kangaroo*, and its attempts to expand the geographic reach of the western, would mainly be remembered – like Warner Bros.' *The Sundowners*, another American 'updated western' utlising Australian locations – as a work 'quaintly counted by some as "Australian film[s]", [but] not Australian in the sense that matters [because] the background was exactly that – background' (Lawson 1965: 30). This view of *Kangaroo* was expressed most emphatically, at the time of its first release, in a *Meanjin* opinion piece entitled 'Kangaroo Tripe' (Grant 1952). In the article, Bruce Grant argued that for all the publicity – the fanfare of the premieres, the sensational posters and taglines, 'and heaven knows how many kangaroos . . . hopping around in the United States breathing out their lives in the cause of entertainment' – *Kangaroo*, 'the first Technicolor feature film made in Australia is not even "good enough"' (1952: 411). This was, in Grant's estimation, not simply for it being 'an episodic melodrama which deals in flabby values and petty predicaments', but for the sad fact that director Milestone had 'come so near the physical heart of Australia and not capture[d] so much as a beat' (1952: 412).³

Wild Turkey: *Kangaroo*'s Legacy

This overtly negative perspective on the film and the experience of making it was returned to later in the 1950s with the publication of Max Brown's novel, *Wild Turkey* (1958). Brown's roman-à-clef is full of barely disguised references to the making of *Kangaroo* – for example, there is a wage dispute involving Indigenous participants in the international film production; the outback town the production crew builds is called Glitzburg rather than Zanuckville; the film they are making is initially known as 'The Down Under Story' in contrast to *Kangaroo*'s 'The Australian Story'; a figure very reminiscent of Dora Birtles (who undertook research for *The Overlanders* and wrote the novelisation, and who is claimed as the author of the very successful *Cattle Drive* rather than the quite similar *The Overlanders*) arrives on location – as well as the conditions it was produced under, and the lost opportunities and finances it represented for truly local film production. Brown had filed reports from the location shooting of both *Kangaroo* in January 1951 (1951a: 2) and Cecil Holmes' *Captain Thunderbolt* (1953) in April of the same year (1951b: 1), demonstrating a patrician's concern with Aboriginal rights and living conditions. He even narrativised his own publicity report on Aboriginal actors and extras being used for *Kangaroo* as part of the rich background detail claimed for the making of the truly lamentable, 'Wild Turkey'. Brown was also a publicity officer for the production and promotion of *Kangaroo* in Australia and his subsequent novelisation and fictionalisation of that experience provides a fascinating insight into the conditions facing Australian cinema in the 1950s, the legacy of Milestone's film, as well as the emerging cultural nationalism of that period.

In respect to the criticism of both Grant and Brown, the real 'lesson' of *Kangaroo* – the unintended long-term value of the 'Australian Story' – was that it emphasised 'the need for Australians to make their own films', to tell their own stories (Grant 1952: 412). In closing, Grant concluded that the 'more subtle lesson' of the 'super-western' *Kangaroo* was to show that money is not everything. That is, in anticipation of debates around the feature-film 'revival' of the 1970s, the runaway productions of the postwar 'interval' demonstrated that what was 'required [in Australia] was not so much a rejuvenated industry as a renaissance of spirit' (1952: 413). And, emphatically, *not* more kangaroos.

Notes

1. See, in particular, the twenty-six-page *Kangaroo* Special Report (1952a) in *Film Weekly* devoted to the production and reception of the film.
2. The press release, from Henry Brand, Director of Publicity at Twentieth Century-Fox, attempts to make sense of the film's title: 'The name "kangaroo" brings to mind a unique Australian animal, bearing its baby in pouch, which smells the wind for danger and bounds off on powerful legs ... And the film "Kangaroo" is a film about danger – about the devastating 1900–1903 drought which brought death and poverty, and yet romance also, to a family on a large "cattle station" or ranch called "Kangaroo Downs"' (Brand 1951).
3. For a broader discussion of this context see O'Regan (1987).

4. ON THE BEACH (1959)

Ground Zero: Australia at the End of the World

The short spike in international film production in Australia at the very end of the 1950s saw a partial shift of focus to urban settings. Three of the four major British and US productions made during this relatively brief moment in time – *Summer of the Seventeenth Doll* (*Season of Passion*, Leslie Norman, 1959), *The Siege of Pinchgut* (Harry Watt, 1959) and *On the Beach* (Stanley Kramer, 1959) – eschew the 'outback' for contemporary or marginally futuristic stories set within the expanding metropolises of Sydney and Melbourne. Yet only one of these films, *Summer of the Seventeenth Doll*, provides a vibrant, energetic vision of the close living characteristic of the inner city. Both *The Siege of Pinchgut* and *On the Beach* use their respective cities as staging grounds for dramas that progressively depopulate their urban environments. *The Siege of Pinchgut* was made on a smaller scale and on a more mundane theme than *On the Beach*, yet its generic crime drama largely staged at Fort Denison in Sydney Harbour shares some interesting commonalities with its more famous and prestigious cousin. It must have been striking indeed to view these two films on first release in Australia and compare their stark representation of two 'rival' cities that had, to this point, only very occasionally appeared in international or transnational productions.

In fact, aside from brief appearances in movies like *The Road to Bali* (Hal Walker, 1952), Melbourne had never been the focus of such a fiction feature before. Nevertheless, it is the city's palpable and actual sense of isolation, as well as its capacity to be rendered as both a specific place and a generic 'anywhere', as a modern metropolis and a colonial backwater, as both familiar (English-speaking but also an important base for US soldiers in World War II) and slightly exotic, that made it an appropriate geographic location for this widely publicised and discussed end-of-the-world drama. This was, of course, also justified by the pointed setting of the film's source novel as well as the ongoing if peripatetic practice of filming US and international productions in Australia throughout the 1950s. As Ben Goldsmith, Susan Ward and Tom O'Regan have argued, Melbourne's use in *On the Beach* jigsaws into Australia's larger historical role 'as a generic location', 'a distant "down under" setting for staging apocalypse and its aftermath' (2010: 203). In the process, this 'tyranny of distance' granted Australia a dubious competitive advantage: 'as the last habitable continent, Australia is suddenly the most important place on Earth, at the very moment of its greatest impotence and ignorance, awaiting dooming winds from an incomprehensible war in the northern hemisphere' (Haigh 2007).

THE GRADUAL APOCALYPSE: THE ARRIVAL OF *ON THE BEACH*

On the Beach was the largest-scale film production made in Australia up to this point in time. The importance of it in an Australian context is illustrated by the significant pre-publicity that preceded filming as well as the extraordinary level of public and press interest in its shooting across a total of sixty-three days in the first three months of 1959. It is also demonstrated by the diverse locations in and around Melbourne that were used such as the Williamstown Dockyard, Canadian Bay on the Mornington Peninsula, Point Lonsdale at the heads of Port Phillip Bay, Steavenson River near Buxton, Frankston Railway Station, the Royal Melbourne Showgrounds (where soundstages and offices for the production were constructed) and the exteriors of the State Library of Victoria and Flinders Street Railway Station, along with the considerable assistance granted by the Royal Australian Navy as well as various branches of local government and business. This municipal fascination and assistance is reflected in the review of *On the Beach* that appeared in *The Sydney Morning Herald* the morning after its glittering Melbourne premiere: 'The making of the film was an overnight sensation in staid conservative Melbourne, with much effort expended by authorities to assist the production' (L. B. 1959: 7).

This notoriety was, of course, fuelled by significant public awareness of the much-debated source novel by Nevil Shute, first published to massive popular success and some critical acclaim in early 1957. According to Gideon Haigh (2007), who calls it 'arguably Australia's most important novel', *On the Beach* sold over 4 million copies, 'had [already] been serialised by no fewer than

40 American newspapers' by September 1957, and went on to become a significant influence and point of discussion for activists, scientists and politicians around the globe. A socially conservative British expatriate and tax exile who moved to Melbourne in the early 1950s, Shute was one of the world's most successful writers and was earning royalties in excess of £80,000 per year prior to the publication of *On the Beach* (Harris 1960: 8).

Producer-director Stanley Kramer reportedly purchased the rights for the novel for US$100,000 and quickly moved into pre-production in early 1958. It was to be the first mainstream, prestige Hollywood film to deal directly and soberly with the aftermath of nuclear war, even if its sense of immediacy was diluted by a focus on the effects of radioactive fallout gradually drifting south after a nuclear exchange involving the mass detonation of 'hypothetical' cobalt devices in the Northern Hemisphere. This carefully maintained element of Shute's narrative and flat style allows the film to deal with the important theme of humanity's destruction while staging its last days in a reserved, character-centred and non-hyperbolic fashion. Although the novel more fully details the gradual effects of radiation sickness, the film retains little that musses up the visual perfection and composure of its glamorous stars, Gregory Peck and Ava Gardner.

The plot of the film and novel focuses on a period of seven to eight months before the arrival of lethal doses of radiation in southern Australia. The film opens with the approach of the nuclear submarine USS Sawfish in Port Phillip Bay, on its way to the Williamstown Dockyard, seven or so kilometres from the centre of Melbourne. It consistently returns to discussion of the relentless progress of radiation and the sketchy details of the nuclear war that took place. It does this while introducing us to various characters who help personalise the effects of this calamity. The narrative is partly centred on the burgeoning relationship between Captain Dwight Towers (Gregory Peck) and a local woman (Moira Davidson, played by Ava Gardner) he meets when visiting the home of Mary (Donna Anderson) and Peter Holmes (Anthony Perkins), the Australian Lieutenant Commander who will serve under him on the penultimate voyage of the Sawfish. We are also introduced to a range of other minor characters from the Navy, the local establishment and various local communities, as well as a British nuclear scientist, Julian Osborne, played by Fred Astaire (and much was made of this being Astaire's first serious dramatic role). The narrative contrasts the daily impact of an increasingly dire situation in Melbourne with the efforts of the Navy and the crew of the submarine to investigate whether life has survived elsewhere in the world. This involves a journey by the crew to the Arctic and a hauntingly depopulated but otherwise 'intact' San Francisco. Other moments take in various domestic scenes between the Holmes family, the trips by Dwight to outer suburban Frankston, Berwick and to the beach, a date in Melbourne's CBD between Moira and Dwight, the last Australian

Grand Prix won by Julian and held at Phillip Island, and the early opening of the trout fishing season near Buxton, amongst others. The film's final scenes show the last parting of Moira and Dwight, Peter and Mary, and return to haunting images of Melbourne's city streets devoid of any human activity.

Local and Global: Hollywood Independent Production in Australia

In terms of its thematic and narrative focus, its emphasis on the hot-button issues of the day, its deployment of numerous major Hollywood stars, and its relative scale and US$3 million budget (Pike and Cooper 1998: 228), *On the Beach* represents a globally significant and highly illustrative instance of transnational film production during this period. Also, unlike many of the other international productions shot in Australia during this era, it made significant attempts to utilise local production facilities, crews and actors, as well as to communicate a relatively accurate sense of the geography and cartography of its southeast Australian locations. According to E. S. Madden, a local historian and film critic who was attached to the production, *On the Beach* employed 110 Australians, twenty-five Americans, two Britons and one Italian (the cinematographer Giuseppe Rotunno), as well as over 450 local extras (1959: 317). Although the crew was numerically dominated by Australians, none of the major departments other than set construction was managed by them.

Despite Shute's displeasure with the subsequent adaptation – which mostly revolved around his aversion to the overly sexualised and cheapened relationship between Peck and Gardner's characters (Harris 1960: 10) – the film is largely a very faithful, if highly condensed, adaptation of an often prosaic novel. It is also highly attentive and sympathetic to the topography and rhythm of Melbourne life as well as Shute's often conservative vision of 'settler-colonial' Australian values and demographics. Shute's Melbourne is largely monocultural, and despite the fast-changing make-up of the city's population under the hefty weight of large-scale Southern and Eastern European migration, the movie only vaguely references this burgeoning multiculturalism. The world of *On the Beach*, despite being a tale about the end of *all* human life and its various civilisations, is overwhelmingly white or Anglo even in the make-up of the submarine crew. This is a particularly surprising colour-blindness for a work helmed by Stanley Kramer, a director who had recently completed *The Defiant Ones* (1958), a landmark if overly schematic treatment of southern US bigotry and segregation in which the two central characters – one black (Sidney Poitier) and one white (Tony Curtis) – are literally chained together.

On the Beach was also a production that had a deep sense of its own significance. Kramer was already well known for making liberal films that explored arguably divisive or controversial subject matter, but his critical reputation and schematic approach to movie-making have long been questioned and critiqued. David Thomson grumbles about the overall 'limitations of his entrepreneurial liberalism' (2002: 477) and Pauline Kael complains of him being 'unusual in publicizing himself no matter *what* the film' (1987: 203), while director Norman Jewison claims Kramer '"was a better producer than he was a director", and once he was in the director's chair, he continued to think like a producer, concentrating on the overall package rather than the shaping of individual scenes, performances, and moments' (Harris 2008: 112). This emphasis on the 'overall package', as well as the mind-numbing consistency of *On the Beach*'s intimate, buttoned-down tone and style, endows Kramer's adaptation with both a dramatic inertia and a fully appropriate sense of deflation. Kramer announced his intention to make a film of Shute's novel on 9 September 1957, with the outlandish and outsized proclamation that it would be 'a concept of hope on celluloid . . . to reach out to the hearts of people everywhere that they might feel compassion – for themselves' (Poe 2001: 93). This is despite the fact that it was based on a novel of ideas with questionable artistic and literary merit. Nevertheless, as Max Harris has harshly written, despite having 'no powers of characterisation in his novels, no gifts of phrasing at all', Shute does have an 'uncommon knack for following through the consequences (usually disastrous consequences) of contemporary developments; they weighed him with a sense of responsibility and indeed of mission' (1960: 9).

But as Jewison suggests, Kramer was a more pragmatic producer than director who also recognised the need to leaven his lesson with a raft of commercial concessions:

> The story challenged the essential values of people everywhere. Its subject was as serious and compelling as any ever attempted in a motion picture – the very destruction of mankind and the entire planet. That's why I cast it so heavily with big, popular stars. Though the public might not like the subject, they wouldn't ignore a picture starring Peck, Gardner, and Astaire. (Kramer 1999: 14)

It is the appearance of these stars, including a quietly mannered Anthony Perkins in an early featured role, that both undermines the drama's small-scale realism and helps assure its deeper exposure and wider significance. The presence of these stars also preoccupied much of the press coverage, both in Australia and overseas. There were endless reports about the particular clothes that Gardner wore, who she was seen with – at this time it was Italian actor Walter Chiari, later to star in Michael Powell's *They're a Weird Mob* (1966) – how she interacted with the public and press, and the manner in which these intersected with accepted understandings of her career and tempestuous stardom. For example, Freda Irving's profile for the *Australian Women's Weekly* is fixated on the minutiae of an insignificant moment captured at the Williamstown Dockyard. Although her article describes the endless takes of a simple walk along Gellibrand Pier, it builds into it a highly descriptive account of Gardner's gestures, the use of a stand-in, a rundown of her various personal assistants, her remarkable earthiness and the kind of insinuating gossip-mongering that hounded the actor wherever she went: 'Miss Gardner's friend Walter Chiari – in black-and-white-striped royal-blue satin trunks and gold chain and disc – joined Miss Gardner, but beat a hurried retreat at the sight of a roving camera' (Irving 1959: 5). This focus on such superficial elements further pinpoints the limitations and contradictions lying at the heart of the 'entrepreneurial liberalism' of Kramer's adaptation (Thomson 2002: 477).

'THE END OF EVERYTHING PERHAPS, BUT THERE IS ALWAYS AVA GARDNER': PROMOTING ON THE BEACH

On the Beach also needs to be placed within its particular moment in political and social history. As Helen Grace has claimed, 'between 1947 and 1962 the United States carried out 107 nuclear tests in the Pacific, with fallout blowing across Australia on a regular basis' (2001: 300, n27). 'Secret nuclear tests' were 'also carried out by Britain' in Australia from 1952, and at the Maralinga test site from September 1956 (Grace 2001: 300, n27). This was also a moment when the US military and government were settling for a policy of 'mutually assured destruction' that would nevertheless 'allow' the survival of populations in 'countries not attacked or not in the downwind fallout patterns' of any such exchange (Broderick 2013). A key contribution of *On the Beach* – both novel and film – is to quietly but firmly undermine such survivalist 'civil defence' narratives. This led to the film receiving little support from the US military and being the subject of negative discussions and interference at Cabinet level. As Mick Broderick (2013) has revealed, the United States Information Agency, for example, 'dismissed formal cooperation with Kramer on the project at *any* level', asked diplomatic posts to file reports on the film's reception in their region, and more generally ran a disinformation campaign aimed at nullifying and questioning the film's defeatist message, overt pacifism and scientific credentials. Although *On the Beach* has some of the trappings of science fiction – it is set in 1964, hypothesises about the use of cobalt technology in nuclear weapons, and provides a minorly speculative and sombre account of the last days of humanity – it is grounded in the quotidian realities faced by those left to expire as the result of gradual radiation drift. It is the film's perceived sense of hopelessness, as well as its failure to concede ground to satiric *Dr. Strangelove*-like visions of a post-apocalyptic future that most alarmed authorities in the US. For many, the mundanity of *On the Beach* was its most disturbing characteristic.

This campaign of interference was, in turn, countered by the film's publicity and marketing on first release. Opening with an ambitious 'simultaneous' premiere in seventeen cities on six continents, the publicity for *On the Beach* was aimed at communicating the film's global importance and reach as well as the ways in which it transcended national borders and identities. Much was made of its screening in places like Moscow and Tokyo – potent locations in terms of past nuclear episodes and possible future exchanges – as well as the attendance at screenings by various dignitaries and people who worked on the film. The subsequent long-form trailer included significant footage from many of these premieres – 'Flash: Motion picture history is made as Stanley Kramer's production of *On the Beach* opens all over the world' – while also laying down a deliberately provocative challenge: 'If you never see another motion picture in your life ... YOU MUST SEE ... ON *THE BEACH*.' As is obvious from these hyperbolic proclamations, *On the Beach* was promoted as no mere movie but as an urgent public-service announcement, one that transcended any other motion-picture experience: 'THE BIGGEST STORY OF OUR TIME!' This promotion positioned *On the Beach* less as an entertainment – despite the trailer's inclusion of copious footage culled from its staging of the world's last motor-racing Grand Prix at Phillip Island (though mostly shot in California) and its careful positioning and promotion of Peck, Gardner, Astaire, Perkins and newcomer Donna Anderson as the attractive stars of the film – than as a duty of care for *any* citizen of the world.

As we'll go on to argue, no film could withstand the level of expectation and aggrandisement raised by this publicity, particularly one staged on the surprisingly intimate scale of *On the Beach*. Predictably, several subsequent reviewers negatively commented on the film's lack of significant action, honing in on a sensibility and approach that takes gravely to heart the famous quotation from T. S. Eliot's 'The Hollow Men' that prefaces Shute's novel: 'This is the way the world ends, Not with a bang but a whimper' (Eliot cited in the epigraph of Shute 1957: n.p.). The great challenge for Kramer's film, as a work nevertheless designed as a large-scale production and made on a relatively high budget, was how to create or communicate both a 'bang' and 'whimper', and to move categorically beyond the pall of superficiality suggested by prominent British critic Penelope Houston in her subsequent review: 'The end of everything perhaps, but there is always Ava Gardner' (1959–60: 38). These contradictory elements and demands are also picked up on by Graham Shirley and Brian Adams in their brief discussion of the film's wider place in Australian cinema: 'Although some impact springs from individual moments of truth and the scenes of a population forming long queues in the desolate city for suicide pills, the novel's chilling quality is lost when the film becomes an all-star "problem" movie' (Shirley and Adams 1989: 208). It is this precarious balancing act between a large-budget independent Hollywood production designed to maximise global film revenues and operate within generic conventions, and a work raising serious arguments about the urgent need for nuclear disarmament and the closeness of global catastrophe, which makes *On the Beach* such a deeply schizophrenic experience.

There is a strong sense of this schism in reports of *On the Beach*'s world premiere in Melbourne. While local critic for *The Age*, Colin Bennett, applauded the film's bold and relatively unwavering portrayal of the inevitable and melancholy extinction of humanity (1959a: 2), copious other reports honed in on the appearance of celebrities and dignitaries at the various screenings taking place around the world as well as the peculiar novelty of some of the promotional gimmicks that were staged for the event. For example, an account of the Melbourne premiere in the same edition of *The Age* as Bennett's grave review lists the attendance of various dignitaries such as Sir Dallas Brooks, then Governor of Victoria, and the managing director of the Australian film exhibitor Hoyts (alongside noting Shute's absence), precisely describes some of the clothes worn by chosen female guests, details the appearance of a replica of a nuclear submarine carved in ice, and notes that 'This was one of the "dressiest" premieres seen in Melbourne for a long, long time. As the audience streamed up the steps of the theatre, it was a memorable scene of color and sparkle' ('Governor at *On the Beach* Premiere Last Night' 1959: 10). A report on page one of the same edition also described the gathering of 500 people outside the Regent Theatre in Collins Street to great the 3,200-strong audience, a guard of honour formed by forty naval ratings, the playing of 'Waltzing Matilda' – the iconic tune given multiple, often-mournful variations across the film's inventive but too insistent score – and 'one touch of novelty . . . the arrival of several guests in two horse-drawn cabs' ('*On the Beach* Premiere in Melb.' 1959: 1). Typically, this final gesture reframed a serious narrative element from the film and book – the reversion to earlier forms of transport due to a global petrol shortage – in a more palatable, even glamourous fashion.

The relative frivolity of these accounts, partly reflective of the endless local press coverage of *On the Beach*'s making in the first three months of 1959, sits in stark contrast to Bennett's highly attentive review. Diverging from dominant accounts of the glittering premiere, he argues that '[t]his is no fashion-plate view of our city, nor is it unfair to our business and beach life. We quickly accept this barren place of brick and concrete, with its horses, buggies, trams and bicycles, as a symbol of Anywhere' (Bennett 1959a: 2). He also praises *On the Beach* as a 'film of tremendous power and impact' and argues that '[t]owards the end, it becomes so real that when you emerge into the traffic it is the bustling life of Melbourne's streets which looks artificial'. These diverse and even contradictory responses are attentive to the local *and* international aspirations of *On the Beach*, its attempts to capture the specificities of Melbourne as the geographically remote 'last' city on Earth, while, as Bennett suggests, also picturing it 'as a symbol of Anywhere' (Bennett 1959a: 2). Melbourne's somewhat less-than-distinctive late Victorian and Edwardian architecture, as well as its cultural, social and architectural fusion of suburban and urban Europe and the US, help communicate a heartily Western universality, one that would have been easily recognisable and relatable to audiences in, let's say, the Midwest of America. This is reinforced by the gilded presence of US stars playing a combination of Australian, British and American characters with little calibration of things like accents. In this regard, *On the Beach* stands as a truly transnational production that uses Melbourne and a wider Australia as both locations to exploit and as geographically, scientifically and thematically necessary places to stage a film about the very human end of the world.

'Attractive and ordinary, foreign and local': Melbourne on the International Stage

On the Beach is highly attentive to the characteristics of Melbourne that render it as a generic 'Anywhere', a stand-in for other second-string cities and towns across Europe and the US. But it is also responsive to its peculiarities. As Federico Passi has argued, the choice of Italian Giuseppe Rotunno as director of photography contributes substantively to this bifurcated perspective. Rotunno brings to *On the Beach* something of the mobile viewpoint, sensibility and 'theatrical' staging of urban European environments that mark his work with Luchino Visconti and, later, Federico Fellini. Analysing a remarkable if unostentatious tracking shot of Peck's and Gardner's characters as they walk down the pavement of a wide city street at night-time, Passi argues that

> the way the scene establishes a 'movement image' in connection with Melbourne's urban space was ... both in terms of the scale of production and the style of filming, quite new and foreign [for Australian cinema]. The by-product is an image of Melbourne that is attractive and ordinary, foreign and local at the same time. (Passi 2017: 201)

Even the gradual arrival of increasingly lethal levels of radiation is pictured in a modest and relatively indemonstrable fashion. As Rotunno claims, this grim reality was visually suggested by the use of lenses that granted a subtle awareness of increasing heat and glare – a 'dirty' effect – especially when combined with highly reflective light. Describing the final scene between Peck and Gardner on the Williamstown docks, Rotunno outlines this technique:

At the moment of parting, Peck's face slowly moves away from Gardner's face, letting the sunlight filter through giving the impression of real atomic radiations and increasing even more the drama of the situation. This was one of the scenes where we used the special filters. (Davey 2005: 106)

As with much of the rest of the film, the audience is left to register the subtle implications of such devices and narrative occurrences.

On the Beach commenced filming on 15 January 1959 in the outer Melbourne suburb of Berwick. Shooting completed – other than the San Francisco-set scenes and the staging of much of the wild, stunt-heavy action of the Phillip Island-set Australian Grand Prix at the Riverside Raceway in California – with some minor retakes featuring several actors in Williamstown on 27 March and shots of a deserted Swanston Street from the roof of the buildings of the Carlton United Brewery on 29 March (Davey 2005: 177). These came just after filming wrapped on the soundstages at the Royal Melbourne Showgrounds in Ascot Vale, evocatively described by Graham Perkin in his report on the end of production: 'Easter at Mr. Kramer's Showground studios was the fag-end of the adventure. And as T. S. Eliot predicted much earlier, the world ended with a whimper' (Perkin 1959: 2).

On the Beach is remarkable in an Australian context for the fact that almost all of the material filmed was captured 'on location', in contrast to contemporaneous international films such as *The Sundowners* and *The Shiralee*, both of which completed most of their interiors in English studios. This is also significant because *On the Beach* is dominated by scenes featuring two or three characters expressing and explaining their various feelings and responses to their predicament, the majority of which are shot and staged within very confined and often claustrophobic interiors. These are, of course, set in contrast to the exterior shots of Melbourne, San Francisco and San Diego (the oil refinery at Geelong's Corio Bay acting as a stand-in for the latter) that are remarkable less for their outward signs of apocalypse than their eerie, uncanny depopulation. In this respect, *On the Beach* stands alongside other apocalyptic fictions of its era – such as Richard Matheson's novel *I am Legend* (1954) – that imagine the end of the world less in terms of the planet's outright destruction than a pointed absence of humanity. This absence includes such iconic and ubiquitous Hollywood stars as Gardner, Astaire and Peck. Even if the film of *On the Beach* survived this 'apocalypse', who would be left to view it?

The filming of *On the Beach*, and the impact it registered on Melbourne, should also be examined alongside a series of other events. The frenzied local reaction to the presence of the cast and crew was perhaps inevitable in such a large, parochial city mostly isolated from film production and geographically distanced from the global centres of screen culture. The second half of the

1950s is also a period in which Melbourne makes a claim for its status as a major international destination, an ambition fuelled by the city's successful staging of the 1956 Olympic Games and the memory of its legendary status as one of the world's fastest-growing and wealthy cities in the second half of the nineteenth century. The late 1940s and 1950s is also a key era in the development and institutionalisation of film culture in Melbourne with the formation of the Melbourne Film Festival, the State Film Centre of Victoria (now ACMI) and various other organisations. At a time when the filming of scenes around the State Library for *On the Beach*'s final onscreen moments drew a significant number of onlookers, evangelist Billy Graham was also speaking to crowds of over 65,000 at Melbourne's newly opened Sidney Meyer Music Bowl ('5000 Watch Filming in City Streets' 1959: 3). Graham also made direct reference to Shute's novel in his sermon while brandishing copies of both the *Bible* and *On the Beach*: 'If a minister got into the pulpit and said some of the things in the book he would be accused of being a sensationalist . . . He would be accused of trying to frighten the people. Yet this book has been a success and the film will be a success' ('Graham Compares *Bible* with *On the Beach*' 1959: 9).

The fevered responses of locals to these international 'events' – 1,500 or so were reported during filming in the outer suburb of Frankston ('1500 See Filming at Frankston' 1959: 3) – speaks volumes about the city's aspirational *and* parochial nature at this time. But as Davey accurately claims, in contrast to many local commentators and business interests who argued for the film's value as a means of promoting the city, '[t]he international reception mostly failed to mention Melbourne' at all (2005: 217). This is hardly surprising considering the film's grave subject matter. But for many local audiences and commentators the appearance of Melbourne onscreen – even if pictured as a demure setting for the demise of humankind – was indeed novel. For example, Davey's painstakingly researched and voluminous account of the making of *On the Beach* is largely fuelled by the wonder of seeing and imagining such Hollywood icons walking the city's streets and suburbs. This was particularly pointed for a country that, in the late 1950s, had little of its own feature-film industry and very little previous feature-film 'experience'. It is unsurprising, therefore, that locals latched onto a prestigious large-scale international production being filmed on their streets.

A Bang and a Whimper: The Impact of *On the Beach*

From its very first moments, it is clear that *On the Beach* will communicate a measured response to global catastrophe. Although there are out-sized emotions expressed by several characters throughout – particularly those played by Astaire, Gardner and Anderson – the novel and film are dominated by a stiff-upper-lip and quietly mad determinism that insists upon the continuation and continuity of life in the face of annihilation. In the film, this is mainly dramatised through Dwight's plans for his already dead children's future and Peter's and Mary's discussions about their young baby, but in Shute's novel such small-scale planning for a time beyond inevitable death is endemic to almost all of the characters. Although the US military and government considered the film dangerously pessimistic, its message is actually strangely sanguine, showing the good behaviour of those left to suffer at the hands of the nuclear madness unleashed in another hemisphere. This is also linked to the strong anti-war message the film communicates. As the writer for the *Tribune* argued: '*On the Beach* is the last word in defeatism. Yet, despite this, it is indirect propaganda for peace and political sanity in the mad, dying years of capitalism. No one who sees it can refuse to support any effort for peace' (A. C. 1960: 6). Unsurprisingly, a peace rally supported by various trade unions was also heavily publicised at some screenings in Australia, borrowing the still hopeful if deafeningly ironic message that can be seen plastered on the drooping banners of the dwindling numbers of the Salvation Army outside the State Library in the melancholy last moments of the film: 'There is still time, brother' ('*On the Beach* Spurs May 15 Peace Rally' 1960: 2).

On the Beach begins with a low-angle medium close-up of Peck's Dwight Towers as he gravely intones: 'prepare to surface'. It proceeds in a highly functional and procedural fashion that leisurely introduces its audience to a sensibility, geography and situation. The location is ushered in by the movement of the submarine past the heads of Port Phillip Bay, before it surfaces to the melancholy strains of 'Waltzing Matilda', a leitmotif that constantly reminds us of the haunting nature of the unfolding story as well as its peculiarly Antipodean inflection. In keeping with the film's low-key tone, the first indication we get of the impending apocalypse is a radio report sent from a local lighthouse, matter-of-factly detailing the background radiation levels found in the atmosphere. The gradual emergence of the 'nuclear' submarine also symbolises the imminent arrival of invisible forces that have been unleashed in the Northern Hemisphere. Although this credit sequence does include a measured array of interior and exterior shots, as well as several composed using a Dutch angle, it also establishes a sense of intimacy and claustrophobia that will go on to dominate much of the rest of the film.

This is reinforced by the first post-credits scene set in the cluttered outer-suburban home of Peter and Mary, an exchange that heartbreakingly details the everyday task of preparing bottled milk for their young baby, but also the feelings of acceptance and denial that will characterise their shared and contrastive responses to humanity's approaching mortality. But this scene is equally illustrative of the 'anywhereness' mentioned earlier. This small-scale moment is confined to the interior of an indistinct house and is meant to communicate a sense of universalism, one that is reinforced by the indistinct accents of a supposedly typical Australian couple played by American stars (though the relative flatness and honesty of Anderson's performance, as well as her lack of previous exposure, aid this). The scene set in the Holmes' nondescript house shows the insidious daily impact of the fallout from these forces. But this opening exchange also highlights a generalised preoccupation with scale. The monumental if insidious impact of nuclear annihilation, as well as the open horizons that surround the submarine as it makes its way towards Melbourne, sit in contrast to the very gradual release of fear, passion, emotion and acceptance by most of the central characters. It is not until a scene staged at a hastily convened party at the Holmes' abode, some way into the film, that this pent-up tension finds its expression. In a heated exchange between Mary and Julian, in which he breaks her rule by discussing the inevitable, Julian provides a kind of timeline of the events that have led to this moment.

'Heavy as a leaden shroud': Fallout

As is probably obvious from our analysis, *On the Beach* presents a particularly resonant viewing experience for Australian and Melbournian audiences. Although we may recognise the low-lying and unspectacular topography of outer suburban Melbourne and its surrounds in the opening credits, the shock of recognition truly arrives in the third scene that starts with Peter crossing a still highly identifiable Elizabeth Street on his way to the offices of the Department of the Navy situated in what was then the General Post Office. This was a site later revealed as 'ground zero' for any targeted Soviet missile attacks on the city. This moment is quietly remarkable for the ways in which it evokes both a very familiar viewpoint of Melbourne and one that is partly transformed and rendered uncanny through small details like the lack of cars and the ease of Peter's movement across the street. We have written elsewhere about the ways in which *On the Beach* plays with common views of Melbourne as a relatively staid and conservative city – particularly at this time – a centre for finance, the establishment (symbolised here by the Commercial Travellers' Association posing as the Pastoral Club) and large institutions. It was also perceived as overwhelmingly monocultural despite large intakes of Southern and Eastern European migrants from the late 1940s (see Danks 2011). This lack of diversity is reflected in a Cinesound newsreel report on the filming which suggests Melbourne was 'transformed' into a 'dead' city, as if this was an astute piece of typecasting that just captured the metropolis on a particular day and at a specific time. Gardner's much-reported, though apocryphal comments on the suitability of Melbourne for its set task – '*On the Beach* is a story about the end of the world, and Melbourne sure is the right place to film it' (Wilson 2019: 6) – reinforce this notion of Melbourne's typecasting as a damningly appropriate place to see out such a 'cool' and gradual apocalypse.

But Melbourne is also positioned as a broad symbol of Western civilisation that provides continuity with the Midwest of Dwight's upbringing as well as the astonishing images of San Francisco we see when the Sawfish travels to the US to trace the random source of a Morse code signal, check radiation levels and confirm the country's demise. Apocalyptic fictions are commonly marked by an 'imagination of disaster' that shows us large, familiar cities obliterated or overwhelmed by catastrophe. *On the Beach* insists on a strong continuity between Melbourne and San Francisco by communicating this catastrophe through their shared depopulation, not the kind of inundation or destruction commonly found in movies like *When Worlds Collide* (Rudolph Maté, 1951). There is something deeply uncanny about these images of San Francisco – a city much more familiar to film audiences – denuded of humanity. As Murray Pomerance has argued, '*On the Beach* is a film that invokes and also examines despair', partly through a fixation on meaningless objects and worlds and things that survive human participation and perception (2008: 114). Writing of the moment the crew discovers that the signal they have travelled so far to source is merely created by the accident of a Coke bottle caught in the cord of a window shade, Pomerance summarises: 'It is a very brief moment, a flash, but in that flash we understand the sadness and vacancy of death ... with its gravity and its objectivity, the sunlight, the cord of the blind, the glass of the window, the Coke bottle *partly full of Coke*, tap tap tap ... there is *only This*' (2008: 115). Pomerance's account of this characteristically non-demonstrative moment highlights the importance of the mundane as well as the culturally specific in communicating existential loss.

Early in Shute's novel there is an exchange between Peter and Mary that helps summarise the heady confluence of expectations and emotions that greeted Kramer's film. Discussing Peter's invitation to Captain Towers to spend the weekend with them at their family home, Mary suggests that they could possibly 'take him to the movies' (Shute 1957: 24). Peter questions this suggestion: 'It might not be so good if it was about America ... We might just hit on one that was shot in his home town.' Stunned by this revelation, Mary admits '[w]ouldn't that be *awful*!' (Shute 1957: 24). It is unsurprising that this small moment does not appear in Kramer's film as it would bring an inappropriate reflexivity to its deadly serious and profoundly grounded drama. But, of course, in retrospect it also provides a commentary on the book's subsequent adaptation. These are precisely the mixed feelings that Melbourne audiences would have experienced when finally seeing their city writ large across a large-scale, self-consciously important transnational feature film about the end of humanity.

This ambivalence is reflected in the initial critical responses that greeted *On the Beach*'s Australian release, as well as the absence of any detailed discussion of the film's setting in international reviews. Many of these reviews also questioned the commercial imperative of such a large-scale film. Bennett opens one of his reviews in *The Age* with a statement of surprise that 'Hollywood is now prepared to spend three million dollars on a pacifist film', while finding it 'a film to be lived and experienced and appreciated, certainly not enjoyed' (Bennett 1959b: 11). In the US, *The New York Times*' influential critic Bosley Crowther (1959) led the way with his highly positive review, but *Variety*'s reviewer set the tone for what became a common critical response:

> it might be good to note that *On the Beach* is a solid theatrical film of considerable emotional, as well as cerebral, content. It will need all possible emphasis on this fact, as well as on the star names involved, to make it a success . . . Because the fact remains that the final impact of *On the Beach* is as heavy as a leaden shroud. (Powe 1959: 6)

Variety's common focus on both the artistic qualities and commercial potential of films they review immediately establishes the partly contradictory forces that tear away at *On the Beach*. The film's marketing drew on this generally positive critical response, with the trailer including quotes from Bennett and Crowther and generally emphasising its cultural and social significance. It is only in the second half of the almost five-minute trailer that attention becomes focused on the dramatic elements of the film's narrative. The trailer, along with the rest of the marketing, highlights the global implications and ramifications of *On the Beach*, as well as the important contributions made by stars such as Peck and practitioners like Kramer who 'CLIMAXES his brilliant career with a motion picture that has startled film-goers all over the world!'

In its own wistful manner, *On the Beach* nails the crepuscular, insidious and all-encompassing realities of nuclear warfare. Its lack of overt or direct representation of calamitous destruction is a subtle critique of the widely circulating propaganda of the time that suggested the possibilities of winning or surviving nuclear conflict. The film's vision of a post-apocalyptic world makes little sense in terms of the broad effects of radioactive fallout for most life on the planet – even if generated by a 'theoretical' weapon, the fallout intensifying cobalt bomb – but rings poetically true in terms of humanity's idiotic self-destruction and its seeming lack of consequence or weight (other than for *us*). *On the Beach* is a peculiar vision of the aftermath of nuclear warfare and the end of humanity, and a haunting fantasy of the end of human consciousness. Although it is now difficult to even imagine how such a global catastrophe could play out in a filtered and whimpering fashion, we are after all a generation that prides itself on connectivity and the 'borderlessness' of contemporary consumer life, this would have made more sense in the somewhat cosmopolitan but still largely isolated Melbourne of the 1950s.

On the Beach was certainly the most 'significant' feature made in Australia in the thirty years after World War II. It was also the most discussed and debated outside of the channels of film culture. Its relative failure at the box office and in terms of industry awards was both a significant disappointment and a sign of the discomfit the film induced. *On the Beach* also highlights the possibilities of making films in Australia that while attentive to the specificities of place could imagine the country as part of a wider global or international network of filmmaking and commerce. Although much of this was determined by the happenstance of geography, the idiosyncrasies of the Trade Winds drifting gradually down from the North, and the localised setting of Shute's 'isolating' novel, the film insisted on the connections between Melbourne and the rest of the world rather than the rarely 'seen', novel and strange continent pictured and promoted in movies like *The Sundowners*, *Kangaroo*, *The Drifting Avenger* and *The Overlanders*. It is therefore ironic that such a globally focused film should be one of the last made in Australia before the significant downturn in feature-film production in the first half of the 1960s.

5. THE SUNDOWNERS (1960)

'Peak' Production

Between 1958 and 1959 four significant international feature films were shot in Australia: *On the Beach* (Stanley Kramer, 1959), *Summer of the Seventeenth Doll* (*Season of Passion*, Leslie Norman, 1959), *The Siege of Pinchgut* (Harry Watt, 1959) and *The Sundowners* (Fred Zinnemann, 1960). In many respects, this represents a period of peak production 'down under' prior to the near cessation of feature filmmaking in the early to mid-1960s. The final of these films, Fred Zinnemann's episodic pastoral, *The Sundowners*, released in the US in early December 1960, is the last large-scale feature made in Australia prior to Michael Powell's *They're a Weird Mob* in 1965–6 and represents the final completed attempt to make a high-budget, mainstream and multi-star-driven popular success in Australia – other than the very differently appointed *Ned Kelly* (Tony Richardson) in 1970 – until the tax concession driven push of the early 1980s.

Three of the four films mentioned above are based on significant and highly successful Australian literary properties. They reflect a maturing of 'locationist' and transnational film production practices as well as the broader trend of independent production companies, with the support of major Hollywood or British studios, optioning bestselling novels and widely performed plays. For example, the decision to relocate Ray Lawler's ground-breaking and distinctively Carlton-set play, *Summer of the Seventeenth Doll*, to the more cosmetically attractive hot-house climes around Sydney Harbour, drawing on an array of performance styles and starring a startling mix of American and British actors – Anne Baxter, Ernest Borgnine, John Mills and Angela Lansbury – was predicated on the international exposure of the source material and its apparent correspondences with thematically and stylistically equivalent US models such as *Marty* (directed by Delbert Mann in 1955, and also starring the Oscar-winning Borgnine) and the work of Tennessee Williams, then a highly popular source for screen adaptations including *A Streetcar Named Desire* (Elia Kazan, 1951), *Baby Doll* (Elia Kazan, 1956) and *Cat on a Hot Tin Roof* (Richard Brooks, 1958). This small 'boom' is also symptomatic of the increased desire of Hollywood-based actors, writers, directors, producers and other significant filmmaking personnel to seek control of development and production and make films largely outside of immediate studio jurisdiction.

Although *The Sundowners* was made for Warner Bros. – with combative studio head Jack Warner even visiting the southern New South Wales (NSW) locations early on in filming, after initially requesting that the movie be made in Arizona with a few kangaroos and other Australian fauna flown in (Zinnemann 1992: 174) – it was also designed as an independent production. It reinforced a shift in celebrated director Zinnemann's filmmaking practice to a peripatetic form of transnationalism; a production mode he never subsequently retreated from. This is illustrated by his ensuing films *Behold a Pale Horse* (1964), set in Franco's Spain but shot in southwest France, the multi-award-winning 'British' production, *A Man For All Seasons* (1966), and various subsequent works. This transnationalism is reflected across the production of *The Sundowners*. The choice of locations illustrates a genuine attempt to represent a range of novel Australian settings alongside the geographic necessities of reining in the scope of production: Cooma, Nimmitabel and Jindabyne in the NSW Highlands, south of Sydney; Port Augusta, Hawker, Whyalla, Quorn, Iron Knob and Carriewerloo in South Australia; and the subsequent interiors shot at Elstree Studios in Borehamwood, just outside London. Like each of Zinnemann's films from the previous year's *The Nun's Story* (1959) onwards, *The Sundowners* illustrates the filmmaker's desire to move beyond a mode of production confined to California and the broader US. In this regard, *The Sundowners* is both a distinctive film and very much a reflection of dominant production methods developing at this time and fully embraced by Zinnemann.

Setting the Wheels in Motion

The Sundowners features a leisurely, almost itinerant narrative set in the mid-1920s that follows the trials, tribulations and daily activities of the Carmody family as they travel across parts of NSW and South Australia – though the actual locations are fictionalised. Although a deep sympathy between

Ida (Deborah Kerr), Paddy (Robert Mitchum) and their son Sean (Michael Anderson Jr.) is emphasised, the narrative's major conflict revolves around the characters' competing desires for and definitions of home and place. On their journeys, the Carmodys meet up with a range of characters including Rupert Venneker (Peter Ustinov), an English remittance man who becomes their travelling companion and fellow drover. Amongst the episodes of the loose narrative are various scenes set in small-town pubs, featuring brawls and various forms of gambling, a raging bushfire, the recurring temptation of a riverside farm, the pregnancy of the wife of a young shearer (John Meillon's Bluey), the difficulties confronted by a property owner's upper-class wife to adjust to life outside of the city, and the two situations that become the film's major structuring elements: the itinerant life of the shearing season and Paddy winning a racehorse in a game of two-up. The change of the horse's name from the novel's 'Our Place' to the film's 'Sundowner' marks a partial shift of focus in the adaptation away from the underlying familial tensions and onto broader conceptions of belonging and community. This is also highlighted by the film's more incorporative vision of family and community. For example, Venneker takes his leave from the family in the novel but continues to ride with them into the 'sunset' at the end of Zinnemann's film.

Like *On the Beach*, based on Nevil Shute's deflating international bestseller, *The Sundowners* represents a nuanced and faithful adaptation of its source, especially when compared with the somewhat histrionic, narratively compromised, overly melodramatic but still often affective adaptation of *Summer of the Seventeenth Doll*. *The Sundowners* was based on the fourth novel published by then US-based Australian author Jon Cleary.[1] Although Cleary continued to write popular novels until the early 2000s, *The Sundowners* was by far his most commercially successful work, becoming a significant bestseller in the US and across the world. A sign of the novel's Australian success was its weekly serialisation in *The Sydney Morning Herald* in late 1952 and its 1953 adaptation as a radio serial starring Rod Taylor. It was also selected as a 'book of the month' in the US and went on to sell several million copies worldwide. Cleary's novel has undergone numerous editions and has rightly received acclaim for its distinctive and detailed rendering of environment, situation and the Australian vernacular.

The screen rights were initially sold to US producer Joseph Kaufman as a key plank in an ambitious production slate planned in the wake of the first CinemaScope feature to be shot in Australia, *Long John Silver* (Byron Haskin, 1954), and its simultaneously made TV series (Pike and Cooper 1998: 219). The relative commercial and critical failure of *Long John Silver* quickly undermined the possibility of future film production by this company. The rights to Cleary's novel were subsequently picked up by Zinnemann at the suggestion of Oscar Hammerstein's Australian-born wife, Dorothy, around the time of the director's commercially successful, though somewhat ill-matched, adaptation of Rodgers and Hammerstein's *Oklahoma!* (1955) (Zinnemann 1992: 173).

Initial plans for Zinnemann's production started to emerge in early 1957 with the announcement of Deborah Kerr and Gary Cooper in the lead roles ('Deborah Kerr in Australian Film' 1957: 3). At this point in time, other actors such as Errol Flynn were suggested for the main supporting parts eventually taken up by Peter Ustinov and Glynis Johns (replicating the mix of British and US talent found in *Summer of the Seventeenth Doll*). At this stage, the plan was to start production in 1958, prior to Zinnemann embarking on the highly ambitious *The Nun's Story*. This earlier date would have positioned *The Sundowners* as the first of this small group of 'Australian international' films, but a range of delays, including Cooper's continued ill-health, led to production being stalled until late 1959. This delay allowed Zinnemann more time to survey potential locations, undertake significant research into period detail, contract other actors and spend time capturing footage of the landscape and the droving of sheep prior to the full production crew's arrival in October 1959.

In regard to this careful attentiveness to filming in Australia, and how it sits in pointed contrast to films such as Lewis Milestone's very opportunistic *Kangaroo* (1952), Zinnemann should be placed alongside Harry Watt, Michael Powell and even Stanley Kramer as 'sympathetic outsiders' who spent considerable time and effort to authentically capture the Australian idiom and environment. This attention to detail is reflected in the subsequent decision to send a number of the Australian actors such as Chips Rafferty and John Meillon, as well as six actual shearers, to London for the studio-shot interiors at Elstree Studios ('Six Shearers Get Film Trip to U.K.' 1960: 7). This division between location staged shooting in Australia up until mid-December 1959 and UK-based studio production in early 1960, helps place *The Sundowners* within the mainstream of transnational movie-making in this period. The combination of US, British and Australian actors and production personnel also reflects these broader practices. Nevertheless, in contrast to an expertly synthesised film like *The Shiralee* (Leslie Norman, 1957), which uses doubles, carefully disguised framing and clear demarcations between exterior and interior locations to minimise the transcontinental movement of actors, *The Sundowners* aims for a more lived-in, immersive and porous sense of space and place. This is further reflected in *The Sundowners*' core theme revolving around the notion of home as well as the decision to send a rogue's gallery of Australian actors and types to Britain to 'authentically' populate and thicken the interior scenes.

An Australian Film?

Like many of the feature films made in Australia during the quarter of a century after World War II, *The Sundowners* is a difficult work to place in relation to broader understandings of Australian and international cinema. It has many correspondences with earlier British films such as *The Overlanders* (Harry Watt, 1946) and *The Shiralee* that deal with itinerant outback life. It is also an important precursor to the distinctive focus on recessive masculinity in many of the films of the 1970s 'revival'. As Quentin Turnour has argued, *The Sundowners* has particular affinities with *Sunday Too Far Away* (Ken Hannam, 1975), a truly seminal film of the 'revival', and was even partly shot in some of the same locations, including a specific shearing shed in the South Australian town of Quorn. But as Turnour has also claimed, the two films vary in their representation of space and place as well as the ways in which character and community are situated within each: '[The] *Sundowners*' town streets, public bars and even private rooms are populated in a way no Australian film ever was' (1998: 68). Whereas *Sunday Too Far Away* is marked by a melancholy and laconic sense of solitariness and emasculation, while still giving some sense of the shearers' shared community and mateship, *The Sundowners* gives us little sense of the vast distances between places or the depopulation that defines them. For example, aside from a somewhat stunted staging of a bushfire, a potentially spectacular action set piece severely compromised by the unseasonably wet and cold weather encountered while filming these sequences in the Southern Highlands of NSW, the droving of the sheep is largely elided. The focus on back-breaking labour and the arduous repetition of work that dominates *Sunday Too Far Away* and *The Overlanders* is also little in evidence.[2] As Turnour argues, *The Sundowners* tends to over-populate both exterior and interior locations such as the shearing shed, the rowdy and crowded pubs and the main streets of towns. This crowdedness is also uncharacteristic of one of the key visual touchstones consulted in preparations for the production, the sparsely populated and haunted paintings of Russell Drysdale. But rather than seeing this as a fault, these qualities emphasise the film's and novel's distinctive focus on community, domesticity, home and family. Zinnemann claimed he was attracted to the novel as it 'had the feelings of a love story between two people who had been married a long time. I thought it was marvellous to see, for once, people who've been married for fifteen or eighteen years and stayed in love with each other under very rough circumstances' (Zinnemann in Silke 2005: 13). In this regard, the film underplays this conflict and, as clearly claimed in some of the Australian publicity appearing during production and on initial release, delivers a 'story that's heart-warming and exciting – full of the tingle of adventure and the very breath of life itself'.[3]

Like many of the films made during this period, *The Sundowners*' critical reception is often ambivalent about its representation of Australia and Australianness. Although it was generally well received within Australia and on international release, criticism was raised about the episodic and leisurely qualities of its narrative, its curious mixture of heightened realism and broad comedy, and its lack of dramatic incident and somewhat clumsy emphasis on stereotypical fauna such as kangaroos, wombats, parrots and galahs, especially in its earlier sections. The last of these elements was even highlighted in the title, 'The Sight of Green Galahs', of Sylvia Lawson's review when *The Sundowners* finally received its Australian release in December 1961 – oddly, Australia was one of the last major territories to release it, a year after its US premiere (1961: 22). Lawson's astute critique of the film in *Nation* is an important precursor to her later calls, in seminal essays such as 'Not for the Likes of Us' (Lawson 1965: 27–31), to establish a truly Australian mode of filmmaking unbeholden to the favours and whims of international film production companies and studios:

> It is horrifying – that we should have to be so touchingly grateful to Warner Brothers for giving this continent a pat on the head, for throwing a few pink galahs on the screen, for showing us ourselves, or our country cousins, in terms proper to folksy radio-serial or the domestic comic strip. Those gasps of joy were the clearest possible demonstration that we need our own film industry to show us who and what we are. (Lawson 1961: 22)

Despite such understandable criticisms, *The Sundowners* was generally praised and went on to be nominated for five Academy Awards: Best Film, Director, Adapted Screenplay, Actress and Supporting Actress. It has subsequently been singled out for the honesty and experiential emphases of its lead performances, particularly those of Kerr and Mitchum, as well as the careful attention to detail found in Zinnemann's fastidious direction and Jack Hildyard's bucolic cinematography. It is also remarkable, in the broader context of transnational film production in Australia in the 1940s, 1950s and 1960s, as a work signed by a director at the peak of his career starring actors of significant box-office allure at the time the movie was made.[4] The only comparable film is the much more sombre and explicitly self-important, *On the Beach*.

Lawson's critique does raise more important questions about the validity of the film's treatment of landscape and environment: 'One might regret more the way the outback seems to be gentled, scaled-down and tidied up. Encountering such distances, most people are challenged and altered. The landscapes could have been used with so much more intensity, they could have been images of inner space as well' (1961: 22). These criticisms are relatively inarguable, but they also misread the film's and book's intentions. Although the three central characters' lives are tough, wearing and physically difficult, the key tension in both film and novel is between different conceptions of community and home, not the faltering of these ideas against the outback's bitter isolation. In some respects, this offers a refreshing vision and even domestication of the Australian landscape that has closer affinities with the backwoods comedies and melodramas of Ken G. Hall than heightened psychological 'landscape' dramas like *Sons of Matthew* (Charles Chauvel, 1949), *Jedda* (Chauvel, 1955), *Walkabout* (Nicolas Roeg, 1971), *Wake in Fright* (Ted Kotcheff, 1971) and *Picnic at Hanging Rock* (Peter Weir, 1975). Cleary's novel does give a fuller sense of the growing bitterness and weariness of Ida, her and Sean's need to tie themselves to a more grounded conception of home, and the mindless distances travelled between gleanings of a broader communal existence, but both novel and film are ultimately triumphant portraits of the resilience of character and community. While the inner and outer conflict between the three characters *is* emphasised – and also placed into relief by the serial dalliances and romances of Venneker, the various women condensed into the single figure of Mrs Firth (Glynis Johns) in the film – there is little sense of a broader existential battle between figure and environment. Cleary's novel does present a stark reminder of the Australian landscape's hostility in the burning out of the Batemans' property, but this family's hardy response reinforces a deep connection to the land as well as the specificity of place. *The Sundowners* is a work profoundly concerned with the diurnal patterns of everyday life and the relationship of character to environment.

Lawson's critical approach to *The Sundowners* needs to be seen in the context of an emerging cultural nationalism as well as arguments for a truly 'Australian' mode of feature-film production. The film's reception in the early 1960s and beyond should also be viewed in light of the rising tide of auteurist film criticism and, more specifically, director Zinnemann's fate at the hands of influential writers like Andrew Sarris who damned him to the category of 'Less Than Meets the Eye' in his taxonomy of American cinema (1996: 168–9). Although these emerging analytical frameworks didn't have a large impact on the film's initial reception, one can sense a negative critical consensus hardening around Zinnemann in reviews by important critics like Penelope Houston in specialist film journals such as *Sight and Sound* (1960–1: 36–7). Zinnemann was one of the most respected and awarded Hollywood directors at the time of *The Sundowners*, but his subsequent critical reputation has been devalued due to what is often regarded as an overly fussy and even 'academic' focus on detail, the lack of a distinctive visual style, and a quietness, coolness and reticence with regards to the outward expression of emotion (see Horton 1997: 64).

Zinnemann himself has expressed an antipathy towards the excesses of auteurism – while still very much putting himself forward as the author of his films – emphasising his ability to adapt to a particular story, environment, collaborative team or sensibility. Nevertheless, over the last twenty years, a number of attempts have been made by fine writers such as Robert Horton and J. E. Smyth to rehabilitate Zinnemann's reputation and position him as a director with a distinctive set of thematic preoccupations (centred around notions of resistance and the relation of personal morality and ethics to broader communities) and a fastidiously attentive approach to the details of gesture, action, environment and performance (see Smyth 2014). Although *The Sundowners* is often discussed as one of Zinnemann's most successful and nuanced films, it is generally placed outside of his key works. For example, Smyth's focus on the theme of resistance, a concept that characterises Zinnemann's personal experience as a Jewish émigré with extended family in Europe along with specific films like *The Seventh Cross* (1944) and *The Nun's Story*, leaves little space for discussion of a seemingly peripheral and less outwardly personal film like *The Sundowners*. It is only when placed within the broader practice of transnational filmmaking – an approach and sensibility integral to Zinnemann's work since making the documentary drama *Redes* (*Waves*) in Mexico with Emilio Gómez Muriel and photographer Paul Strand in 1936 – that *The Sundowners* moves to the centre of his oeuvre. But *The Sundowners*' focus on 'individual conscience' (Fitzpatrick 1983: 379), personal choice and the ramifications of a specific 'philosophy of life', unbendingly expressed by Paddy through his refusal to settle down, also draw it closer to the mainstream of Zinnemann's output.

'Bush week': Travelling Back in Time

The Sundowners opens with a leisurely long shot of a horse and carriage trundling towards the camera before panning to the right to register the gentle movement of the characters through space. The opening three shots, over which the credits appear, accompanied by Dimitri Tiomkin's folksy but effective score, matter-of-factly establish location, scale, period (as a 1920s-era car passes the anachronistic horse-drawn carriage), character, pace and sensibility. There is no sense that what we are about to experience will be rushed or even tightly framed or organised, though it will have a composed and burnished pictorial beauty. Although the film's period is established in these shots and following scenes – by the car, an offhand reference to Buster Keaton, and so on – a sense of unhurried timelessness and even solipsism is established here. This sense of going back in time was central to the film's marketing to American audiences and Zinnemann's own impressions of Australia:

> I found the Australians at that time [1959] to be like the Californians in my time thirty years earlier, very simple people with a primitive, very

warm sense of humor. You couldn't call them naïve, but they were very insular. And they knew what they were about and were very honourable. (Zinnemann in Nolletti 1994: 25)

Although basking in a kind of bucolic naturalism or realism, *The Sundowners* communicates a sense of insularity from the outside world. There is little sense given of broader national or even global concerns, and the legacy of World War I, the ingrained racial policies of 'white Australia', and emerging workers' rights have little impact on the episodes and conflicts depicted. In contrast to *Sunday Too Far Away*, which was mostly set just prior to the 1956 shearers' strike, unionism and workers' rights are only briefly touched upon – in the comic scene where the shearers are chauvinistically deciding whether to take Ida on as a cook, a moment directly referenced in *Sunday Too Far Away* – and are largely discounted by the breezily utopian but highly segregated vision of gender, labour and benign management that develops at the station. Although there is space and time given to the depiction of labour and the mutually desired separation of workers and bosses, much of the daily grind of droving, shearing and life on the road is elided by the narrative's focus on stereotypical Australian elements and events such as a two-up game, further practices of gambling, horse racing, a shearing contest, numerous bouts of drinking at the pub, a young expectant mother who travels to the shearers' camp and tests the mettle of the women she finds there (all of whom rise to the task) as well as her husband. For a film aiming at the diurnal rhythms of the real life of the sundowner, it communicates little of the isolation, physical hardship and true economic deprivation that underline this existence. Unlike *The Shiralee* or *The Overlanders*, both of which are suspicious of fixed notions of community, the city and the exploitation of the land, *The Sundowners* emphasises the importance of home and the various ways it can be configured, situated and reframed.

Immediately following the credits, and after a brief set of exchanges that help situate the specific locale the characters are about to enter as well as the attitudes they hold towards it, Sean, Paddy and Ida set up camp on a riverbank overlooking the verdant spread of an idyllic farm nestled in the Southern Highlands near the Snowy Mountains. The following scenes reinforce many of the values highlighted throughout, particularly the warm sense of humour and ease of relationships between the characters. These scenes also set up the clipped, gently mocking tone of conversation, alongside the peculiarities of the Australian vernacular. Both Mitchum and Kerr manage to approximate, throughout, the modulations of the Australian accent and speech patterns, and the dialogue is peppered with distinctive slang and colloquial expressions. These include the liberal use of words and terms like 'flamin'', 'darl', 'g'day' and 'beaut', and less straightforwardly translated expressions like 'cow cockies', 'bush week' and 'shickered'. The dialogue closely follows that found in Cleary's novel and furnishes evidence of his role as a script consultant or editor instructed to reintroduce the Australian vernacular to Isobel Lennart's 'mid-Pacific' script. Cleary was plainly on set for much of the shooting as evidenced in various production stills and contemporary accounts of the filming. Although lively, affectionate and leisurely, these opening scenes establish and reinforce the carefully crafted nature of the film.

These opening passages also bring to the fore other themes, conflicts, visual preoccupations and physical relationships that will preoccupy the film. As already mentioned, *The Sundowners*' portrait of a married couple is quite remarkable and although the strength of their bond is tested by different desires and hard-won expectations, the resilience, carnality and physicality of the union is never placed in serious question. This marital bond is demonstrated in a remarkable later scene at the shearing station when Ida warns her son to not take sides against his father: 'Sean, you've got your whole life to live. We're half way through ours, your Dad and me. There's other people waitin' for you but there's no one waitin' for us except each other. Don't ever ask me to choose between you and your Dad, because I'll choose him every time.' This exchange highlights the tripartite nature of the film's narrative, its focus on the dynamic of a small, unevenly formed family, the particular journeys taken and tests faced by each of its members, as well as its matter-of-fact emphasis on generational change and the process of ageing. This is clearer in the novel, where Sean's journey from childhood to the cusp of adulthood is explicitly set up as a key narrative thread, the one mostly keenly observed by the alternative father figures (Venneker and Bluey) offered to Sean. That said, there are still significant remnants of this comparison in several of the film's exchanges, including the final parting between Bluey and Sean where the former expresses his hope that his newly born son will grow up to be like young Carmody.

Although not overemphasised in either film or novel, the passing of a particular way of life is documented and nostalgically remembered in *The Sundowners*. It is fairly clear that the Carmodys will someday need to settle down, though their home may be no less precarious than their tirelessly moving wagonette. As Venneker loquaciously states in the final passages of the novel:

> You've been on the road a long time, but I don't think you'll finish up like most sundowners. Most of them never reach the end of their road. But you will, Sean. Just keep plugging away. Never mind the disappointments you've had . . . just go your own way with your eye on what you want, and you'll get there. (Cleary 2013: 317)

There is also a grounded nostalgia for a lost time and place that is highlighted in the novel's spare dedication: '*Long Island, Sept. 1950–Aug. 1951*' (Cleary

2013: 319). This closing line, a subtly smuggled in declaration of time, place and distance, recognises the novel as a memory work written from a vastly different point in time and place. It also helps to further situate and justify the nostalgic perspective of Zinnemann's film, its potential appeal to an increasingly urbanised American and international audience, and its transnational qualities and characteristics.

Hollywood-Australian Pictures:
Men and Women; Mitchum and Kerr

Zinnemann's film also shifts further emphasis onto Ida while generally and more pointedly observing the place of women. The carnality and physicality of Ida and Paddy's marriage is established in these early scenes, somewhat crudely but efficiently introduced through a set of exchanges about Ida's backside. *The Sundowners* is clear-eyed and upfront about establishing the healthy sexual relationship between the couple. This is reinforced by the expression of a clear mutual respect and comfort between the two actors who had previously worked together on John Huston's *Heaven Knows, Mr. Allison* (1957) and co-starred in two further productions: the considerably less salubrious *The Grass is Greener* (Stanley Donen, 1960) and the TV-movie *Reunion at Fairborough* (Herbert Wise, 1985). Some reviewers found Kerr miscast as the earthy, unvarnished and confidently sexualised Ida (see P. J. D. 1961: 21). But this limited understanding of Kerr's prim star persona, pointedly dissected in Otto Preminger's *Bonjour Tristesse* (1958), discounts the sexual yearning bubbling just beneath the cloaked exterior of Sister Clodagh, her breakthrough role in *Black Narcissus* (Michael Powell and Emeric Pressburger, 1947), and forgets the harder-edged sexual frankness of her portrayal of the worldly but vulnerable Karen Holmes in Zinnemann's *From Here to Eternity* (1953). Kerr singled out her role in *The Sundowners* due to its departure from the typical characters she had previously played: 'She's a typical female really, no sentimentality at all. I haven't had a part like this before; it's quite new. Oh, I know I've played dowdy people, but the sheer physical roughness of this part is something different' (Capua 2010: 127). Kerr's performance as Ida is upfront, no-nonsense and relatively undemonstrative. She is the one who initiates sexual relations with Paddy and her desires are naturalised rather than overly erotised. They become a necessary and ritualised part of daily life – nothing more or nothing less.

The one aspect of the film that has received almost universal acclaim is Mitchum's performance. This is reflected in the sometimes-surprised contemporaneous reviews, but can be neatly summarised by the following appraisal by Mitchum's biographer, Lee Server: 'As Paddy Carmody, a living, breathing creation without a hint of artifice or theatricality, Mitchum gave perhaps the greatest demonstration of his supreme command of a naturalistic acting technique that was as rare as it was – generally – underappreciated' (2001: 352). This view of Mitchum's grounded, unfussy, laconic qualities as an actor, and how they are embodied in his performance as Paddy, was shared by both Cleary – 'Robert Mitchum is anything but a droopy-eyed slob once you get to know him. He is extremely well read and writes beautiful poetry' (Cleary in Server 2001: 350) – and Zinnemann: 'Bob is one of the finest instinctive actors in the business' (Zinnemann in Eells 1984: 221). These appreciations of Mitchum's performance sit in contrast to many reports on the film's production that highlighted the actor's demonstrable unease with the overbearing attention showered on him by a clearly star-struck Australian public and the difficulties associated with the locations used and the climate encountered. Mitchum's apparent problems on location reflected popular preconceptions of his combative star persona. This is demonstrated and somewhat questioned by the publicity interview appearing in the *Australian Women's Weekly* during production: 'When I went to see Mitchum, I expected I might find someone boorish and uncooperative, I found instead someone just the opposite – helpful, polite, and extremely intelligent' (Frizell 1959: 5). Mitchum's reputed dislike of his time in Australia was capped off by his hounding by the Australian Taxation Office in relation to his earnings on the film (Server 2001: 353).

The opening scenes set up the core theme of home and the various ways it can be defined. At this juncture, Paddy's reluctance to settle down is seen as a minor point of conflict. The characters look across the river to the idyllic farm that is evidently available for sale. But rather than this being set up as a contrast between the sedentariness of the farm beckoning across the ceaselessly flowing river and the itinerant lifestyle of the sundowners, we are shown, instead, two different ideas of home and community. Paddy's flight from the financial burden of a mortgage and the spatial restrictiveness of a bordered property is not a retreat from his family, his responsibilities or the concept of home. Home for him is the camp the three of them set up every night and that dominates the film much more than their itinerant life on the road. There are also things to commend, particularly from a contemporary environmental viewpoint, about Paddy's refreshing desire to only ever tread lightly on the land. For a film about characters who supposedly live their lives on the road between sunrise and sundown, *The Sundowners* spends an awful lot of time in camp, in town or with its characters gathered together in conversation. As Paddy openly suggests, their home *is* the landscape.

As we have emphasised throughout this chapter, *The Sundowners* is a transnational film that aims to address a wide potential audience and meet its narrative expectations. This is reinforced, of course, by the decisions made to cast internationally recognised American and British actors in the main roles (and only Ustinov's Venneker matches the nationality of character and actor). The film also contains elements that are reminiscent of the western and specific domestic frontier films like *Friendly Persuasion* (William Wyler, 1956). But *The Sundowners* exploits its exoticism as a rendering of the under-represented landscape. The initial moments do not provide a clichéd or even particularly characteristic image of this Australian landscape – the environment is largely green and shot in the mountain areas of NSW around Jindabyne – and the use of the Australian vernacular is evident but not overly pronounced or self-consciously explained. But such stereotypical images and sounds do start to creep in, though they are largely isolated to the earlier scenes. The decision to string together a series of shots of birdlife including cockatoos, galahs and kookaburras, soon to be followed by kangaroos, koalas and wombats either mixing with the sheep or fleeing a raging bushfire, self-consciously addresses the desire to distinguish and exploit the identifiable local fauna. But unlike *Kangaroo*, for instance, this does not extend to the Indigenous owners of the land. Aboriginal characters are largely absent from *The Sundowners* and only appear briefly when bringing the sheep into the shed or interacting with each other in the background of shots at the shearing station. This is both a strength and a weakness. These isolated and unheard figures are 'normalised' and not exoticised, but there is also no curiosity towards these 'backgrounded' characters. This stands in, largely grateful, contrast to the earlier *Kangaroo*. Although the early shots of various Australian animals and habitats suggest that *The Sundowners* will wearily display a cornucopia of stereotypical Australian elements and icons, these clear markers of nationality, origin and place are de-emphasised in the film's later sections.

A 'RICH LUSTY LIFE YOU'VE NEVER KNOWN BEFORE': SELLING *THE SUNDOWNERS*

The true novelty of filming in Australia was highlighted in the film's marketing, along with the personas of its various stars, its appeal to character-based realism and Zinnemann's track record as a director of highly awarded films sometimes shot in exotic or at least 'foreign' locations (such as Hawaii for *From Here to Eternity* and the Belgian Congo for *The Nun's Story*). This somewhat muddled collection of selling points can be traced back to the theatrical trailer. In a very noticeable American accent, the voiceover opens by proclaiming: 'This is down under, the fascinating continent of Australia. And these people [accompanied by brief shots of Kerr, Mitchum and Johns] are of that rare breed you'll find nowhere else: the sundowners'. Elsewhere, the novelty of the setting is explicitly emphasised: an 'untold story of a new kind of people ... [a] new kind of motion picture experience'. This way of promoting the film highlights the uncommonness of its setting and the diurnal rhythms of its tight-lipped, laconic drama. Although the epic nature of its setting and narrative is emphasised here and in the main US release poster, this claim that it provides a 'new kind of motion picture experience' also prepares audiences for the peripatetic journey of its characters and the 'drama' of their daily existence. Kerr has suggested that part of the reason for the film's relative failure at the US box office was its prescience in terms of this dramatic emphasis – though these elements did not stop the film achieving significant box-office returns in Britain and Australia. In this respect, Kerr compares *The Sundowners* to the emerging European art cinema of its era as well as the more episodic and de-dramatised Hollywood movies that appeared in the mid-to-late 1960s: 'It was a little before its time. It was a no-story movie – an observation of life, with a marvellous cast' (Kerr in Braun 1977: 175).

This brings us back, though through a more positive frame, to the 'gentled, scaled-down and tidied up' outback landscape opined by Lawson (1961: 22). This is the personalised realm that the film unapologetically deals in. A great illustration of this dramatic economy is found in its most remarked-upon scene. For instance, the highly enthusiastic reviewer for *Variety* hyperbolically called it a 'fleetingly eloquent scene at a train station ... that ranks as one of the most memorable moments ever to cross a screen' (Tube 1960: 6). This brief moment features an exchange of furtive glances between Ida, grimy faced and perched on a wagon, and an elegantly dressed woman travelling to the city, or a larger town, on a train. The novel's original dialogue exchange covering several pages is transformed into a simple contrast between the costume, situation, spatial confinement and mode of transport of these two never-introduced characters. It is very difficult to read the response of the woman on the train to Ida's studied gaze or to her appearance, but Kerr gives a wonderfully subtle expression of both defiance and extreme longing. It is as if she sees the memory of another kind of life pass by.

While the trailer introduces each character in terms of the physical sensation they will generate in the audience – 'You'll bask at the warmth of Ida. With all that beauty under a coat of dust' – it also highlights the novelty of the physical environment we will experience: 'for two unforgettable hours you'll go along with *The Sundowners*, living a rich lusty life you've never known before'. The trailer's tone and mode of address suggest that the studio and the filmmakers were fully aware of the experiential and immersive portrait they had on their hands. The trailer does show us some of the scenes featuring local flora and fauna, but it also emphasises the naturalistic and physical relationships between the characters: 'Glowing with the flavour and excitement of special people and real passions.' In its understandable attempt to appeal to both male and female audiences, the trailer concludes with superimposed titlecards riding roughshod over the subtler dimensions of the film's careful staging, plotting and even promotion: 'For every man who ever wanted to wander and every girl who wanted to follow him ... until she could pin him down ... this is the motion picture!'

These overly dramatic and clichéd elements are equally emphasised by the film's key US release poster. This highly synthetic image combines multiple shots of incidents from the narrative against the background of the shooting flames of a bushfire. The poster also highlights the erotic and sexual nature of Kerr's character and the actor's broader star persona (she is shown in bed and wearing a slip in two of the separate images that make up this collage, a somewhat unrepresentative vision of her character). Meanwhile, the hyperbolic lead tagline is not afraid to overstate the drama of the narrative or the felt distance that the characters travel: 'HERE COME "THE SUNDOWNERS"! They're real people, fun people, fervent people. They have a tremendous urge to keep breathing. Their rousing story comes roaring across six thousand miles of excitement....' We guess this was indeed a welcome contrast to those films that featured characters who didn't 'have a tremendous urge to keep breathing'. Though, perhaps, that was a genuine point of appeal after the creeping nuclear annihilation of the previous year's *On the Beach*.

An 'untold story of a new kind of people'

Although *The Sundowners* features familiar and even clichéd flora and fauna, landscapes, character types, colloquial expressions and slang, it is still not commonly regarded as a key work of Australian national cinema. For example, in his survey of the sparsely populated terrain of Australian feature filmmaking between 1930 and 1960, Bruce Molloy offhandedly devotes just half a paragraph to Zinnemann's film, merely claiming it 'ranks as one of the more successful attempts by foreign filmmakers at evoking a genuinely Australian atmosphere, possibly due to its setting in the bush ... and to its concern with distinctively Australian occupations such as droving and shearing' (1990: 38). In contrast to other significant international productions of the postwar era such as *The Overlanders*, *Bitter Springs* (Ralph Smart, 1950), *They're a Weird Mob* and *Wake in Fright*, *The Sundowners* is considerably more reserved in its exploration of national character, identity and the drama of the Australian landscape. It stands as a genuinely mature and transnational film that draws significantly upon the expertise of American, British and Australian personnel and reflects dominant trends in large-scale international production at the time it was made. As is evident from its somewhat schizophrenic marketing campaign, it was and has been a difficult film to place within broader understandings of Australian and international cinema. Promoted as portraying 'a rich lusty life you've never known before', it is equally remarkable for its sympathetic depiction of the rhythms of everyday life and the 'tremendously good-natured' quietness of its narrative and central performances (Bennett

1961: 11). Although it is highly responsive to the essence of environment, situation and character, it also works hard to universalise these localised elements while respecting the special demands placed upon it by Australian audiences. *The Sundowners* reflects the care and attention to detail characteristic of Zinnemann's internationally focused and produced work, but still sits a little precariously between the demands of international and national cinema. As Graham Shirley and Brian Adams matter-of-factly claim about this balancing act: 'With *The Sundowners* . . . came a worthy successor to *The Overlanders* as a visitor's film that captured some genuine national sentiment without appearing to overreach itself' (1989: 208). These are qualities that we should not undervalue.

NOTES

1. Cleary worked on the scripts of *The Sundowners* and *The Siege of Pinchgut*. A large part of his role on *The Sundowners* was to reintroduce the distinctively Australian atmosphere and laconic dialogue to the shooting script. The sole-credited scriptwriter, Isobel Lennart, had downplayed these elements in her adaptation (Cleary 2013: xi).
2. The bushfire has a more devastating effect in Cleary's novel. On their travels, the Carmodys visit with another family, the Batemans, whose property is subsequently burned out by the bushfire. This traumatic event, and what it communicates about the harshness of the Australian landscape and human claims to it, does not carry over to the film.
3. This tagline was used to promote *The Sundowners* in some of the Australian newspaper advertising appearing on first release.
4. Though it should be noted that neither Kerr nor Mitchum were ever listed amongst the top ten Hollywood stars in terms of box office, they both featured in a large number of commercially successful films and sustained A-list careers for significant stretches of time.

6. THE DRIFTING AVENGER (1968)

Toei, Nikkatsu and Toho Down Under

Despite vociferous calls for increased support to the Australian film industry by practitioners, cultural commentators and some politicians, 1968 and 1969 were still largely fallow years for local feature-film production (see, for example, Thornhill 1985: 166–70). Of the eight features made across these two years, none made a significant impact at the Australian box office, though *You Can't See 'Round Corners* (David Cahill, 1969), *Age of Consent* (Michael Powell, 1969) and *The Intruders* (Lee Robinson, 1969), a quickly made attempt to exploit the phenomenal recent international success of the television series *Skippy the Bush Kangaroo*,[1] featuring almost all of the same personnel in front of and behind the camera, did well in specific locations.[2] Aside from, arguably, *Age of Consent*, which was also the biggest commercial success of this ragtag group, none of these 'local' productions left a lasting impression on Australian audiences or its national cinema.

The most intriguing and surprising 'Australian' films made across these two years were stand-alone productions completed by three different major Japanese studios (in the order of their completion: Toei Company, Nikkatsu Corporation and Toho Co.) and exploiting their host country's natural resources, locations and filmmaking facilities. News of this surprising spate of regionally specific international production emerged in early 1968 when the Sydney press announced that 'A MAJOR Japanese film company plans to shoot a $200,000 colour movie in Australia this autumn', exploiting the backdrop of 'the search for Bass Strait oil' ('Bass Strait Oil Hunt Inspires a Japanese Film' 1968: 6). It would feature 'an Australian female lead' and was plainly aimed at highlighting Australia's mineral wealth, a core platform of the emerging cultural, geopolitical and economic relationship between the two countries ('Bass Strait Oil Hunt Inspires a Japanese Film' 1968: 6). It was to be made by Nikkatsu, Japan's oldest major film studio. The finished movie ultimately shifted its focus to a young advertising illustrator who comes to Sydney, Newcastle, the area around Tamworth in northern New South Wales and, as originally planned, Fiji, seeking inspiration for the tourism campaign he is contracted to work upon.

A seemingly perfect combination of the whirlwind, dynamic, '"borderless action" (*mukokuseki akushon*)' movies Nikkatsu was noted for (Schilling 2007: 7), and a set of exotic locations very distinct from those found in Japan, production on *Moeru tairiku* (*Blazing Continent*, Shogoro Nishimura, 1968) was stalled. Initially slated to start filming in mid-April, after a four-month hiatus its key settings and story changed, but not its title nor star (Tetsuya Watari). This allowed another studio, the famously economical Toei, to be the first to complete and release a Japanese-produced film shot almost entirely in Australia: *Koya no toseinin* (*The Drifting Avenger*, Junya Sato, 1968). According to Joseph L. Anderson and Donald Richie, Toei concentrated on juvenile-oriented period drama and modern thrillers for children and rural audiences (1982: 260). This, along with its very robust 104 films a year production slate, routinely low budgets, integration and hybridisation of 'Hollywood's formulas' (Kitamura 2020: 526), industry-leading shift to widescreen in the mid-to-late 1950s and control of a vast array of cinemas, accounted for its postwar 'rise to power and fortune' (Anderson and Richie 1982: 420).

In many ways a highly conventional western shot in the New England area of northern New South Wales, filmed largely in English but subsequently dubbed into Japanese, and located in an understandably ill-defined period and American West setting sometime after the conclusion of the US Civil War (1865) and the start of the Meiji Restoration (1868), *The Drifting Avenger* leaned heavily on the seasoned expertise of its fifty-strong Japanese production crew, various Sydney-based suppliers of equipment, workers and facilities, and a mostly Australian cast. The production also received significant local support from around the central location of Nundle, a small town approximately 50 kilometres southeast of the regional centre of Tamworth and about 400 kilometres from Sydney. Astonishingly, *The Drifting Avenger* was released into Japanese cinemas in mid-June 1968, less than two months after filming had commenced.

Blazing Continent was subsequently filmed in the late Australian winter of 1968 before being released on 14 December of the same year ('*Blazing*

Continent' 1969: 14). The budget for this production was reported at approximately 200 million yen, commonly converted to around AU$200,000 (see 'Another Film Here by Japs' 1968: 33). Although considerably more ambitious in its use of diverse and widely dispersed locations, its limited budget and over-extended mode of production are clearly evident in the finished film's incoherent coverage of various scenes and the often wild transitions between one moment and another.

The third and final film, *Nyu jirando no wakadaisho* (*Young Guy on Mt. Cook*, Jun Fukuda, 1969), was, as its title clearly indicates, a less geographically contained movie produced by Toho, and is rarely mentioned in any discussion of this small group of films. It has almost no place in the writing about Australian cinema more generally, even that focused on international location-based production. A key exception is Andrew Pike's well-researched early account of the production of all three films (1971: 15). This was the first time that these movies received substantive discussion in Australia beyond fairly generalised and often inaccurate press reports. But even Pike's article only devotes a couple of short paragraphs to this final film. An entry into a long-running series featuring the 'young guy' of the title travelling across an array of exotic foreign locations, it was partly shot in Australia with more substantive filming undertaken in New Zealand and elsewhere. *Young Guy on Mt. Cook* (it is also sometimes called *Young Guy in New Zealand*) was released in Japan on 12 July 1969, but there is no evidence of any Antipodean screenings. This broadly defined and varied series of youth movies (*seishun eiga*) extended across multiple episodes between the early 1960s and the early 1980s.

'For the first time, a samurai western filmed in Australia': Japanese International Pictures

It is difficult to fully determine – beyond an apparent openness to overseas production by various Australian governments – why three different Japanese studios independently moved into location-based film production in Australia across a very short period of time. Although it was suggested that these would be the first of a larger slate of Australia-shot Japanese movies, no more were subsequently made.[3] None of the three has ever been screened commercially in Australia, though *The Drifting Avenger* was shown on television in the late 1970s, and repertory screenings of the first two films have occurred very occasionally across the last thirty years.[4] They did also receive very limited international releases in places with significant ethnic Japanese populations, like Hawaii. When shown in Honolulu in mid-1969, *The Drifting Avenger* was promoted in the following way: 'FOR THE FIRST TIME, A SAMURAI WESTERN FILMED IN AUSTRALIA'; an emphasis on novel filming location, the hybridisation of genre and firstness that was not stressed for the Japanese release, where the 'Americanness' of the setting and story was the more remarkable and promotable feature. Promotion in the US and Japan also highlighted the Australian stars of the film, all of whom were only recognisable within Australia and, even there, had only received limited exposure on radio and television. For example, the trailer for the Japanese release introduces J. Roberts, K. Cooney, K. Goodlet, R. Lea and J. Sherwood as if this would actually mean something to audiences. Of these, only Ken Goodlet had a substantial career in film and television, though Judith Roberts and John Sherwood did appear in a number of other productions. Several news stories in the Australian press did speak of the favourable conditions for production facilitated by national, state and local authorities at the time, and, at least in the case of *The Drifting Avenger* and to a lesser extent *Blazing Continent*, the secondment of highly professionalised but underemployed local production facilities such as Ajax Films and Supreme Sound in Sydney.

These three films also need to be placed in the broader context of Japanese film production during this time. Although feature-film exhibition and distribution reached a peak in Japan in the late 1950s and early 1960s with the release of over 500 titles per year, the introduction of television and other factors had a massive impact on cinema attendances and, ultimately, on the production and financing of films (Yomota 2019: 163). For instance, between 1958 and 1963 cinema attendances in Japan dropped vertiginously by almost half (Yomota 2019: 127). By the late 1960s, several of the major studios – as was also true in Hollywood at the same time – were facing bankruptcy, a fate accentuated by the high levels of vertical integration found across the industry.[5] These Australia-shot films should also be examined in relation to a broader tendency throughout the 1960s for shooting to take place in a wide variety of locations outside of the studio, both around regional Japan and in various international settings. In a crowded market, and within a still highly efficient but financially straitened and unsustainable system of filmmaking, this was one means of attempting to differentiate film products from those made for television.

All three films are very different in terms of the ways in which they represent and interact with these international or 'foreign' locations. For example, *Blazing Continent* is preoccupied with showcasing and swiftly transitioning between a wide array of different environments, from outback Australia to modern, night-time Tokyo, from a strikingly modernist and bustling Sydney to the 'kitsch' touristic locales of Fiji, from the industrial port-scape of Newcastle to the rolling, bucolic New England countryside. The often incoherent story, characterisation and mash-up of genres and performance styles is largely an outcome of these globetrotting demands as well as the overriding style and form of Nikkatsu's 'borderless action' movies, as mentioned previously. In this respect, the nevertheless inferior *Blazing Continent* has much in common with the contemporaneous work of the now widely celebrated Nikkatsu director, Seijun Suzuki. It also features major roles for two of the stars – Tetsuya Watari and Chieko Matsubara – of one of Suzuki's most admired and visually striking crime movies, *Tokyo nagaremono* (*Tokyo Drifter*, 1966).[6]

The Drifting Avenger sustains a considerably more coherent sense of place than *Blazing Continent*, despite it being set in one country while being filmed in another. But it is this broader practice of 'locationism' that is central to the place of all of these films within Australian, Japanese *and* transnational cinema more broadly (see Cunningham 1991: 162). As Olivia Khoo has argued, in the only previous substantive account of the film written in English, although *The Drifting Avenger* 'might be considered international, in the sense that it can travel and translate, it is not *global*, that is, homogeneous and non-specific through its setting or location' (2010: 233). When watching *The Drifting Avenger* we routinely accept its simulation of the American West, its place within the international circulation and practices of adaptation characteristic of its genre, but also its setting within a very distinctive and identifiable Australian landscape. Though it can be seen as symptomatic of a 'borderlessness' characteristic of globalisation, the marks of translation, adaptation and textual accommodation, as well as the specific material conditions of the film's production, are everywhere evident. For example, in an early scene detailing the central character's inculcation into the ways of the gunslinger, a coin is tossed into the air for target practice. As a close-up fills the 'scope frame we can clearly see that it is a penny from the reign of King George VI (1936–52). If we recognise the origin and era of this currency, coined in Australia in the 1930s or 1940s, we are immediately alerted to the mixed origins of the film we are watching, as well as a degree of carelessness in relation to questions of authenticity. Of particular note in this regard are the various ways *The Drifting Avenger* combines the generic accoutrements and story events of the western – bar-room brawls, a simple revenge narrative, gunfights, a cattle stampede, the relationship between a master and a younger protégé, the core elements of costuming including ten-gallon hats, gun belts, chaps, and so on – with 'out-of-place' flora and a melange of American, Australian, transatlantic and Japanese accents. Of course, these variations in accent are only evident when watching the English-language release. The Japanese version dubs all of the characters into the local language, erasing (but also reinforcing at particular moments) this aspect of the film's practices of hybridisation. In the process, *The Drifting Avenger* plays equally as a generic but 'genuine' western, a minor samurai variation, and a Cobb & Co.-style simulation.[7]

As we will further argue later in this chapter, these qualities also position *The Drifting Avenger* clearly within the overwhelmingly impure economy of the international western in this period, a form that incorporates, amongst others, 'spaghetti', 'paella', 'sauerkraut', 'borscht' and 'noodle' variations (that is, culturally stereotypical food types that signpost westerns of Italian, Spanish, German, Eastern European and Asian origins). The use of Australia to stand in for the US in *The Drifting Avenger* also parallels Italian productions shot in Spain but set in the US or Mexico. Even a passing knowledge of the broad scope of westerns produced throughout the 1960s and beyond must recognise the capacity for global audiences to successfully negotiate multiple local and regional variations upon this ubiquitous genre across languages, locations, iconography, narrative conventions, histories and even ideologies. An interesting instance of this is Nikkatsu's nine-film Wataridori (Wanderer) series. It was produced between 1959 and 1962 and placed a conventionally attired singing cowboy within a range of contemporary regional contexts and conflicts in Japan. This popular figure illustrates the capacity of Japanese audiences to read, integrate and accept particular and sometimes isolated conventions and iconographies of the western across and within a range of other genres, contexts, periods, narrative forms and settings.

Emerging Allies and Lingering Stereotypes: Japan-Australia Relations in the 1960s

The production of these three films should also be discussed in relation to the broader history of Australia-Japan relations. At the time they were produced, the draconian and explicitly racist White Australia Policy was still in operation. Although its application was, by this time, significantly tempered, it would not be fully dismantled until 1973.[8] World War II had also only concluded a little over twenty years earlier. Of course, relations between Japan and Australia developed significantly after the war, fuelled by the Allied Powers' occupation between 1945 and 1952, the common adversary of communism they faced throughout the Cold War, the increased availability and commercial success of Japanese cultural and consumer products in Australia including anime (*Astro Boy*, *Kimba the White Lion*, and so on), arthouse films, toys, household appliances, Toho monster movies and *The Samurai* TV series. The substantial exportation of Australian mineral resources and primary produce to Japan is also central.

But there was still a significant level of distrust, misunderstanding and condescension that existed between the two countries. This mindset, and even openly expressed conflict, is reflected in some of the press reports covering the production of the first two films. For example, under the headline '*Blazing Continent* is Real Hot Stuff', a reporter from the *The Sydney Morning Herald* filed a condescending review of the film's shooting script, pointing out various nonsensical scenes and language contained within it such as: 'A half-blooded high-teen boy sitting on an empty case only a few steps away from the fruiterer's [sic] playing a guitar. The town is so quiet that that sound is heard clearly. The music being played is Waltzing Matilder [sic]'; and 'A sandstorm then blows him over. A helicopter and flying doctor come to the unconscious hero's rescue. He makes up in "Melbourne"' (Frizell 1968a: 6). The reporter concludes her story by adding that she hopes nothing is altered when this illogical script finally makes it to the screen. As with many other reports filed in the Australian press across 1968, this story reveals an obstinate lack of interest in the actual content and form of these Japanese film productions. This article also fails to concede that the writer is discussing a very rudimentary English translation of a Japanese script. Unlike *The Drifting Avenger*, *Blazing Continent* features few significant non-Japanese roles and was filmed almost entirely in Japanese.

An equally Orientalist perspective is taken up by Nan Musgrove, a writer for the *Australian Women's Weekly*, when reporting on the press conference that preceded filming of *The Drifting Avenger*. Complaining about the paltriness of the snacks on offer, and the smallness of the press contingent gathered for the announcement, she then outlines various other details of the event including the 'good, white teeth and long-fingered, narrow hands' of actor Ken Takakura: 'an elegant man ... [who] wore an elegant wristwatch and cufflinks' (Musgrove 1968: 4). Although this report does include some useful information about the scale of the production, where it will be filmed, the studio that was making it – in fact, it is surprisingly accurate in this regard – and the wearying stupidity of many of the questions posed by other reporters (about whether the movie will feature any kangaroos, gumtrees, Australian accents, and so on), it still retreads racist stereotypes of supposed Japanese inscrutability. Nevertheless, one of the important pieces of information it does reveal is that a key shooting location was to be Goonoo Goonoo Station, a setting previously used in Ken G. Hall's seminal but stridently eugenicist nationalistic epic, *The Squatter's Daughter* (1933). A story of rival sheep stations, *The Squatter's Daughter* troublingly narrativises and splices together concepts of 'pure breeding', 'natural' selection *and* nation building. If nothing else, there is some poetic justice in seeing this iconic location relocated – as seen through the gaze and expert actions of a highly professionalised Japanese film crew – to another continent.

Samurais, Cowboys and Gumtrees

The inherent imperialism and even colonialism that characterises many international or transnational productions is, as suggested earlier, both reinforced and questioned by the complex interweaving of the general and the specific, generic 'no places' and very particular locations across these three films. But *The Drifting Avenger* is also fascinating for its use of Australia as a *location* as well as a site of cultural appropriation. These qualities relate to a more widespread Japanese practice of producing and consuming what are sometimes seen as 'culturally odourless' texts carefully tailored to travel across borders and boundaries while erasing or minimising identifiable features (such as audiovisual typologies of race), sources or origins; this is a characteristic that is particularly evident in anime like *Astro Boy*, *Kokaku kidotai* (*Ghost in the Shell*, Mamoru Oshii, 1995) and some of the films made by Studio Ghibli, particularly those that adapt Western sources (Khoo 2010: 234). But the significance of *The Drifting Avenger* lies in how it dramatises this narrative of cultural appropriation and adaptation through the story of a young Japanese American who retrains his body and mind to become a western gunslinger in order to mete out revenge. The abrupt reappearance of a samurai sword at intermittent points in the narrative acts as a synecdoche for how this character will adapt to his environment and its cultural practices while still drawing upon ancient and inherited cultural traditions.

The Drifting Avenger opens with a zoom out to a stagecoach recklessly careening through the (Australian) landscape. This opening scene also introduces us to the film's protagonist toiling in the fields as the stagecoach passes by, before swiftly transitioning into one of its many action set pieces as Ken (Ken Takakura) reacts quickly in order to bring the stagecoach under control. This scene is also a harbinger of the violence that will unfold as Ken discovers that everyone aboard the stagecoach has been murdered; knowledge that will seal the fate of his own family when the killers arrive at his home. Over the next three years, Ken sets out to avenge his parents' deaths, relentlessly tracking down each member of the gang. He also befriends an older professional (Marvin played by Ken Goodlet) who tutors him in the arts of gunplay (and is, coincidentally, the father of one of the outlaws he is tracking), as well as the wife (Judith Roberts as Rosa) and child (Kevin Cooney as Mike) of the gang's leader.

This basic plot situates *The Drifting Avenger* solidly within the tradition of the revenge western, a form that was particularly dominant in Hollywood in the 1950s across, for example, such actor-director collaborations as those between James Stewart and Anthony Mann (for example, *The Naked Spur* [1953]) and Randolph Scott and Budd Boetticher (for example, *Ride Lonesome* [1958]). But it is also a defining narrative component of the contemporaneous spaghetti western. The soundtrack reinforces this set of allegiances and antecedents by drawing on Japanese, American and Italian musical styles and instrumentation. The film also relies upon other key narrative conventions of the genre including the burgeoning but complicated relationship between an aged professional and the younger protégé he takes under his wing. It also dramatises the hard work Ken undertakes to change his appearance – the credit sequence features him trying on the conventional attire of the genre – and radically improve his abilities with a gun.

The film's second half deals with the complications that arise when Ken becomes attracted to the wife and then widow of the leader of the gang, as well as the conflicted emotions then felt by her young son. This ultimately leads to an explicit reworking of the concluding scene of George Stevens' *Shane* (1953), as Mike calls out for Ken to 'come back'. But despite Ken's self-evident 'otherness' in appearance, not much attention is actually paid to his ethnicity. His ancestry is mainly drawn upon in an early scene between Ken and his father, in which the latter explains how he came to settle in the US before outlining the traditional values associated with the figure of the samurai. Further direct reference to Ken's Japanese origins is chiefly restricted to his intermittent use of a samurai sword, as mentioned earlier. But it is only at the conclusion of his quest that he reverts to this more ritualistic and traditional form of combat. Nevertheless, as Khoo has claimed, what 'remains invisible' in *The Drifting Avenger* is indeed 'Ken's otherness'. Ken is 'not represented by any of the stereotypes generally associated with (diasporic) Asian masculinities . . . In fact, he is not recognized (or recognizable) at all' (Khoo 2010: 239). But this is, of course, a matter of perspective. Within the context of a Japanese western shot in Australia in the late 1960s but set in the US in the second half of the nineteenth century and made for local consumption, Ken's 'otherness' is perhaps not much of a consideration at all.

The Drifting Avenger is both an idiosyncratic exception to, and a blatant inheritor of, a broader set of filmmaking practices and tastes. As Stephen Teo argues, '[t]he Western is a popular genre that is produced in all the major Asian film industries', including those of Japan and Australia (2017: 1). As Meaghan Morris also claims, the 'regionally dominant cinema in the 1960s was Japanese', and the western genre – or variations upon it – represented a recognisable and marketable form to sell to these diverse Asian audiences (2004: 245). The careful mixing together of the conventions of the American western with partly Japanese (and more broadly Asian) themes focusing on the moral and communal codes of loyalty, fidelity and family is also significant here. As Hiroshi Kitamura argues,

> this 'learning' from the US Western did not come to mean the blind consumption of 'foreign' behaviours. Japanese viewers often associated the social practices of American frontiersmen with values of their own, such as the notion of 'obligation and human feeling' (*giri ninjo*) – a common trope in Japanese period dramas (*jidaigeki*). (2020: 520)

The western itself was very popular in Japan before and after World War II. For example, John Ford's *Stagecoach* (1939) 'was [finally] released in 1951 and was the fourth most successful foreign film that year', reflecting a pattern of restricted and delayed releases heavily controlled by the Central Motion

Picture Exchange administered by the occupying forces (Raine 2019: 130). In part, according to Kitamura, the western also tapped into 'a cultural longing for a distant "Japanese past"' that also 'invoked a sense of *furusato* [homeland] that seemed to disappear in the face of modernisation' (2020: 518–19). Therefore, the popularity of the western and its many Japanese variants and hybrids partly reflects a nostalgia for a time before rapid economic growth and industrialisation and exploits an ongoing fascination with the frontiers of regional Japan (particularly Hokkaido). Japanese films made within or influenced by the genre also reflected local variations in the timing of release for specific westerns and the sustained popularity of singing cowboys such as Roy Rogers on Japanese television. Aside from *Stagecoach*, five other Hollywood westerns also appeared in the top ten in 1951. This popularity was still evident sometime after the Occupation ended, with the genre 'taking the top three slots in 1959 (with *Rio Bravo* at number one) and placing three more films in the 1960 top ten. Even though Hollywood's market share was in decline at the end of the 1950s, westerns were surging' (Raine 2019: 130). This was further reinforced by the success of American westerns on Japanese television from 1956, the production of numerous local variations on the genre and the direct influence of several key samurai films – such as Akira Kurosawa's *Shichinin no samurai* (*Seven Samurai*, 1954) and *Yojinbo* (*Yojimbo*, 1961) – back upon American and Italian westerns made in the early-to-mid-1960s. For example, *Seven Samurai* was famously remade as *The Magnificent Seven* (John Sturges, 1960) and *Yojimbo* was the uncredited source for Sergio Leone's *Per un pugno di dollari* (*A Fistful of Dollars*, 1964). In turn, many of these samurai films were themselves significantly influenced by the American western.

Local production of westerns, generally shot in regional Japan, often set in contemporary times and fused together with elements of the yakuza film, also reached a peak in the early 1960s with, as mentioned earlier, the production of the Wataridori series. Featuring Akira Kobayashi as a wandering singing cowboy, these films were 'modelled on Hollywood Westerns, right down to Akira's guitar, boots, fringes and horse', but generally transferred their narratives to a modern Japan that 'resembled, in its wider reaches, the mountains and plains of the Old West' (Schilling 2007: 16–17). Alongside this series, which often featured the wandering protagonist protecting the interests and rights of villagers and Indigenous inhabitants, and assayed themes of loyalty and fidelity, a considerable number of other Japanese westerns were filmed elsewhere in Asia and in places such as Mexico. An illustrative example of this practice is Koreyoshi Kurahara's *Mekishiku mushuku* (*Mexico Wanderer*, 1962).

'Japan rolling oater on Aussie location': Making *The Drifting Avenger*

Nevertheless, the production of *The Drifting Avenger* in Australia was still unprecedented, particularly in a country where few Japanese films were released or even known of and which did not have a significant homegrown feature-film industry. The amazement expressed by local commentators at the seeming anomaly of a Japanese film studio making a US-set western in Australia, largely for its own audience, but with some ambitions for wider release, was therefore hardly surprising. Locations were scouted in early April 1968: 'Director Junya Sato is now surveying rural Aussie locations. Two assistant directors, Hisashi Yabe and Shinji Sawai, are handling additional production details with three local studios . . .' ('Japan Rolling Oater on Aussie Location' 1968: 30). Amongst other things, arrangements were made for the shooting of several action scenes including 'a stampede by 1,000 cattle on the property, Goonoo Goonoo' ('Wild West – By Japanese' 1968: 3). Though it should be added that, onscreen, the cattle stampede appears to be of a significantly smaller scale than that announced in this report. The metropolitan Australian press did not report on the film's imminent production until mid-April 1968, and the filming itself was mainly undertaken in rural locations far from the beat of most reporters. Production commenced on 29 April and location shooting in Australia was completed by 21 May. Beyond some unfulfilled ambitions for future production and the smooth facilitation of filmmaking in the chosen locations, Toei wasn't overly concerned with enchanting or even informing the broader Australian public or potential audiences.

The cast itself featured only two Japan-based actors, the star Ken Takakura and US-born child actor, Kevin Cooney. Takakura was a major box-office draw at this point in time. He starred in a further nine features that were released in 1968 and went on to appear in Hollywood movies like *Too Late the Hero* (Robert Aldrich, 1970). The production also relied heavily on the participation of the local community, as is evidenced by the wide ranging access attained by the crew to varied locations including assorted homesteads and the main street and buildings of Nundle. In fact, although the production added various period and genre trappings to these buildings (such as bat doors for the saloon) and the town's streetscape (hiding its bitumen road with layers of gravel), little effort was made to disguise the town's true identity, with many of the featured buildings and businesses still including the name 'Nundle' in their signage. As we argued earlier, this is characteristic of a synthetic or schizophrenic filmmaking practice that attempted to partly disguise the actual locations being used while, at the same time, noting or flaunting their provenance. This somewhat contradictory use of Australian locations is supported by comments made by Sato about the key reasons they decided to shoot the film in Australia: 'Australia's regulations are the easiest and there seemed to be some similarities between Australians and Americans . . . There were also the landscape and the climate and both countries were settled by cattlemen, drovers, cowboys . . . In Japan there are not enough cowboys' ('Japanese Oater Ready to Roll on NSW Locations' 1968: 3).

Filming in Australia was completed on a tight three-week schedule, with further interiors shot at studios in Tokyo and involving nine of the Australian cast (O'Brien 1968: 56). Remarkably, *The Drifting Avenger* was released into Japanese cinemas on 15 June, less than four weeks after filming in Australia had completed (see '*Drifting Avenger*' 1968: 24). This brief window after the conclusion of Australian location shooting incorporated the filming of various interior dialogue and some action scenes, dubbing of the soundtrack into Japanese, the editing of the entire film, the striking of prints and other post-production requirements. At a length of 107 minutes, *The Drifting Avenger* is plainly designed as an 'A' feature and only in some moments does it fully betray its overly rushed production schedule, particularly compared to other Japanese studio films of the time. Its streamlined, if highly generic qualities are testament to the skills and highly professional, efficient filmmaking techniques of its widely experienced production crew.

Although self-evidently a Japanese production shot in Australia, *The Drifting Avenger* does also embrace some qualities of co- or transnational production. For example, Toei worked closely with three Sydney-based production companies: Ajax Films, Artransa Park Studios and Supreme Sound. They also employed an Australian production manager, Roland Litchfield, to coordinate the contributions of these three companies and help negotiate and work with local communities and authorities. In a report published in *The Sydney Morning Herald* immediately after the completion of filming in New South Wales, Litchfield speaks very positively about the experience of working with the seasoned Japanese crew, claiming '[t]hey were amazing' and that despite the fact that the 'weather was foul' these conditions 'never discouraged the Japanese' ('Jap Western Dead on Schedule' 1968: 45). He also discusses the possibility that the film's premiere would take place in Tamworth (it didn't), that they would definitely be 'coming back to Australia this year' (they didn't) and 'have already announced they intend to make a film about the mass escape of Japanese P.O.W.s at Cowra during World War II' (it wasn't made) ('Jap Western Dead on Schedule' 1968: 45). As in most other accounts of the production, Litchfield also overstates the budget by around AU$500,000 (he claims it was AU$720,000).

This interview with Litchfield is also remarkable for the precise details it gives us about an otherwise little-documented film production, including some information about the set building undertaken (a saloon, a barbershop and an insurance office), the locations used (such as the 'Vickery family's old property, Beehive'), the close working relationships between Japanese and Australian crews and the unexpectedly bad weather suffered on location: 'One day it snowed, so they simply changed the script' ('Jap Western Dead on Schedule' 1968: 45). Unlike most of the other press reports, which are generally patronising towards both the production and to the western genre more generally, this interview speaks glowingly of the ingenuity and adaptability of the Japanese filmmakers, the overriding spirit of co-production and the economic possibilities and shared opportunities suggested by these vanguard filmmaking practices.

An 'Instant Western': The Questionable Legacy of Transnational Film Production in Australia in the Late 1960s

But we also need to keep sight of the international, regional and local contexts in which the film was produced and released. *The Drifting Avenger* was just one Japanese movie made as part of a vast production slate across half a dozen or so major studios in 1968. It was quickly released into Japanese cinemas, fostered no further productions by its studio in Australia or sequels, and has been widely forgotten beyond a small number of repertory screenings in Australia and a low-profile Japanese DVD release in the early 2010s. The other two Japanese films shot 'down under' have even lower visibility. This is also a sobering reminder of the dangers we face when viewing international and transnational cinema, and Australia's place within both, through a predominantly solipsistic and parochial local lens. Undoubtedly, *The Drifting Avenger* appears to be far more significant when viewed from an Australian rather than a Japanese perspective. This lack of a truly international outlook, understanding or context is also symptomatic of the local press response at the time, the interview with Litchfield cited above included. As Pike states, the Japanese crew's 'level of experience ... was noted with incredulous bemusement by the Australian press, which has little concept of the size of the Japanese film industry' (Pike 1971: 12). It was also characterised by the easy application of largely unfounded stereotypes across many of these accounts. For example, one commentator merely described *The Drifting Avenger* as an 'instant western', self-evidently aligning it with then popular preconceptions (relating to miniaturisation, efficiency, volume, quality and immediacy) of Japan's key contribution as a cultural and industrial powerhouse in the postwar era (Frizell 1968b: 6). Although Khoo has suggested that both *The Drifting Avenger* and *Blazing Continent* 'have been more or less erased from the scholarship on Australian cinema', it is more accurate to say that they were never considered part of it in the first place (Khoo 2010: 236). This attitude towards international production and co-production arrangements, amplified in response to these unfamiliar, 'foreign' and largely unseen films, was also central to the arguments then gaining ground for a truly homegrown and explicitly nationalist Australian cinema (see Lawson 1968: 18).

Although *The Drifting Avenger* has rarely been discussed in relation to either Australian national cinema or international production 'down under', it is nevertheless a fascinating example of transnational filmmaking linked to broader practices of genre cinema circulating globally. Along with *Blazing Continent*, it sets an important precedent for later regional filmmaking in Australia that embraces collaborations with various Asian film industries including those of India, Hong Kong and China. But it is also an interesting example of 'locationist' filmmaking that deploys many of the colonialist, diplomatic and economic strategies we more commonly associate with Hollywood and British cinema, particularly within Australia. *The Drifting Avenger* emerges as a model of adaptation and hybridisation, as well as one of a vast number of international westerns produced in the 1960s and 1970s. As we've discussed, an examination of its production and release, as well as the various contexts in which it was made, illustrate the possibilities *and* limitations of making films in Australia during this period.

Notes

1. In his article 'Tchk, Tchk, Tchk: *Skippy the Bush Kangaroo* and the Question of Australian Seriousness', Mark Gibson gives an evocative account of the popularity of the show and its role as a cultural ambassador in late 1960s Japan (2014: 577). The airing of the show on Japanese television in the late 1960s provides a further context for the three Japanese-Australian films discussed in this chapter.
2. For example, *You Can't See 'Round Corners* was distributed by US company Universal and 'broke records in Perth' before going on to moderate success elsewhere (Pike and Cooper 1998: 242). Like *The Intruders*, it was also a spin-off of a television show and was adapted from a novel by popular author Jon Cleary who also wrote *The Sundowners*, amongst many other novels.
3. Only a small number of further Japanese-led productions have filmed in Australia over the following fifty years.
4. The earliest television listing we could find is for a screening of what is described as a 'Japanese western filmed in Tamworth, NSW' on ATN 7 in Sydney on Saturday, 8 October 1977. It is suggestively included within a programme called 'Bill Collins' Golden Years of Hollywood' ('Herald TV Guide' 1977: 73). Collins was one of the most widely travelled and beloved presenters of films on Australian television for fifty years from the mid-1960s until 2018 (appearing on almost all of the free-to-air networks).
5. Ownership of cinemas was highly lucrative when attendances were robust, but a significant financial burden for studios in a rapidly changing and declining industry. Nikkatsu was particularly affected by these conditions and closed down production completely in August 1971 before reopening and largely shifting to the making of '*roman poruno*' (romance pornography) in November of the same year. This led to the departure of many of its key actors and directors. See Schilling (2007: 26).
6. *Tokyo Drifter* is a definitive and highly illustrative mash-up of genres and styles and features a wandering, singing 'cowboy' and an incongruous western-style bar-room

brawl alongside and within a brutal and sometimes soulful rendering of the modern yakuza film.
7. The transportation stagecoach company Cobb & Co. is one of the most recognisable and widely remembered brands and institutions of nineteenth-century Australia. Despite these popular associations, it was a company of US origins.
8. This starts to take place from the late 1940s and is most clearly motivated by the changing immigration practices and demographics of a rapidly expanding and diversifying Australian population. But economic and trade considerations were also significant.

7. AGE OF CONSENT (1969)

ESCAPING ENGLAND: MICHAEL POWELL IN AUSTRALIA

Celebrated English filmmaker Michael Powell's career in Australia is a tale of considerable tenacity, pragmatism and, ultimately, missed opportunities. Amongst his mooted projects were films based on Arthur Upfield's popular Bony novels, Joan Lindsay's *Picnic at Hanging Rock* and Norman Lindsay's *The Magic Pudding* (Powell 1992: 508–509). The two films that he did make in 1960s Australia – *They're a Weird Mob* (1966) and *Age of Consent* (1969); also adaptations – are amongst a small number of features produced in Australia during that leanest of decades. For example, *They're a Weird Mob*, a significant box-office success in Australia and New Zealand but nowhere else, was the single Australian-made or -filmed feature to be commercially released in 1966. Powell's two features are also amongst the highest profile and budgeted 'Australian international' co-productions of their era.

Though they are, in some ways, studies in contrast – *They're a Weird Mob* working to embrace and reflect upon the Australian idiom and character while signalling significant demographic changes in its population; *Age of Consent* labouring to escape the pressures, increased cosmopolitanism and transformations of modern Australia on the tropical idyll of Dunk Island in North Queensland – both films feature outsiders or exiles learning or relearning the rhythms and nuances of daily, Australian life. Although shot many thousands of kilometres from Britain, these films are as responsive to place as the filmmaker's more celebrated works, and reflect Powell's genuine commitment to working in Australia during this period. While various writers have claimed that Powell's subsequent 'exile' to the Antipodes marked a significant downturn in his work's quality and level of engagement, and represents a kind of purgatory to be endured after the scandal of *Peeping Tom* (1960), his efforts in the largely moribund Australian feature-film industry of the 1960s still draw upon his maverick personality, as well as his truly adaptive and responsive filmmaking practice. This is reflected in Powell's accounts of his time in Australia in the second volume of his autobiography, *Million-Dollar Movie* (see Powell 1992: 436–55, 472–88, 509–15). Powell has very little to say about the day-to-day realities and challenges of shooting either *They're a Weird Mob* or *Age of Consent*, or their aesthetic achievements and thematic continuities with his earlier work, but he writes expansively of his physical and endlessly mobile encounter with Australia and the various personalities he met and worked with including actor-producer John McCallum, film and theatre entrepreneur Sir Frank Tait and novelist John O'Grady. Most revealingly, he documents his emergence as a producer negotiating difficult personal and business relationships, hard-won financial arrangements and precarious co-production deals in a very reticent filmmaking environment. Powell's autobiography shows him engaging directly with the very forces – the largely internationally controlled exhibition, distribution and financial sectors – that had stymied the Australian feature-film industry since at least the late 1930s.

It is plainly evident from even a cursory reading of *Million-Dollar Movie* that Powell regarded *They're a Weird Mob* as a reawakening: 'here was such a chance for me, not in America, but in Australia' (Powell 1992: 438). It followed the critical and commercial disaster of *Peeping Tom* mentioned above, the supremely underwhelming *The Queen's Guards* (1961), the one-off, low-budget, if startling, adaptation of Béla Bartók and Béla Balázs's *Herzog Blaubarts Burg* (*Bluebeard's Castle*, 1963) made for German television, and the dissatisfying piecework Powell had begun to undertake in British television on shows such as *Espionage*, *The Nurses* and *The Defenders*. Thus, the making of *They're a Weird Mob* represents both a retreat from and an embrace of new challenges, core ideas that are coincidentally at the centre of *Age of Consent*, the tale of an expatriate Australian painter burnt-out by his experiences in the New York art scene who returns 'home'.

Powell's two films largely sit in contrast to the majority of internationally funded productions in Australia in the late 1950s and 1960s. They are also markedly different from the final movies made by the Rank Organisation and Ealing Studios, the two British companies most committed to producing films in Australia during the postwar era: *Robbery Under Arms* (Jack Lee, 1957) and *The Siege of Pinchgut* (Harry Watt, 1959), respectively. Powell's dedication to filmmaking in Australia, and his painstaking efforts to understand its cultural, social and filmmaking landscape, find their closest parallels in the peripatetic work of Harry Watt in the mid-to-late 1940s: *The Overlanders* (1946) and *Eureka Stockade* (1949). But *They're a Weird Mob* and *Age of Consent* were produced in a vastly altered cultural, social and industrial context, and reflect Powell's status as both a veteran of European cinema – he was sixty-three when he filmed *Age of Consent* – and a filmmaker with broadly international-ist concerns. It is a long way from the hard-won documentary realities and explicit nationalism of *The Overlanders* to the exotic Pacific-Island idyll and soft-core nudity of *Age of Consent*.

A Sympathetic Outsider: Powell as a Sojourner Filmmaker

Ultimately, Powell should be seen as an embodiment of the 'sympathetic outsider' or 'sojourner', an overseas filmmaker committing the time and effort needed to make two popular features in Australia during one of the most difficult and unproductive periods for local film production. Jane Mills has theorised the 'sojourner', citing Powell specifically, as a figure who explores 'a sense of "at homeness while abroad"' (Mills 2014: 147). Powell journeyed to Australia five times over three years during the long planning and production of *They're a Weird Mob*, did much groundwork to court financiers and significant collaborators such as John O'Grady and Norman Lindsay, fully completed the production of both films within the country, and also committed himself to the establishment of his youngest son's (Kevin Powell) life and career in Australia. Although there is some residual disappointment that these films never reached – or in any way aimed at – the artistic level of Powell's earlier work on the films he made in collaboration with Emeric Pressburger such as *A Matter of Life and Death* (1946) and *The Red Shoes* (1948), they should now be regarded, and even celebrated, in terms more appropriate to their production circumstances. They are pragmatically visionary and commercially ambitious transnational works completed in a country just starting to make its own feature films again.

The often gentle, parochial, broadly comic but surprisingly cosmopolitan *They're a Weird Mob* has since emerged as a key instigating work of the Australian film 'revival', setting an important example in terms of the financial model it drew upon as well as its caricatured approach to subject and character. Its dependence on a combination of private, corporate and international financing – an initial model and impetus Powell himself saw as necessary (1992: 446–7) – was often seen as anathema to those pushing for a government backed and subsidised film industry. While seeing merit in the importation of Walter Chiari for the leading role of *They're a Weird Mob*, Sylvia Lawson saw little else of value in a work 'better described for many reasons as a British film made in Australia' (Lawson 1968: 18). Nevertheless, it does 'introduce' and popularise an approach to Australian culture and masculinity taken further in the more extreme, insular and less whimsical 'ocker' comedies of the next decade, most notably *Stork* (Tim Burstall, 1971), *The Adventures of Barry McKenzie* (Bruce Beresford, 1972) and *Alvin Purple* (Tim Burstall, 1973).

In contrast, *Age of Consent* is a more confident, relaxed and typical work of its time. But, like *They're a Weird Mob*, it largely survives in the public and critical imagination as a film directed by Michael Powell. This is both to its detriment and advantage. It has also received some fame for granting Helen Mirren her first significant film role, and is equally notorious for the actor appearing *en plein air*.[1] It was made in the transitional period between the very late 1960s and early 1970s and released alongside a motley array of international productions and co-productions generally exploiting Australia as a location. This piecemeal 'industry' saw the creation of a schizophrenic slate of ultra-low-budget local features, runaway productions made by a small number of countries including the US, the United Kingdom and Japan, and a smattering of films now regarded as seminal works of Australian national cinema: most prominently and lastingly, Nicolas Roeg's *Walkabout* (1971) and Ted Kotcheff's *Wake in Fright* (1971).

Age of Consent straddles a number of these categories, and has struggled to gain a significant critical reputation despite its distinctive pedigree. As we will go on to discuss, this 'failure' is partly the result of the film's botched international distribution as well as the fall from critical and popular favour of its source novel's author, Norman Lindsay. But *Age of Consent* has always been difficult to place, despite its clear alignment with specific models and trends in transnational and international filmmaking. It was also produced during a period of significant transition and financial difficulty for many of the Hollywood studios, including its distribution company and chief financier, Columbia Pictures.[2]

'A BUSMAN'S HOLIDAY ON THE BARRIER REEF': REVIEWING *AGE OF CONSENT*

Although they were never intended as final works – and Powell continued to dream of further features up until the 1980s, most notably Shakespeare's *The Tempest*, with James Mason as Prospero – both of his Australian features display a more relaxed and accepting tone than many of his more celebrated films. As Scott Salwolke has claimed, *Age of Consent* 'serves as a fitting finale to Powell's cinematic career, providing him a chance to lay to rest many of the demons that had haunted his earlier characters. The portrait of an artist rediscovering his passion ultimately foretells Powell's own career was over' (1997: 248). Nevertheless, as a result of this lack of intensity, as well as the relative invisibility of these two Australian co-productions on the world stage, both films have been critically undervalued, routinely regarded as directorial afterthoughts of one of the greatest filmmakers of the mid-twentieth century. Aside from a small range of articles published during his period of critical and commercial success with collaborator Emeric Pressburger in the 1940s, Powell wasn't widely discussed as a significant auteur until his 'rediscovery' by figures like Ian Christie and Martin Scorsese in the 1970s (see Scorsese in Christie 1994: xv–xx). His relatively low ranking and perceived decline is reflected in many of the articles published in Australia during his stay there in the mid- to-late 1960s (see, for example, Lawson 1966: 17–18; Bennett 1966: 23). For others, Powell's mere presence in Australia was ample evidence of his decline.

This relative neglect can also be traced to the circumstances surrounding both films' initial releases. Although *They're a Weird Mob* generated significant pre-publicity, and a generally very positive critical reaction from the Australian popular press, *Age of Consent* was received much more matter-of-factly. This is true within Australia and internationally. For example, prominent and often sympathetic critic Colin Bennett, writing in Melbourne's *The Age*, called the film 'an unspectacular co-production' and 'a busman's holiday on the Barrier Reef for James Mason', while further gently damning it with very faint praise: '*Age of Consent* is competently put together – the veteran Powell probably does it now with one eye shut' (1969: 2). The international reviews in influential outlets like *Variety* (Stanley 1969: 32) and *Monthly Film Bulletin* were also dismissively positive, while highlighting the lack of ambition evident in what ended up on screen: 'Given the convincing and humorous development of this island duo [Mason and Mirren], it is only a pity that the film's side-line sketches are meagre distractions rather than embellishments' (Combs 1969: 256).

The overall Australian critical response to *Age of Consent* was mixed. Somewhat gossipy and even distracted accounts of the filming appeared in various magazines, but overall press and public interest was considerably tempered in comparison with *They're a Weird Mob* (see Keavney 1968: 8–9; Guinness 1968: 9–10). The *Australian Women's Weekly*'s Kay Keavney provided a lively and positive, if superficial, account of filming on Dunk Island, while the *Bulletin*'s Daphne Guinness presented a more deflating account of the filming of final scenes at Sydney's Bonython Gallery (Keavney 1968: 8–9; Guinness 1968: 9–10). This limited coverage was partly due to the film's remote locations, but also the decreased novelty of a second Powell production. The subsequent reviews that appeared in two prominent Sydney-based publications characterise this often dialectical response. The *Bulletin*'s Bev Tivey places *Age of Consent* within the context of a faltering Australian film 'renaissance', before dismissing it as an 'enfeebled vision of Norman Lindsay's robust comic novel'. She also singles out Powell's 'ham-fisted direction, bits of frantic overacting and a general lack of comprehension of how Australians talk and behave' (Tivey 1969: 45).[3] In contrast, the *Sydney Morning Herald*'s

Charles Higham praises a director who 'at his best is a poet of nature. And in Norman Lindsay's novel, for the first time in 20 years, he has found a subject to excite the poet in him' (1969: 8). Higham's generally enthusiastic review is also the first to place *Age of Consent* within the context of the recurrent thematic preoccupations, autobiographical concerns and emerging legacy of Powell's work: 'It will be recalled for the evocation of a whole self-contained world, and for its perfect matching of the director's own rediscovery of himself as an artist; unwittingly, perhaps, the film becomes a kind of autobiography of relived experience' (1969: 8). Andrew Pike, writing in the *Canberra Times* a few months later, also praises the film's romantic and poetic impulses, alongside the contributions of composer Peter Sculthorpe and editor Anthony Buckley, while recognising the limited scale of its achievements: '*Age of Consent* is not a return to the standard of *The Red Shoes* or *I Know Where I'm Going* [sic], but it is a strong and positive film' (Pike 1969: 13).

Highly influential Australian cultural commentator Sylvia Lawson was far blunter in her assessment of the transnational hybrid represented by Powell's second Australian-made film:

> The overstrained, manufactured Australianism of *Age of Consent* should be enough to convince any adult filmgoer of the total inadequacy, so far as Australian self-interpretation is concerned, of the British- or American-based project which uses Australia as a location. (Lawson 1985: 180)

Although Lawson was plainly disenchanted with the film, and was writing more generally about the tepid state of the Australian industry, her comments also need to be contextualised within the growing push for local production and government support gathering pace at this time.

'You only want me for the pitchas': Making *Age of Consent*

Age of Consent was made on a larger scale than *They're a Weird Mob* and was intended for a more general international audience than its predecessor – even if it did not end up finding an audience in anything like the numbers desired. The budget of AU$1,200,000 is closer to the kind of sum typical for films of its kind internationally (Pike and Cooper 1998: 243).[4] It was also largely funded by Columbia Pictures' arm in the United Kingdom, made under the auspices of Nautilus Productions, and only green lit on the insistence that an actor of James Mason's stature was engaged to play the central role. As we will go on to discuss, *Age of Consent* also directly addresses these issues of internationalisation, as well as its status as a transnational film funded by overseas interests. It is also not too difficult to see explicit parallels between the retreat of the artist to Australia that propels the narrative and Powell's own 'rebirth' in the mid-to-late 1960s. Even the paintings produced by the artist-protagonist when he returns home, and their more elemental, figurative and human dimensions, can be compared to Powell's embrace of a broader, less intense and freer mode of colloquial filmmaking.

Production began in early March 1968 with the arrival of around sixty cast and crew on Dunk Island (Buckley 2009: 109).[5] The two months of filming would take in six weeks on the island, ten days around Cairns and Green Island, and smaller amounts of time spent in a range of other locations including Tully, Cardwell, Brisbane and finally Sydney. As Buckley remarked, the production entourage, including complete editing and screening facilities, travelled between most locations (2009: 109). Production was plagued by hot and humid weather, which made the loading and editing of celluloid difficult, the loss of a generator early in the shooting, and significant periods of wet, squally weather. The evidence of the latter is seen across the tempestuous finished film despite its generally sun-kissed demeanour. The limited production accounts that are available suggest it was generally a happy shoot – with rushes screened to an enthusiastic cast and crew every night once they started to arrive from Colorfilm in Sydney – as reflected in the on-set report published in the *Australian Women's Weekly*: 'Their mood was victorious. They seemed to feel they were on a winner. And so, over the next few days, did I' (Keavney 1968: 9). This story is preoccupied with profiling various personalities, but also highlights the significant and rare opportunities offered to underemployed Australian film workers on a relatively large international production with noteworthy local contributions: editor (Buckley); associate producer (Michael Pate); art director (British migrant Dennis Gentle); music (Sculthorpe); make-up (Peggy Carter); casting (Gloria Payten); alongside most roles 'beneath' the three stars and the other principal production personnel. Shooting concluded in Sydney in early May with the finished film's initial scenes set in New York but staged at the Bonython Gallery. This preceded the completion of the rough cut by Buckley, the recording of Sculthorpe's score and the looping of dialogue. According to Buckley this led to one of the finished film's 'serious flaws' when Mason insisted on trying to master the Australian accent (2009: 112).

Age of Consent received its premiere run at Brisbane's Odeon from 27 March 1969. According to a writer for the *Bulletin*, during this initial engagement it was 'reported to be limping through a "simultaneous world-premiere release" season in such widely scattered Queensland locations as Mackay, Brisbane and Toowoomba' ('The Flickering Flame' 1969: 42).[6] Despite what it claimed was a 'critical reaction to the movie in Queensland ... [that] ranged from chauvinistic indulgence to savage distaste' ('The Flickering Flame' 1969: 42), *Age of Consent* went on to successful runs in large cinemas in Melbourne (the Forum), Sydney (the Rapallo) and various other locations. After opening in Melbourne on 9 May, its premiere Sydney engagement was held up by the runaway success of Franco Zeffirelli's *Romeo and Juliet* (1968) at its designated first-run downtown theatre. Finally opening in Sydney on 27 July, it ran for seven months before moving on to suburban theatres (Buckley 2009: 117). The much less successful UK release, shorn of around seven minutes, commenced in mid-November 1969 before its American bow on 8 March 1970 (*'Age of Consent'*). As was the case with *They're a Weird Mob*, local success did not translate into significant international box office.

Girl Friday: Exploiting the 'Age of Consent'

The plot of *Age of Consent* is very simply structured, and primarily works as a means of getting the film and its central characters into its elemental tropical settings. An expatriate Australian painter, Bradley Morahan (James Mason), becomes disillusioned with the international art scene and decides to return to Australia and his home state of Queensland to rejuvenate his love of painting. After arriving in Brisbane and reacquainting himself with various lovers and hangers-on, Brad retreats to the beachcombing life of Dunk Island, north of Cairns on the Great Barrier Reef, holing up in a rustic beach shack awaiting inspiration. This inspiration arrives in the form of the natural world surrounding him and in the guise of a young woman, Cora (Helen Mirren), a free spirit dogged by her deceased mother's 'loose' reputation and her grandmother's (Neva Carr-Glyn) insinuating barbs: a figure who represents a garish and unnatural presence in such a beautiful and harmonious environment, but who also appears to emerge from it.

Despite the disturbing implications of the burgeoning sexual connection between painter and model – Cora is seemingly only *about* to reach the 'age of consent' – and the reasonably frank but tasteful nudity dotted throughout, *Age of Consent* is a surprisingly chaste and disconcertingly innocent movie. As more than one commentator suggested, the most disturbing implications of this May–December romance are to be found in the film's closing song, whose lyrics longingly spell out the paedophilic implications of the relationship we've seen blossom: 'Cora, I've loved you so / As I've waited, my Cora, and watched you grow' (see Jones 2009). This troubling dimension is also hinted at in the film's publicity. The British poster, for example, outlined the simple pleasures promised by this confection: 'How to have a great time on the Great Barrier Reef: Comb a beach . . . Catch a bird . . . Guzzle a pint . . . And paint the lovely nature-girl who's just reached the "*Age of Consent*".'

Possibly played too often for broad comedy, rather than truly felt emotional affect, the episodic but wistful narrative leisurely develops this 'romance' while providing numerous asides to other, often grotesque and cartoonish supporting characters, as well as an engagingly performative dog: Godfrey. The interactions with several of these characters also help to displace the indecency of

Brad and Cora's bond. The 'distracted' and even chivalrous intentions of Brad are contrasted with the fumbling advances of Ted Farrell (Harold Hopkins), the incessant lasciviousness of celebrated Irish actor Jack MacGowran's Nat Kelly, an old friend of Brad who well and truly outstays his welcome, and the pent-up sexual aggressiveness of Brad's next-door neighbour, Miss Marley (Antonia Katsaros). Brad's 'healthy' sexuality is further contextualised by an early scene in which he admits to having spent almost an entire week in bed with an old girlfriend, a character played by Mason's future wife, Clarissa Kaye, who he met on the production.

Nevertheless, the relative delicacy with which the relationship between Cora and Brad is developed, and the film's focus on Brad's gradual re-emergence as a driven and intuitive artist, almost makes us forget, or at least partly disregard, the plot's sordid implications. This is despite Cora's gin-soaked grandmother intermittently accusing Brad of being a 'perv' and threatening to call the police. Even scenes featuring Cora discovering her own body, after viewing Brad's painterly representation, communicate a self-awareness that decentralises Brad's eroticised vision. As Dave Kehr playfully and perceptively argues, '*Age of Consent* seems about as likely to be remade today as *The Birth of a Nation*, yet the picture doesn't feel unhealthy' (2009).

Age of Consent needs to be placed in the broader context of late 1960s international film production and be appraised in relation to the more sexually explicit and often titillating work exploiting changing censorship regulations and the boundaries between the 'continental' art movie and (very) soft-core eroticism. At times, particularly when we view Cora swimming amongst the coral, or when the camera holds a little too long on a cloud formation, *Age of Consent* has some of the qualities of an exotic travelogue (see Bennett's 'busman's holiday', mentioned earlier). It precedes a string of more sexually explicit and controversial home-grown movies exploiting the increasing relaxation of censorship in Australia in the late 1960s and early 1970s including *The Set* (Frank Brittain) and *The Naked Bunyip* (John B. Murray), both released the following year.[7] Although Powell's film downplays its focus on the 'age of consent', as well as its boundaries and policing, it would be highly inaccurate to suggest it doesn't also exploit this troubling notion.

The 'Australian *Lolita*'

Audience expectations were also central to the decision to adapt Norman Lindsay's source novel, first published in New York (Farrar and Rinehart) and then London (T. Werner Laurie) in 1938 but banned in Australia until 1962. It had gained a reputation in some circles as the 'Australian *Lolita*', but by the time of its belated publication this once-salacious work was regarded as an antiquated time capsule of pre-World War II Australia (Hoorn 2005: 76).

The novel is actually set in the 1920s, so it was a period piece even when first published, and its view of sexuality, and even art, was decidedly quaint by the 1960s. Although Lindsay's work as a writer did achieve significant success, he is more popularly known and remembered as a painter, illustrator and cartoonist. For example, John Baxter argues that Lindsay was largely responsible for creating the popular image of the 'digger' during World War I, as well as the 'archetypal Hun', and that his work during this period was '[f]anatically nationalist' and that '[b]igotry came naturally to him' (Baxter 2014: 114 and 115). This is some distance from the relatively benign and seemingly libertarian figure Sam Neill plays in John Duigan's *Sirens* (1994), but both representations favour him as a figurative artist. As novelist and essayist Kylie Tennant stated at the time of *Age of Consent*'s belated Australian publication:

> It has been a standing joke that ever since the 30's any book with the name Norman Lindsay on the cover, even if it was about raising Persian cats, was automatically banned. Now the laughter is louder as this pretty little mouse of a book creeps in. The very title must have thrown the Customs House into a panic: 'Age of Consent' indeed! It is a delicious book – all the quainter for being so dated with the usual Lindsay stock characters. (1962: 379)

Powell was even more dismissive of the novel's pedigree: 'I had never done one of those Girl Friday stories, but that was no reason I shouldn't make one, now that I was in my dotage. Norman Lindsay had obviously written the book for money, but that was no reason it shouldn't make a film' (Powell 1992: 509). Powell's comments link Brad and Cora's relationship to Daniel Defoe's *Robinson Crusoe* and the colonialist castaway and South Seas Island fiction it inspired (see Craven 2016: 58).

In his autobiography, Powell provides a somewhat incoherent view of the film's gestation. Although Powell states that it may have been Chips Rafferty who made him aware of the novel, and the director's interest in *The Magic Pudding* would suggest some prior knowledge, other, likely more accurate sources suggest that the key instigators of the project were Mason (its co-producer) and the rights holder, actor and associate producer, Michael Pate (Pike and Cooper 1998: 243). No matter the case, the novel was largely seen as a property with marketable notoriety. Unlike in Australia, it had been published in the US and Britain in the late 1930s when Lindsay had a significant international reputation.

Importing Stardom: James Mason and Helen Mirren in Queensland

The choice of actors to play the central roles in *Age of Consent* was equally significant. Mason's darkly charming if irascible presence brought to mind other recent films in which he had played a middle-aged man attracted to a much younger woman or girl. This was perhaps less troubling in a film like *Georgy Girl* (Silvio Narizanno, 1966) – lyrics like 'It's time for jumping down from the shelf – a little bit', notwithstanding – but is fully exploited in his extraordinary performance as Humbert Humbert in Stanley Kubrick's fascinatingly compromised adaptation of Vladimir Nabokov's *Lolita* (1962).[8] Not surprisingly, Mason's performance in the latter film was often mentioned in relation to *Age of Consent*, and even exploited in the pre-publicity. Therefore, by the time of the making of *Age of Consent*, Mason had developed a shifting screen persona that moved well beyond, while playing with, his popular image as a dashingly attractive if often dangerous or troubled romantic lead in early films like *The Seventh Veil* (Compton Bennett, 1945) and *The Wicked Lady* (Leslie Arliss, 1945).

Age of Consent draws on some of these elements of Mason's star persona, but they partly operate in contradistinction to Brad's character and his relationship with Cora. Whereas Humbert first sees Lolita sprawled out on a blanket in her backyard, flamboyantly and coquettishly looking up at him wearing a bikini and sunglasses, and is immediately enraptured, Brad initially seems to only see Cora's glorious potential as an artistic subject and for giving him back his 'eyes'. Lindsay's novel is, considering its controversial reputation, surprisingly in tune with Powell's adaptation, suggesting that there isn't much more to the relationship than that between artist and model. But there is a large shift between the novel's portly, rough-bearded and almost anti-social Bradly Mudgett and the character's habitation by an actor of Mason's presence, voice, reputation, brooding sexuality and screen history. The bringing together of Brad and Cora in the final moments – as they cavort in the water after Cora has sullenly blurted out that 'you only want me for the pitchas' – was largely at the behest of Mason, Powell favouring a melancholy and wistful conclusion merely showing Brad wandering after her. The contrast between these two views of the character and his motivations has a curious effect on the film's overall tone.

The casting of Helen Mirren as Cora is also noteworthy. Although Mirren had started to gain a significant reputation as a member of the Royal Shakespeare Company, she had little experience in feature filmmaking. Nevertheless, while she is playing a character in her mid-to-late teens, and is often very good and intuitive in the role, her actual age (she was twenty-four when the film was released), as well as the growing sexual confidence of the character she plays, has a significant impact on our view of her character's actions. We would also argue that although it is difficult to watch *Age of Consent* now without thinking of these troubling implications, the subsequent career and fearless sexuality of Mirren in a range of roles also acts to de-emphasise these concerns. *Age of Consent* establishes a clear set of parallels between actress and character. As Jeanette Hoorn has argued, Mirren's partial discomfort with her nude scenes – though sometimes using a body double – is mirrored by Cora's initial resistance to posing for Brad (2005: 81). This also sets up clear parallels between Powell, Brad and Lindsay and their exploitation of youthful female sexuality.

Artists and Models: The Fate of *Age of Consent*

Powell's *Age of Consent* is, inevitably, a loose adaptation of Lindsay's novel. Full of minor references to the work of various Australian and international artists, it departs significantly from the source by shifting the action from the south coast of New South Wales (Batemans Bay) to North Queensland, more fully emphasising Brad and Cora's emerging relationship, making its central character a *successful* artist, and updating its setting to the present day. As we've discussed, in contrast to *They're a Weird Mob*, Powell himself was quite dismissive of his source. He considered the film's main attractions the picturesque, largely pristine and isolated surroundings of Dunk Island – having previously visited with his partner Pamela Brown and actor Walter Chiari around the time of making *They're a Weird Mob* (Powell 1992: 515) – the star power of Mason, the fulfillment of his long-held desire to work with Jack MacGowran, the congeniality and professionalism of the shoot, and the corporeal beauty of a young Mirren. To be fair, Lindsay's novel is most impressive in its focus on the small details of the artist's life and its exploration of his gradual emergence as a more expressive, intuitive artist. Although the drawings by Lindsay that illustrate the novel show clearly why he was very pleased with Mirren's casting, they also suggest a parochial and down-at-heel environment that contrasts with the more worldly Brad and the exotic, touristic locations of Powell's adaptation.

Shot almost entirely on location, with some interiors filmed at Ajax Film Studios in Bondi Junction, Sydney, *Age of Consent* is a picaresque and intermittently arresting contribution to the tradition of the film and novel that dramatises the relationship between a fading artist and the muse who rejuvenates his – and it is almost always 'his' in works of this kind – creativity. In this regard, it is a sun-kissed and somewhat benign 'final' work in the career of a director often preoccupied with the lives of artists, patriarchs and visionary autocrats who attempt – and often gamely fail – to command and control the worlds around them. Although a significant departure from the darker realms of *A Canterbury Tale* (1944), *The Red Shoes*, *The Tales of Hoffmann* (1951) and *Peeping Tom*, *Age of Consent* is nevertheless an intriguing late entry in this encompassing 'series' that also provides one of its few truly happy and romantic endings. Brad is able to reinvigorate his art and eye, retreat from the pressures of the commercial world and also win the girl.

The international release of *Age of Consent* was hampered by the heavy-handedness of Columbia Pictures. Featuring an often beautiful and quite sophisticated Balinese-inflected score by noted Tasmanian composer Peter Sculthorpe, its international release was marred by trims to the nude footage, significant changes to the credits and the opening New York-based gallery scenes, and the replacement of Sculthorpe's music by a more hackneyed, if still pleasing score by Stanley Myers. Like *They're a Weird Mob*, *Age of Consent* is a relatively unsophisticated, often broad and laconic entertainment, but it trades in Powell's characteristic preoccupation with place, the world of artists, and the conflict between the ethereal domain of ideas and the corporeal demands of the body. Like *They're a Weird Mob*, it is also an unevenly paced work that shifts significantly in tone between the often lyrical scenes featuring Cora, and the more grotesque and exaggeratedly physical moments showcasing MacGowran, Carr-Glyn and Andonia Katsaros. Although often over-the-top, MacGowran's performance is an adept piece of physical comedy, his accent appearing unforced and never as variable as the still laudable efforts of Mason and Mirren. But Carr-Glyn blights the film in her unsubtle and hysterical performance as Cora's grandmother. Ultimately, the key pleasures of this Powellian idyll are found in Mason's and Mirren's performances, as well as the exquisitely captured flora, fauna, beaches and cloud formations of Dunk Island and its surrounds. This gave Powell and his crew the opportunity to focus – though never abstractly – on the colour and light afforded by the environment. This focus upon composition and the sculptural qualities of light is evident in many of the film's shoreline compositions. This emphasis on colour, environment and visual style is prioritised from its very first moments.

As suggested above, *Age of Consent* was compromised by the cuts and changes performed on it for international release. Some of these changes were due to privations against nudity in the US and Britain but also reflected the difficulties the studio had in fully accepting the film Powell delivered. After being restored to close to its original Australian cut in the mid-2000s, it is now possible to better understand the important shifts of tone and colour that structure it. A central element of this is the contrast between the pictorial style of the paintings we see under the film's cursive credits, meant to correspond to that of Lindsay as well as Brad once he starts to work on Dunk Island, and the abstract, largely brown, red and orange canvases and tapestries Brad commercially exhibits in New York. The opening credits suggest that the film will be both an adaptation of Lindsay's novel and his artistic practice or style, an aspect downplayed in the titles for the original international release. This direct reference to Lindsay's work speaks to an Australian and international audience familiar with the artist's oeuvre. Although the credits pan from an image of the Columbia Pictures logo shaped in the odalisque 'form' of Mirren, taking in sketchy paintings of Brad, Nat and the dog Godfrey, as well as the shoreline itself, the film's title is accompanied by a facsimile of the image of a chain of dancing, voluptuous women often associated with Lindsay's art. The paintings included in this credit sequence, and which propagate once we get to Dunk Island, were created by Paul Delprat, while the 'international' work displayed in New York was undertaken by John Coburn. This decision to use the work of two separate, established and quite distinct Australian artists operating in very different registers and both very unlike Lindsay, acts to communicate Brad's varied capacities as an artist as well as the radical break his work makes when he returns to Queensland.

Coming of Age: Local and International Influences

These opening scenes play with this concept of 'internationalism' as they move swiftly, even effortlessly from the Great Barrier Reef to a fish tank in New York and then on to the modern architecture and fragmented spaces of the large metropolis. The fact that Sydney is used as a stand-in for New York, with taxis that don't look quite right, is a sign of the film's freewheeling confidence as well as the artificiality and interchangeability of the modern city. These scenes work to establish Brad's reputation, his disillusionment with the art he is producing, and the distance between the abstract tropical designs of his work and their organic source. The actors in these opening New York scenes, most of which were excised for international release, also highlight the film's transnationalism. Brad's dealer, Godfrey, is played by Frank Thring, one of Australia's most successful theatrical exports in the 1950s and 1960s, and one of his buyers is played by Tommy Hanlon, Jr., an American who made his name on Australian television. These night-time interiors also stand in contrast to the opening credits and the expressively light-sculpted and cloud-capped compositions marking Brad's arrival on Dunk Island. They work very economically to establish the artistic, spatial and economic context of Brad's situation and work. This is even true of the positioning of Brad as an Australian artist working within the framework of modernism. His work is exhibited in the 'Bonython Gallery Penthouse' – transplanted to New York but located in Sydney – a book on painter Sidney Nolan is casually placed behind him as he speaks to Godfrey in his studio, and his work is compared to William Dobell and Paul Gauguin in a television interview playing in the background of the scene featuring Brad and May (Clarissa Kaye) in bed.[9]

But, as Hoorn has argued, 'Lindsay was an implacable opponent of modernist painting, lampooning it ferociously in his novels and cartoons. While in the novel there is no hint of this, [Peter] Yeldham's screenplay highlights an anti-modernist sensibility' (Hoorn 2005: 76). Hoorn is correct in identifying Brad's seeming flight from the 'idiom of the New York School', and the film does rely upon a clear distinction between the work of the two artists tasked with creating his paintings, but I'm less convinced of the absolute break with modernism signified by Brad's shift to Dunk Island (Hoorn 2005: 75). The paintings Brad completes on the island are certainly less abstract in terms of how they represent the natural world and return to the human figure, but the experimental use of colour and more expressionist approach to the subject still sit within particular tenets of modernism. Brad's transition to the human figure occurs gradually and organically: he initially paints the interior of his lodgings in bright colours that pre-empt the ways in which his life increasingly fuses with the environment. His denial of the art world is also very much in keeping with these hardly abandoned modernist sensibilities.

This is a key aspect of the transition from novel to film and from the 1920s to the late 1960s. Although Brad is attempting to escape from the world of international corporate art, he only has the opportunity to do so because of the established market for his work. Brad is a much more confident and easygoing character in the film, a shift of persona and perspective partly necessitated by the sophisticated charm of Mason's star persona. There are, of course, direct parallels between Brad's retreat from the international art scene and Powell's more complicated status as a globally recognised filmmaker 'going native' in far North Queensland. Although, in retrospect, Powell questioned his decision to adapt Lindsay's relatively undistinguished but lively novel as his second Australian feature, the material is a good fit for the leisurely and speculative film he sought to make, as well as the adaptations and innovations it signalled within his filmmaking practice (Powell 1992: 508). In some ways, the problem with *Age of Consent* is one of perspective. The film was an Australian box-office success, but undoubtedly appeared less distinctive, exotic or erotic within an international or transnational context. Although Powell has suggested that Columbia executives baulked at the film's frank nudity – which, considering the cuts made for international release, is likely true – it also suffers from its crude stereotypes, generic story and bold but curiously innocent sexuality. In the context of the common aesthetic and cultural extremes that mark Australian cinema, *Age of Consent* is also something of an outlier.

'Discovering a New World'

The international and transnational dimensions of *Age of Consent* have also made it a difficult film to place historically. This was the first Australia-based film to feature a significant Hollywood star since the appearance of Robert Mitchum and Deborah Kerr in *The Sundowners* in 1960. But, as we have argued, it is also not an exclusively 'locationist' exercise and represents

Powell's bold attempt to foster feature-film practice within a very difficult and often antagonistic production, distribution and exhibition environment. All of these factors need to be taken into account when assessing the film's minor pleasures, understandable limitations and its achievements. In this regard, Powell's identification with the figure of Brad is both touching and somewhat delusional. Like Brad, Powell's 'eyes' were reopened in the Antipodes – 'I went to Australia to see whether it [the world of *They're a Weird Mob*] was true. And I saw it *was* true. I had the impression of discovering a new world. It was enthralling!' (Powell quoted in Lacourbe and Grivel 2003: 64) – but his true contribution is less a matter of aesthetic achievement than the prospective models of production, financing and distribution his films suggested.

Both editor Buckley and Powell's son Kevin have claimed that Powell continued to dream of further and more ambitious Australian projects throughout the 1970s. Although the two movies he did make need to be rethought as key formative works of the Australian film 'revival', they are also idiosyncratic and uncategorisable movies that reflect upon migrant and expatriate experiences of Australian society in the 1960s. Powell is to be commended for turning to Australia during a period in which many significant and ultimately influential cultural figures such as Clive James, Germaine Greer, Robert Hughes and Barry Humphries journeyed in the other direction. It is in this regard that we can think about the film's title and its implications less in terms of the May–December 'romance' between Cora and Brad, and more in relation to the 'coming of age' of Australian cinema itself. Though consciously naïve, *Age of Consent* is also a mature work that recognises the increasingly transnational and transcultural possibilities and realities of Australian feature-film production. It is a film that looks forward to the fitfully cosmopolitan Australian cinema of the 1980s and beyond.

Notes

1. One of the most common stories told about the film's original release involves the gradually decreasing length of release prints as a result of projectionists excising nude footage of Mirren, a fate that playfully mirrors its truncated international version (see Buckley 2009: 117).
2. As mentioned elsewhere in this book, this period was also difficult for established studios in other countries such as Japan.
3. Appearing in 1969, Tivey's comments on the already faltering 'renaissance' of the Australian film industry are fascinating.
4. The *Bulletin* claimed the budget was AU$1,000,000 ('Filming on an Island' 1968: 57).
5. Buckley states that the cast and crew left Sydney for North Queensland on 7 March.
6. This report is another account of the seemingly faltering film 'renaissance', with particularly harsh words reserved for the deflating release of the truly home-grown *Two Thousand Weeks* (Tim Burstall, 1969) in Melbourne in late March 1969.
7. A key development would occur in late 1971 with the introduction of the 'R' certifi-

cate in Australia. *The Naked Bunyip* is a serio-comic 'essay' film surveying sexual attitudes in modern Australia. *The Set* is notable for its 'expose' of Sydney high life and its ground-breaking representation of homosexuality.
8. Although Kubrick's film was released in Australia, Nabokov's novel remained banned until 1965.
9. Kym Bonython established significant contemporary art galleries in Adelaide and Sydney in the 1950s and 1960s and was central in promoting the careers of Sidney Nolan, William Dobell and Brett Whiteley. Bonython Gallery Sydney opened in 1967.

8. COLOR ME DEAD (1970)

Film Noir in the Antipodes

In the late 1960s, producer-entrepreneur Reginald Goldsworthy (of Goldsworthy Productions) brought American television director Eddie Davis to Australia to make three feature films: *It Takes All Kinds* (1969), *Color Me Dead* (1970) and *That Lady from Peking* (1970). Generically similar crime-thrillers, each film was made in collaboration with senior American partner, Commonwealth United Corporation, on a modest budget and with American actors mainly known for their work in television and B-movies in the lead roles (O'Brien 1970b: 35).[1] The second film, *Color Me Dead*, stands apart from the others for being a direct remake of the film noir classic, *D.O.A.* (Rudolph Maté, 1949). Discarding the flashback structure of the original, *Color Me Dead* begins with an atmospheric night sequence, but soon settles into a routine (if convoluted) thriller in which the poisoned protagonist attempts to track down his own killer. While the Davis version closely follows the dialogue and plot of Maté's film, the form and style of the Australian remake owes less to its precursor than it does to post-classical noirs (such as *Harper*, Jack Smight, 1966; *The Detective*, Gordon Douglas, 1968; *Lady in Cement*, Gordon Douglas, 1968) and television noir (*Dragnet*, 1951–9; *Naked City*, 1958–63; *The Fugitive*, 1963–7). In this chapter we look at the Antipodean, cultural remaking of *D.O.A.*, historically situated midway between its classic original (1949) and its second, neo-noir remaking, *D.O.A.* (Rocky Morton and Annabel Jankel, 1988). The Australian remake's television aesthetic – and US cable release – adds weight to the suggestion that, through the 1960s, the noir of the classic sensibility was kept alive mainly through television series and movies, some of which embraced an increased transnationalism. The Australian remake also demonstrates something of the way in which the development and expansion of 'international' film noir – as an 'artistic impulse to represent global modernity and its psycho-sexual anxieties' (Petty 2016: 1) – extends well beyond France and the US.

In *More Than Night*, James Naremore describes the category of film noir not as a set of narrative or stylistic features, but as a discursive formation: 'film noir belongs to the history of ideas as much as to the history of cinema . . . [I]t has less to do with a group of artifacts than with a discourse' (Naremore 1998: 11). In the first instance, American film noir is a *critical* genre, 'a belated reading of classic Hollywood that was popularized by cinéastes of the French New Wave, [and later] appropriated by reviewers, academics, and film-makers, and then recycled on television' (Naremore 1998: 10). Naremore describes a first, 'historical' age of film noir, enabled and made evident by the postwar arrival of Hollywood film into Paris, and a French predisposition to view the form as an 'existential allegory of the white male condition' (Naremore 1998: 26). In the late 1950s and early 1960s, French auteur filmmakers such as Jean-Luc Godard, Claude Chabrol and François Truffaut took film noir as a pretext for reinventing cinema as a mode of self-expression. In the US, the expansion of film noir was assisted by factors such as the importation of the French *la politique des auteurs*, the upsurge of thematically and contextually programmed seasons at repertory theatres, the contribution of broadcast television to film literacy, and the expansion of film courses in American universities. Along with shifts in Hollywood production methods and commercial infrastructure, these factors led to a delayed new wave of American filmmakers whose early films were influenced by the *nouvelle vague* and were 'somewhat noirish in tone' (Naremore 1998: 32–3).

By the late 1960s, the critical appraisal of the form had motivated something of a revival, but film noir did not become an *industrial* genre until revisionist and neo-expressionist productions – such as *The Long Goodbye* (Robert Altman, 1973), *Chinatown* (Roman Polanski, 1974) and *Taxi Driver* (Martin Scorsese, 1976) – helped generate a cycle of noir remakings. 'At this point', Naremore concludes, '[film] *noir* had fully entered the English language, and it formed a rich discursive category that the entertainment industry could expand and adapt in countless ways' (Naremore 1998: 37). Naremore's argument – that film noir is a discursive construct with heuristic value – together with the suggestion that it is not a specifically American form, but rather 'something like an international genre', prompts the treatment of noir (and neo-noir) as a dynamic cultural form, one that exists as a global (or transnational) phenomenon, embracing different media and cultures (Naremore 1998: 277; see also Petty 2016; Spicer 2007). As in other countries with a particularly strong legacy of American cultural influence, Australian film and television is populated by works that betray this lineage from noir and neo-noir. A significant strain of home-grown television production in Melbourne in the 1960s and 1970s – taking in such seminal series as *Homicide* (1964–77) and *Division 4* (1969–75) – shows a strong thematic, narrative and stylistic affinity with noir. This influence can also be traced across various films of the 1960s, 1970s and early 1980s, including significant films of the 'revival' such as *Money Movers* (Bruce Beresford, 1978), *Blood Money* (Christopher Fitchett, 1980) and *Goodbye Paradise* (Carl Schultz, 1983). Australian film culture – particularly the strong film society movement – also betrayed a strong connection to these critical models from overseas, including *la politique des auteurs* and its British and American variations.

Transnational Remakes: *D.O.A.* versus *Color Me Dead*

The complex set of ideas, texts and personnel that characterises the cross-cultural and transnational circulation of film noir is evident in the example of *Color Me Dead* (aka *D.O.A. II*). Filmed at Sydney's Ajax Studios, with exteriors shot around Sydney and the Gold Coast (Musgrove 1969: 8–10), and with American leads (Tom Tryon, Carolyn Jones, Rick Jason), *Color Me Dead* credits only the original screenplay of *D.O.A.* by Russell Rouse and Clarence Greene. *Color Me Dead* additionally inherits from the Maté version what R. Barton Palmer describes as a key theme of Hollywood's 'dark cinema': namely, the understanding that, 'in the noir detective film, death is the final truth of the human condition, the limitation placed on desire and action, the reality we [embodied, especially, in the white male protagonist] all flee from but must finally face' (Palmer 1994: 83). In the Maté version, this theme is forcefully rendered in the opening credit sequence that follows a man, Frank Bigelow (played by Edmond O'Brien), walking through the dark streets of Los Angeles to a police precinct building. He enters and marches through its empty corridors to the homicide division where he asks for the man in charge, announcing that he wants to report a murder. When asked who was murdered, he replies: 'I was.'[2] The detectives are not surprised by the revelation, their colleagues in San Francisco already having issued an all-points bulletin for Bigelow. Invited to tell his story, Bigelow begins: 'I live in a little town called Banning out on the desert, it's on the way to Palm Springs.' As he continues his story – 'I have a small business there . . .' he tells the detectives – a swirling vortex announces the beginning of a flashback (some two days earlier) which shows Bigelow in his office, an attractive brunette perched on the corner of his desk, his girlfriend and co-worker Paula (Pamela Britton) eyeing them with disapproval. As Palmer points out, 'initially, the narrative is melodramatic, concerned only, as the mise-en-scène suggests, with male and female roles' and the 'policing of desire', but as the film progresses it soon demonstrates that the 'real problem life poses . . . is not that the best outlet for the satisfaction of desire must be found, but rather that an unreasoning annihilation may crush dreams and hopes at any moment' (Palmer 1994: 85, 87).

In contrast to *D.O.A.*, *Color Me Dead* begins with the credits superimposed on a single, night-for-night shot, filmed (in Eastmancolor) through the windshield of a convertible crossing Sydney Harbour Bridge. In the mid-1970s, *Taxi Driver*, which starts with a similar sequence, was to become a key marker in film noir's movement from critical to industrial category, providing a link between classical (black-and-white) noir and neo-noir through its rendering of dense and mysterious blacks, and its lurid use of colour (Naremore 1998: 192; Erickson 1996: 314–16). Although *Color Me Dead* soon settles for a vibrant colour pattern closer to something like the 1960s version of the *Dragnet* television series (1967–9), no other sequence evokes the distinctive style (low-key lighting, claustrophobic framing, strong compositional lines) and prototypical setting (dark cityscape, after-hours timeframe, location footage) of noir more strongly than this opening segment. The shot through the windshield – and the use of the motor vehicle as a 'transitive driving force' (Bruno 2001: 57) – is paradigmatic of the genre, from examples such as the opening of the classic noir, *Out of the Past* (Jacques Tourneur, 1947), through the transitional *Taxi Driver* and on to the neo-noir of *Collateral* (Michael Mann, 2004). The retitling of the property– from *D.O.A.* to *Color Me Dead* – at once plays on the predicament of the protagonist – literally coloured to death by the luminous toxin in his bloodstream – but also signals the technological shift from black-and-white original to colour remake. In addition, the film's title – which appears against an optically rendered red gash that irrupts upon the image – together with the jazzy soundtrack act as further generic markers. At the same time, the prominence of the iconic Harbour Bridge and a (redundant) final title, 'SYDNEY, AUSTRALIA', advances a type of 'locationism' – that is, the superimposition of the B-grade protocols of film noir onto a local milieu (see O'Regan 1987: 6–7) – which characterises a number of 'Australian international pictures' of the era, including *The Siege of Pinchgut* (Harry Watt, 1959) which also commences with a segment featuring the Harbour Bridge.

The atmospheric credits for *Color Me Dead* open up to a scene of a shadowy figure entering an office at night. The prowler moves to a wall safe (concealed behind a painting of a modern passenger train) from which he removes an oblong bar of metal, carefully replacing it with a facsimile. The depiction of the crime – the theft of what is later revealed to be a briquette of refined uranium – which will soon entangle the hapless Frank Bigelow, sets up a Cold War theme of espionage, abundantly familiar at the time from such films as the James Bond cycle, especially the contemporaneous *On Her Majesty's Secret Service* (Peter R. Hunt, 1969), and popularised for television by series like *The Man from U.N.C.L.E.* (1964–8), *Mission: Impossible* (1966–73), and spoofed in *Get Smart* (1965–70). At the end of the sequence, the thief (hitherto hidden by dark shadows) turns towards the camera to reveal his identity, just before a shot of the painting on the wall leads (in an overt graphic match) to a near identical train pulling into the station of a small New South Wales town, Mittagong, located around 100 kilometres southwest of Sydney. A single figure – Eugene Phillips (Reg Gillam) – disembarks and is met by the thief – George Reynolds (Michael Laurence) – in a white Mercedes Benz convertible (most likely the automobile seen crossing the Harbour Bridge in the film's opening). Phillips is carrying $50,000 cash payment for the bar of uranium, but before the transaction can be completed the two men make their way to the Village to have the bill of sale notarised.

The next segment picks up the story from where the flashback of the original *D.O.A.* begins, with Bigelow (Tom Tryon) hurrying to finish up business at his office so that he can leave for a bachelor's vacation (in this version) at the subtropical resort town of Surfers Paradise, just south of Brisbane. Bigelow calls out to his co-worker and partner of six years, Paula Gibson (Carolyn Jones), who chastises him for abruptly announcing the vacation, and (more hesitantly) questions why Bigelow feels the need to get away from her for a week. Having worked as an accountant in Mittagong with a partner of long standing, Bigelow evidently requires time away from his routine to re-evaluate and (presumably) confirm his feelings for Paula. The casting – television actors Tryon and Jones in lead roles[3] – together with the flat dialogue and mise-en-scène make for a decidedly melodramatic (and televisual) set-up, the essentially domestic scene interrupted only briefly by the arrival of Phillips and Reynolds for whom Bigelow hastily notarises the bill (a copy of the transaction carelessly left to fall from copier to floor). Jaunty music (Bigelow's 'Vacation Theme') accompanies two brief transition shots of Paula driving Bigelow through Mittagong to the station, the mood abruptly changing upon their arrival at the deserted platform. Bigelow fumbles for small talk, but Paula foreshadows (with clarity) the events to come, telling Bigelow: 'I have a feeling that if you get on that train, you're never coming back.' Bigelow reassures her that he will be back, in just a week, but the music (now playing the melodramatic 'Paula's Theme') swells as Bigelow jumps aboard, leaving Paula to plaintively exit the station alone.

Rather than follow Bigelow directly to his recreation spot (as in the case of *D.O.A.*), *Color Me Dead* detours further in the direction of the crime film (and television series), adding two segments – presumably scripted by Davis himself – to those of Rouse and Greene's original screenplay. The first shows Phillips arriving at the office seen burgled at the film's opening, the painting of the wall that conceals the safe making for its immediate recognition. Phillips is received by the arch villain, Taylor (Rick Jason, in the Majak role of the original *D.O.A.*), and his psychopathic henchman, Chester (Sandy Harbutt). Phillips has come to sell the bar of uranium (which both he and Taylor have yet to realise has been stolen from the latter's own safe) but finds himself out-manoeuvred by the sinister Taylor who pays only $60,000 in cash against the $100,000 that Phillips asks for the metal. The second added segment begins with an establishing shot of the forecourt to the recently (1967) opened Australia Square building, its modernist fifty-storey circular tower – Sydney's first true skyscraper, designed by Harry Seidler & Associates – the location of Phillips' office. Philips asks his secretary, Miss Foster (Penny Sugg), for the whereabouts of his business associate Halliday, places a telephone call to a Marla Stevens, and conceals the brown paper bag carrying the cash payment, along with the notarised bill of sale for the uranium, in the back of a false drawer in his office desk. He has only just left the room when a man – identified only by a jewelled pinky ring – enters through a back door, and steals both.

The International Style: Sydney, Cosmopolitanism and the Globalised City

The modern cosmopolitan lifestyle signalled to this point – most obviously through the international style of Seidler's Australia Square building, but also through the theme and trappings of Cold War espionage – is underlined by Bigelow's arrival at the Chevron resort hotel, the first stage of which was built by entrepreneur Stanley Korman in 1958, and (a decade later) the glitzy location for the 1969 Miss International Air Hostess Quest, Australia's first national, primetime telecast. This type of 'internationalism' – most evident to television and film audiences of the period from the rousing theme and jet-set locations of Peter Stuyvesant cigarette commercials – is evident in such contemporaneous productions as *Moeru tairiku* (*Blazing Continent*, Shogoro Nishimura, 1968), *Nickel Queen* (John McCallum, 1971) and *Bello onesto emigrato Australia sposerebbe compaesana illibata* (*A Girl in Australia*, Luigi Zampa, 1971). Despite their generic trappings and often highly economical mode of production, *Blazing Continent* and *Color Me Dead*, in particular, present striking portraits of a rapidly modernising and internationalising Sydney, with an explicit focus on its modernist architecture. Checking in at the Chevron, Bigelow finds himself surrounded by young, eligible women, most of whom are clad only in bikini swimsuits. Walking to his ground floor room adjacent to the courtyard swimming pool – a milieu something akin to the Fort Lauderdale setting of Elvis Presley's *Girl Happy* (Boris Sagal, 1965) – Bigelow picks his way through a crowd of beautiful vacationers, attracting in particular the attention of a young woman playing beach ball with a group of revellers.

His room open to the pool, Bigelow takes off his shirt, orders a bottle of Scotch, and while answering a call from Paula (who tells Bigelow that a certain Mr Phillips has called) turns to find the girl – Sue (Suzy Kendall) – wriggling half way under his bed, attempting to retrieve the beach ball that has run in from the courtyard.[4] Sue's flirtation with Bigelow, who also climbs in under the bed in an attempt to extract the ball, is interrupted by Sam (Alan Lander), who dryly observes, 'Excuse me, but from here one of you looks like my wife.' Sue, who makes abundantly clear her sexual interest in Bigelow, effusively remarks: 'we're having *a ball*'. They all find the situation good fun, and Sam invites Bigelow to join them for a drink.

That same evening, Bigelow accompanies his new friends, Sue and Sam, to the Pink Panther Club (the exterior, in fact, of a strip joint in Darlinghurst Road in the heart of Sydney's notorious Kings Cross red-light district). The nightclub segment divests itself of the threatening racialised milieu of the juke joint in *D.O.A.*,[5] but (as in the original) does begin to sketch Bigelow's divided state of mind: that is, as a character caught between romantic love and promiscuous sex. It transpires, however, that Bigelow is not much interested in the strippers' routines, and even less in the drunken and increasingly vulgar attentions of Sue, who taunts the strippers: 'Take it off. Go on, take it off!' Turning to Bigelow she adds: 'I can beat that [the strippers' act, and firm bodies]. Ask Sam. He knows, but you don't know. You *could* know. Know what I mean?' Unimpressed by Sue's overly suggestive behaviour, Bigelow moves across to the bar, where he joins an attractive woman (described, by Leo the bartender, as a 'society' type) who frequents the bar, always arriving alone in her convertible, but not leaving without company. Absorbed in conversation with the woman, Bigelow does not notice that the unidentified intruder from Phillips' office – the man with the pinky ring – has tampered with his drink. He does, however, realise that something is amiss when, taking a sip from the glass, he finds the taste irregular. Assuming that Leo has given him the wrong glass he simply asks for a fresh drink, and then moves to leave the club with the phone number of a venue where his new acquaintance might be reached later that evening. As Bigelow walks towards the exit, Sue calls out from across the room, 'Hey Frank, have a look at this.' She steps up onto the stage and effortlessly drops her dress to the floor, leaving poor Sam to drag her drunkenly from the podium.

Next, in another added segment to this version of the story, it becomes evident that Phillips' illicit business transaction with Taylor has become somewhat more complicated. The crime boss has realised that the uranium sold to him was his own product, and Phillips – when pressed to return the cash – finds that the money, along with the bill of sale, has been stolen. Were it not for this (and the earlier) additional scenes that build up the storyline of espionage, the melodramatic line that propels the Bigelow-Paula part of the story would lead the film towards a premature narrative conclusion. Bigelow returns to the Chevron, and begins to dial the society woman's number, but while doing so he observes a vase of flowers, sent by Paula, seated atop the television set. Bigelow reads the attached note and smiles fondly ('Paula's Theme' plays throughout the sequence), and then tears the paper that carries the other woman's number, drops it in the wastebasket, and retires (alone) for the evening. Whatever Bigelow's exact motivation for the week's break in Surfers Paradise, it seems at this point in the story that he will – as Paula had hoped – be returned to her with a greater appreciation for their relationship and resolve to marry after an overly long courtship. However, as Palmer points out (with reference to *D.O.A.*), the true subject of the narrative is yet to fully emerge, even though the actions of Phillips, Taylor and the mysterious figure (with the pinky ring) now stalking Bigelow have already begun to 'hint at the workings of an arbitrary, capricious malevolence' that will recast the narrative and seal Bigelow's fate (Palmer 1994: 87).

Sunshine Noir on the Gold Coast

Waking the next morning, Bigelow feels strangely ill. His first thought is that he has mixed his drinks, but walking through the hard and glary streets of Surfers Paradise – the mise-en-scène recalls the 'sunshine noir' of site-specific television series such as *77 Sunset Strip* (1958–64), *Hawaiian Eye* (1959–63) and *Surfside Six* (1960–2) – he thinks to stop at a local medical centre (see Sandars 2008: 11–12). The initial diagnosis is that Bigelow is in perfect health, but the results of a blood test soon reveal his actual condition; namely, that he has a luminous toxic matter – a deadly poison – in his system. Having already absorbed the substance into his body (and with no known antidote), Bigelow is told that the toxin will kill him within a day or two. Dismissing the assessment as a bad mistake – 'You're telling me I'm dead', he exclaims – Bigelow hurriedly leaves. Crossing the road to the Surfers Paradise Hospital, he consults a second physician, Dr McDonald (Tom Oliver), who confirms the original diagnosis. The doctor explains that the poison has been in Bigelow's system for some twelve hours. McDonald begins to arrange for his admission to the hospital, but when Bigelow admits to not knowing how the poison was imbibed, McDonald declares: 'Then this was no accident. Somebody knew how to handle this stuff. Judging by the amount of alcohol in your system you must have got it in liquor.' Telling the still uncomprehending Bigelow that it is now a case of homicide, McDonald bluntly explains: 'I don't think you understand, Mr Bigelow. You've been murdered.'

Murdered, but not yet dead, Bigelow runs from the hospital. Making his way in a blind panic down the main street of Surfers Paradise – the doctor's words, 'you've been murdered', echoing in his head – Bigelow comes to rest on a street corner, a shop window sign offering an ironic commentary: 'Think of your future. Invest today.' Coming to his senses, Bigelow realises that he has no hope of saving himself, but should he prove equal to the task, he now has the unique opportunity of finding his own murderer.[6] As Thomas Leitch explains, the *D.O.A.* screenplay 'blueprint' offers the most economic encapsulation of the (Hollywood) 'victim film', a subcategory of the crime genre in which an embattled and persecuted protagonist is transformed from passive victim into a far more traditional active hero, one empowered and capable of eliminating his (or her) initially more threatening tormentors (Leitch 2002: 80). As in the case of *D.O.A.*, the fact that 'the inescapable threat of death [is] not merely impending but already accomplished' frees Bigelow of any social inhibitions and institutional restraints, allowing him to freely interrogate suspects, use excessive force, and – ultimately – abandon his reticence in expressing his true feelings for Paula (Leitch 2002: 82). As Leitch puts it:

> As a result of getting murdered but still being alive . . . Frank [Bigelow] not only enjoys a unique indemnity against danger (since there is nothing anybody can do to him that will make his situation any worse) but has the opportunity to occupy all three major positions associated with crime fiction: victim, detective, and criminal (or at least dispenser of vigilante justice unencumbered by the law). In terms of the film's black-and-white morality, Frank's death is none too high a price to pay for the exhilarating privilege of serving as judge, jury, and executioner of the man who killed him. (Leitch 2002: 82)

Dead on Arrival

Bigelow – now cast as a prototypical noir protagonist, trapped with *no way out* – begins his quest for justice by retracing his steps in the hope of uncovering some information from the previous evening's activities. First he returns to the Pink Panther Club only to find it closed, a janitor offering no assistance. At the seedy location, he has hallucinations of the previous evening, tawdry images of the strippers,[7] and of the temptation – sexual urges – that led him to the illusion that there might be something more awaiting him in Surfers Paradise than what he already had in Mittagong with Paula. He remembers, too, Sam and Sue's encouragement (sinister, in retrospect) that he 'have another drink'. Next, Bigelow returns to the Chevron, only to find that his companions from the previous evening have returned to their workaday marriage, and that the torn fragments of the woman's phone number have already been emptied from the wastebasket. Bigelow's fledgling investigative steps have drawn a blank, but a call and chance remark from Paula – that Eugene Phillips, who the day before had been so anxious to contact Bigelow about a business matter, is now dead – gives him a fresh lead. Suspecting a connection, Bigelow immediately flies to Sydney where at Phillips' Australia Square offices he talks first to Phillips' secretary and then to Phillips' associate, Halliday (Tony Ward) from whom he learns that Phillips committed suicide by jumping from a sixth storey window. Desperate and unfettered by any courtesy that he might have shown the widow, Bigelow moves on to immediately interview Mrs Phillips (Margot Reid) at her apartment. Bigelow finds the widow of little assistance, but Phillips' brother, Stanley (Peter Sumner), explains that his sibling was in 'great trouble', driven to suicide by his involvement in some (uncharacteristically) unlawful transaction.

By this point in *Color Me Dead*, director Davis – through his expansion of the Rouse and Greene crime story – has introduced every 'type' and player in this tangled story of theft, murder and intrigue: the instigator (Phillips), the trickster (Reynolds), the crime boss (Taylor), the thug (Chester), the associate (Halliday), the secretary (Miss Foster), the mistress (Marla), the wife (Mrs Phillips), the brother-in-law (Stanley) and the victim-detective-vigilante (Bigelow). Bigelow is already 'dead', Phillips has committed suicide under suspicious circumstances, Reynolds cannot be located, and – soon enough – bodies will start piling up in a situation as complicated as anything from the infamously convoluted *The Big Sleep* (Howard Hawks, 1946). Davis' laboured presentation of what (in Rouse and Greene's script) is dispensable (or at least pedestrian) backstory, together with the appearance of Tony Ward as Halliday – an actor best known to local audiences for his title role in the Australian espionage series, *Hunter* (1967–9) – tags the film generically and routinely as a crime story. At the same time, the film's bizarre scenario – everyman Bigelow's sudden descent into existential crisis and the subsequent tracking of his own executioner – mark it out (thematically) as a close relation to the celebrated television noir of *The Fugitive*, and Richard Kimble's comparable quest 'to establish his innocence and get out from under the death sentence that hangs over his head' (Sandars 2008: 8–9).

ANYWHERE: TRANSNATIONAL GENRE BETWEEN AUSTRALIA AND THE US

Bigelow returns to his hotel – the Menzies Hotel (opened in 1963) in Sydney's Carrington Street – where a call from Paula provides one piece of the puzzle: she has found a copy of the bill of sale that identifies a transaction between Eugene Phillips and George Reynolds. Finally realising his connection to the Phillips case, Bigelow returns with new resolve to Mrs Phillips' apartment to ask why her husband did not use the notarised bill to establish his innocence. She tells him that the bill, along with the bag of cash, mysteriously vanished from Phillips' office drawer and that his attempts to locate Reynolds were unsuccessful. Suspecting that the office secretary, Miss Foster, knows more than she revealed during their initial meeting, Bigelow returns to Phillips' offices. Finding Miss Foster at the Summit Restaurant – a revolving eatery on the 47th floor of Australia Square with panoramic views of Sydney Harbour – Bigelow learns that, on the day of his death, Phillips placed a call to his 'friend', Marla Stevens (Patricia Connolly), the glamorous Ann-Margret-like redhead gratuitously slapped around by Taylor in an earlier scene. Bigelow finds Marla, apparently Phillips' mistress, in the midst of packing her bags for a one-way trip to Buenos Aires. Thinking that Marla has conspired with Reynolds to set up Phillips, and then stage his suicide and poison Bigelow to cover up evidence of the uranium transaction, Bigelow sets out after her assumed accomplice, armed with a photograph of Reynolds, and a revolver that he has fearlessly wrestled from Marla.

Transformed from ordinary man to obsessed avenger, Bigelow hires a car and makes his way to a photographic studio – located in a deserted industrial zone – where he hopes to obtain an address for the man – Reynolds – in the picture. Bigelow does not get the address but, in a further twist, learns that the name 'George Reynolds' is an alias for Raymond Taylor, nephew of arch villain, Bradley Taylor. Earlier, upon realising that the uranium sold to him by Phillips was his own product, Taylor has commented that he suspects that his nephew has something to do with it, and this is now confirmed by Bigelow's discovery of Reynolds' true identity. Returning to his vehicle, Bigelow is ambushed and shot at by a sniper – the pinky ring man, again – perched on a pedestrian bridge overhead. Taking cover in a deserted railway terminus, Bigelow – just twenty-four hours earlier a reserved small-town accountant, but now a condemned man operating outside the law – has no hesitation in exchanging gunshots, eventually driving the gunman from the terminus and allowing Bigelow to make his escape back to his city lodgings.

The Menzies Hotel affords Bigelow his first (brief) respite since arriving in Sydney. In a phone call (and reprise of 'Paula's Theme'), Bigelow finally finds the opportunity to admit to Paula: 'I never should have left you. I just didn't realise how much I love you.' The quiet interlude is interrupted, though, by Chester who enters the room with two of Taylor's henchmen. Playing the part of 'young wild west' – that is, the type of quick to temper young thug immortalised by Wilmer (Elisha Cook Jr) in *The Maltese Falcon* (John Huston, 1941) – Chester tells Bigelow, 'I'd just love to let you have it', and issues a grizzly warning: 'if you so much as look cockeyed at anybody, I'll blow the back of your skull out'. Chester drags Bigelow off to Taylor's office. Also present is Marla, and Bigelow tells them that he believes 'Reynolds' killed Phillips, then poisoned him (to cover up the uranium transaction), and made another attempt on his life only an hour before at the deserted railyard. But Taylor proves Bigelow wrong, pointing out that 'Reynolds' – in reality his nephew Raymond – is dead, fished out of the harbour the previous evening.

Taylor – always the professional – casually (even apologetically) tells Bigelow that because he has learned too much about his own part in the uranium ring he is obliged to have him eliminated, right away. Accordingly, the condemned man Bigelow is sent off on a patented private-eye excursion, a 'last ride' with Chester from which he is not meant to return.

In Taylor's office, Bigelow has already demonstrated that he does not fear Chester, even taking a swing at him when provoked. Chester is now clearly excited at the prospect of a kill, and holding Bigelow at gunpoint as he drives through the Sydney nightscape tells him: 'I'm going to enjoy this . . . I don't like you. I didn't like that puss of yours from the minute I saw it. I'm going to give it to you in the belly: you don't like it in the belly.' When they pull up alongside a police vehicle stopped at traffic lights, Chester urges Bigelow to 'try it', but the accountant holds his nerve, later seizing the opportunity to overpower Chester by grabbing the steering wheel as he is taking a corner. The car crashes into a fire hydrant and, first to recover, Bigelow runs into a busy indoor shopping mall, Roselands, in Sydney's southwest. The recently opened (1965) Roselands was one of Australia's first multilevel shopping centres and (though modest in size by contemporary standards) was, at the time, the largest indoor mall in the Southern Hemisphere. Roselands Mall – along with its centrepiece, the Raindrop Fountain – presents another face of 'internationalised' and corporatised (semi-)urban Australia and provides the setting for the film's largest set piece, Chester's frenzied pursuit of Bigelow through the complex. In a scene that anticipates a similar mall setting, pursuit and outcome – the foot chase through the exclusive mall on Rodeo Drive in the neo-noir, *Body Double* (Brian De Palma, 1984) – Chester sights and takes aim at Bigelow, but is shot dead by a police officer before he can get away a round.

Bigelow – increasingly wearied by his ordeal – makes his way back to the Menzies Hotel, this time to find Paula waiting for him on the street. The sight of his long-time companion brings Bigelow crashing down to the hard reality that he is trapped in a blind alley with no exit: 'All I did was notarise a paper, one paper out of hundreds', he tells her. Paula – still unaware of any of the details of the case, but intuitive of the situation – expresses her deep concern, saying 'I have a feeling that I'm losing you.' Bigelow doesn't tell Paula that he is dying, but urges her to leave, and assures her: 'I love you. I was never so certain of anything in my life. I wasn't sure before. I didn't know what I had.' In the strict moral universe of film noir, Bigelow's attempt to evade the responsibility and promise of small-town married life has come at a heavy cost. In a sequence that rounds out the film's opening, and ties up the Frank-Paula narrative thread, Bigelow adds: 'Sometimes something has to happen to a man . . . to make him realise how much someone means to him. How much he loves someone.' Although consoled by the admission, Paula is left (as in the early station sequence) close to tears, and now for the last time.

With 'George Reynolds' dead, and Taylor only taking a professional interest in Bigelow's fate, Bigelow thinks (incorrectly, as it turns out) that Miss Foster and Stanley Phillips are behind his murder and also that of Eugene Phillips. When Bigelow goes to Mrs Phillips' apartment to confront Stanley, his visit coincides with that of Miss Foster who explains that she has received a call from Stanley saying that he is ill. Together they discover Stanley and Mrs Phillips exhibiting the same symptoms initially felt by Bigelow. Telling Miss Foster to call the emergency hospital for an ambulance before it is too late, Bigelow learns from Mrs Phillips – evidently resigned to her own fate for her own infidelities – that it was Halliday who served the drinks. She goes on to tell Bigelow (and explain to the, by this point, bewildered audience) that Halliday is behind it all: Halliday seduced her with the promise of taking her away with him, set up and subsequently staged Phillips' 'suicide', murdered Reynolds to cover up the deal, and has now poisoned her and Stanley, just as he did Bigelow the previous evening. Upon learning that Halliday is about to depart with Marla for South America, Bigelow heads for the harbour. Aboard an ocean liner (a mildly anachronistic location for the denouement, shot on the Lloyd Triestino liner Galileo at Circular Quay) he confronts and chases Halliday to the bowels of the vessel. A fistfight ensues and Halliday, accidentally opening a steam valve, is burned and falls to his death. A quick shot of his pinky ring confirms (to the audience, at least) that he has indeed been responsible for the theft of cash from Phillips' drawer, the rifle attack on Bigelow earlier that afternoon, and the fatal poisoning of Bigelow the previous night. In a coda – that belatedly replays the famous opening of *D.O.A.* – Bigelow, bruised and bloodied but with his mission now complete, makes his way to a NSW police department building where he asks to see the man in charge. He tells him that he wants to report a murder. When asked who was murdered, Bigelow replies – 'I was' – before collapsing dead (on arrival).

Internationalising Australia

Color Me Dead was sold direct to cable television in the US and released theatrically through MGM in Australia (opening on 5 March 1970) where it screened in Melbourne and Sydney alongside (a record number of) three other Australian-made or co-produced films: *Age of Consent* (Michael Powell, 1969), *Squeeze a Flower* (Marc Daniels, 1970) and *The Set* (Frank Brittain, 1970). *Color Me Dead*'s international credentials and universal appeal were signalled in the local press. A feature article in the *Australian Women's Weekly* predicted the film 'will be a boost to the Australian movie industry ... an accomplishment [that will] more than pleasantly surprise the experts' (Musgrove 1969: 8), and *Film Weekly* described *Color Me Dead* as 'an Australian film you can support without drawing on your patriotism' ('Four Aussie Films Release in Sydney' 1970: 1). These types of comments not only endorsed *Color Me Dead*'s genre credentials, but also the image of an 'internationalised Australia' promoted by the choice of Surfers Paradise and the Sydney location settings. Less encouraging, however, was the US trade journal *Variety* which described *Color Me Dead* as 'a leisurely remake of the 1949 sleeper *D.O.A.*', one that stretched and anesthetised the original's 83-minute running time to a slow 97 minutes characterised by 'a pointless melange of swindlers, murderers and red herrings' (Spil 1970: 38). 'Remaining but little realised', continues the review, 'is the truly unique idea of having a poisoned man search for his own killer' (Spil 1970: 38). According to Pike and Cooper, the film's 'Australian theatrical release through M.G.M. was cursory', going on to detail that a 'poorly publicized week . . . at three Melbourne theatres was scarcely a success' (1998: 248). Despite this, *Color Me Dead* nonetheless signals the presence and historical significance of the hitherto rarely interrogated category of Australian noir, a form seldom examined prior to the release of another international co-production, *Dark City* (Alex Proyas, 1998).[8] Rarely seen and little commented upon since its initial showings, *Color Me Dead* – with its forlorn romanticism, sense of malevolent evil and Antipodean variations on an overly familiar genre – deserves to be remembered, at the very least, as a curious hybrid of crime thriller and television noir that highlights Sydney's increased internationalisation and modernisation. It is also a work that occupies not only the interval between classic and neo-noir, but the neglected interstice of postwar and pre-'revival' 'Australian international pictures'.

Notes

1. Musgrove puts the budget for *Color Me Dead* at $500,000 (1969: 8). O'Brien puts the combined budget for all three films at between $1.5 and $2 million (1970b: 35).
2. The neo-noir 1988 *D.O.A.* remake announces itself as a high-tech noir, complete with a four-minute, black-and-white prologue, brimming with shadows and tilted compositions. It replays the opening of the 1949 original, but in this version it is college professor Dexter Cornell (Dennis Quaid) who staggers into a police station to report that a murder has been committed and that Cornell *himself* is the victim (see Verevis 2004).
3. The casting of Tryon and Jones firmly establishes *Color Me Dead*'s television credentials. Jones began a career in feature films, appearing in noirs such as *The Big Heat* (Fritz Lang, 1953), *Baby Face Nelson* (Don Siegel, 1957) and *King Creole* (Michael Curtiz, 1958), but from the early 1960s she mainly appeared in television series such as *Burke's Law* (1963–6) before landing her signature role as Morticia Addams in *The Addams Family* (1964–6). Tryon's best-known feature-film role was the lead in Otto Preminger's *The Cardinal* (1963), but he was more widely known for his television work, especially in westerns, and notably the title role in the Disney series *Texas John Slaughter* (1958–61) which screened as part of *Walt Disney Presents* (1958–61). Perhaps least recognisable of the three leads was Rick Jason, another television actor known principally for his role of Lieutenant Gil Hanley in *Combat!* (1962–7).

4. Kendall is not the UK star who played in *To Sir, with Love* (James Clavell, 1967) and several Giallo films of the early 1970s, but a little-known Australian actress who appeared in Australian television series such as *Homicide, Hunter* (1967–9) and *Division 4*.
5. In this respect, *Color Me Dead* – like Tay Garnett's version of *The Postman Always Rings Twice* (1946) – is a 'white-washed' noir, removing the jazz club setting and altering the 'foreign' names of characters: Majak becomes Taylor; Marla Rakubian is renamed Marla Stevens.
6. This is the tagline for the US Spotlite video release: 'He's a DEAD MAN . . . But he won't rest until he finds his own MURDERER!'
7. The shots of topless dancers in this sequence landed the film in mild controversy and delayed its Australian theatrical release (see Spil 1970: 38).
8. In a move that is characteristic of the genre more generally, Australian 'noir' has tended to be categorised long after the production of many of its key examples. For example, the recent edited collection, *Australian Genre Film*, includes chapters devoted to the 'New Australian Crime Drama' and 'Sun-Lit Noir: Australian Thrillers' (Dolgopolov 2021: 74–89; Rayner 2021: 186–201). Both of these chapters link contemporary examples to precedents emerging from the 1970s onwards.

9. NED KELLY (1970)

NED KELLY: AUSTRALIA'S FIRST MULTIMEDIA STAR

Any representation of the figure of Ned Kelly (1855–80) – the 'loud-mouthed, law-breaking, swaggering, son of an Irish convict' (McIntyre 1982: 38) – is framed not only by the historical record but also by an intertextual relay that includes a vast array of novels, plays, operas, songs, comics, video games, and a long history of cinematic portrayals of the famed bushranger, beginning with *The Story of the Kelly Gang* (Charles Tait, 1906) and extending through to *True History of the Kelly Gang* (Justin Kurzel, 2019) (see Gaunson 2013). While the depiction of Kelly in each version varies, sometimes considerably, depending on its principal source and approach – from the close attention to specific historical accounts in the TV miniseries *The Last Outlaw* (George Miller and Kevin Dobson, 1980) to outright parody in *Ned* (Abe Forsythe, 2003) – each attests to the cultural resonance, continuing power and local and international recognition of the Kelly myth and its foundational place in popular conceptions of Australian identity and its audiovisual heritage. It is this continued fascination, and the ability to use Kelly's story to address key aspects of Australian history and character, which has led to the production of over a dozen Kelly-related feature films and numerous documentaries, TV movies and series, and short films. The story and character have also proven attractive to filmmakers – both from overseas and locally – seeking an Australian *and* international audience (though, perhaps surprisingly, few of these films have been significant financial or critical successes). The themes of youthful anti-authoritarianism, liberation and social injustice that run through many iterations of the Kelly saga, may also have been particularly attractive to filmmakers in the mid-to-late 1960s aiming to explore revisionist and politically progressive variations on established genres and forms. At this moment, almost 100 years after his death, Ned Kelly may have seemed like a figure whose 'time' had well and truly come.

British director Tony Richardson's interest in making a film about the Australian outlaw was piqued by Sidney Nolan's celebrated series of Ned Kelly paintings that were successfully exhibited in London in the early 1960s. Richardson was likely drawn not only to the poetry, humour, visual boldness and pathos of Nolan's canvases but also to the broader themes of violence, injustice and betrayal across the twenty-seven paintings (1946–7) depicting the main events of the story of Kelly and his gang, from the shooting of constables at Stringybark Creek to the siege at Glenrowan and ending with the trial in Melbourne at which Kelly was sentenced to death. As Justin Corfield describes, the 'simplicity yet overwhelming power' of Nolan's rendering of Kelly, '[the] black helmet – sometimes with the sky beyond visible through the eye-slit, at other times bloodshot eyes – has made it the quintessential Kelly image' (2003: 366). According to Richardson, it was the 'strange image of the home-made suit of armour' that immediately drew him to the outlaw story and character: 'Ned Kelly was a natural anti-authority hero – a bank robber and thief to some; a kind of Robin Hood of the bush to others. His story . . . was a natural for a movie' (Richardson 1993: 221; see also Allen 1969: 9).

Richardson's resulting film also had a much longer gestation. Richardson formed Woodfall Film Productions in 1958 with writer John Osborne and producer Harry Saltzman, and the company went on to produce many of the key films of the British 'new wave', a significant number of them directed by Richardson in an extraordinary five-year run: *Look Back in Anger* (1959), *The Entertainer* (1960), *A Taste of Honey* (1961), *The Loneliness of the Long Distance Runner* (1962), and *Tom Jones* (1963). It also provided an important home for other directors and actors of the 'new wave' like Karel Reisz and Albert Finney. According to Stephen Gaunson, *Ned Kelly* first emerged in 1962 as a project instigated by Reisz and Finney, with an initial script completed by novelist and screenwriter, David Storey (2010: 258). After this was rejected by Columbia Pictures – who were expecting a more generic, western-style treatment – and Finney and Reisz moved onto other projects, Richardson picked up the property (Gaunson 2010: 258). Richardson's career had reached a meteoric zenith with the commercial and critical success of *Tom Jones* (the filmmaker receiving the Academy Award for Best Director and Best Film in 1964) but most of his subsequent features, aside from *The Charge of the Light Brigade* (1968) – a significant box-office failure but well-received critically –

met with little favour. In light of this, travelling to the other side of the world to make *Ned Kelly* probably seemed like a very attractive opportunity for Richardson at this stage of his faltering career.

Outlaw, Rock Star or Rebel? Revitalising Ned

With a budget of around $2.5 million secured from United Artists, Richardson approached Ian Jones, author of the provocative essay 'A New View of Ned Kelly' (1968: 154–89), to collaborate with him on a revised screenplay for the film. Principally known at the time for his television work at Crawford Productions (Melbourne), Jones went on to co-write the screenplay for *The Last Outlaw*, the four-part mini-series mentioned above based on the life of Ned Kelly, as well as key reference books about the Kelly gang including *Ned Kelly: A Short Life* (1995) and *The Fatal Friendship: Ned Kelly, Aaron Sherritt and Joe Byrne* (2003). Meeting with Richardson in October 1968, Jones was encouraged to find that the filmmaker shared his view that Kelly should be depicted as an Irishman: '[Richardson] saw a lot of poetry in Ned and thought, as I did, that the Irish roots were very, very important. He believed that Ned should speak with an Irish accent. This was revolutionary at the time. Ned was always archetypically Australian' (quoted in Stanton 2019). In London, Richardson began the process of casting for the role of Ned, testing several actors including Ian McKellen before turning to the seemingly unlikely option of Mick Jagger: 'Mick was sniffing at a career as an actor. I'd always been a fan of the [Rolling] Stones and was excited by the prospect: the wicked battered "Irish" face was perfect for Ned' (Richardson 1993: 224). Elsewhere Richardson stated that Jagger would 'present the human "reality" of . . . the "justifiably angry rebel" that the historical Kelly really was' (Rawlins 1969: 9): '[I] always thought with Ned that it shouldn't be an actor, but someone who has the inner reality. As soon as I met Mick and got to know him, I recognised this in him' (Allen 1969: 9). Although Richardson later admitted that, 'having gone for Mick, I should have made a very different kind of film' (1993: 224), he initially defended the choice of star, later telling *The Guardian*: 'I became interested in a man [Kelly] who was a criminal, a revolutionary, a dreamer, an idealist, who wrote letters to Members of Parliament from his hideout. In choosing Mick I felt he was absolutely right for the part' (Langley in Shail 2012: 110).

News of Richardson's bold casting decision came to public attention in May 1969 when the *Daily Mail* (London) reported that Jagger was to star as the outlaw in a $2,142,000 film to be shot in Australia, with Jagger's then girlfriend, singer-actor Marianne Faithfull, in the role of Kelly's sister, Maggie ('Mick Jagger "Ned Kelly"' 1969: 3; 'Kelly Roles' 1969: 3). Early the following month, Woodfall Film Productions confirmed that it intended to go ahead with its plans for the singer to star in the film despite Jagger and Faithfull being remanded on a drugs charge (until 23 June) just one month before filming was due to start, and amid increasingly loud protests at the casting from the people of Glenrowan, site of Kelly's last stand, and still home to some of his relatives ('Jagger's Role in Film Confirmed' 1969: 6). The local press reported that 'Mac' Holten, Country Party MP for the Federal Division of Indi 'in the heart of "Kelly country"', had presented a petition and hundreds of letters protesting against the choice of Jagger as lead, asking the Minister for Immigration, Billy Snedden, to refuse Jagger entry into Australia ('MP Acts to Keep Jagger Out' 1969: 3). Urged by residents to take the matter to Canberra and 'drop it in [Prime Minister] Gorton's lap', Holten said he would do whatever possible at a federal level to prevent 'this pop singer fellow' from portraying Kelly ('Trouble in Kelly Country' 1969: 10). The response from senior immigration department officials was to point out that, as a British subject with no criminal record, Jagger required no other authority to enter Australia ('MP Acts' 1969: 3). Moreover, once it was announced that filming would take place not in Victoria but southeast of Canberra in the Tallaganda and Yarrowlumla shires on the Southern Tablelands of New South Wales, local communities embraced the casting choice, reportedly telegramming Jagger: 'if Errol Flynn can play Robin Hood, a pom . . . then you can play Ned Kelly for ours' ('Actors Upset' 1969: 9).

Jagger and Faithfull arrived at Sydney's Kingsford Smith Airport on Tuesday, 8 July 1969 to a small reception of press and fans, with Jagger 'dressed [in clothes least likely for a national folk hero] like an advertisement for Carnaby Street . . . in maroon maxi coat, black-and-white checked flared trousers, high heeled boots, a straw hat, with a long white Isadora scarf around his neck and carrying a fringed leather handbag' ('Braidwood is Laying it On' 1969: 3). Plans to move on to Melbourne the following day to begin filming were, however, immediately thrown into disorder when Faithfull collapsed and was admitted unconscious to St Vincent's Hospital where 'detectives from Sydney's Police Drug Squad maintained a constant vigil . . . waiting to interview Miss Faithfull when she regain[ed] consciousness' ('Jagger's Girlfriend Still Unconscious' 1969: 7; see also Drewe 1969: 1; 'Crisis Over for Miss Faithfull' 1969: 1). Jagger and Richardson attended the Wednesday press conference as scheduled, the former responding to suspicions that Faithfull had overdosed on illegal drugs by attributing her collapse to the long flight from London: 'she's a very delicate woman and the trip just knocked her' (Frizell 1969: 6). Further questioned over his suitability for the role, Jagger admitted that while he bore no physical resemblance, many critics had failed to realise just how young Kelly was and that Jagger himself was just the right age: 'Ned was only 25 when he died – and how old is Chips Rafferty? Ned Kelly was a young guy, and young people will be interested in the film about him' (Frizell 1969: 6). Moreover, appealing to both Richardson's intuition that Kelly should be played as a rebel-hero, and to his own reputation as an iconoclast, Jagger added: 'I'm very excited [for the role] ... It's a good chance to play an individual who kicks the ---- out of the establishment' (Drewe 1969: 1).

The Ned Kelly Drop: Shooting Ned

In Victoria, restorations had been undertaken at the Old Melbourne Gaol in preparation for the shooting of the hanging sequence that opens the film. Built over a period of twenty years in the mid-nineteenth century, the 'hill' on Russell Street was the site of 133 hangings undertaken between 1842 and 1929, after which time capital punishment was relocated to HM Prison Pentridge before finally being abolished in 1967, just two years before the filming of *Ned Kelly*. The Old Melbourne Gaol was cleaned and reconditioned for the film and a replica of the gallows – the original beam and apparatus had been moved to Pentridge – was restored to its previous state ('Preparing for Ned's End' 1969: 3). In Melbourne, Richardson rehearsed the hanging drop with an off-duty policeman, Constable Ken Webb, 'a veteran stunt man [and] former athletics coach and wrestler' who claimed he was 'the only man in Melbourne ... prepared to do the "Ned Kelly drop"' ('She's Still Ned's Sister' 1969: 2). With Faithfull still unconscious and seriously ill (from what turned out to be an overdose of prescription drugs), Jagger left Sydney for Melbourne on Friday, 11 July to undertake, over two days, the scenes at the prison. Appearing publicly for the first time in his 'Kelly face' – his long hair cut and wearing a short beard – Jagger described, 'with feeling', his experience at the gallows of the Old Melbourne Gaol and his thoughts on capital punishment: 'pretty horrible ... I don't think anyone should be hanged' (Beattie 1969: 1; 'Jagger's Locks Gone' 1969: 3). Importantly (even though it did not do much to shift the general public's attitude), those present at the filming reported, positively, on Jagger's commitment to the role. Bonnie Muir, who played the hangman, applauded Jagger: 'I was really impressed with the man. He is a very good actor who sincerely wants to play the role well' (Drewe 1969: 1). And Jones, who always maintained that Jagger did not have the sheer physicality required for the part, conceded upon meeting Jagger at the Gaol that 'Richardson's gamble was paying off ... [At] his execution ... [Jagger] achieved a taut and defiant dignity; [and at] the courtroom scenes, including the last exchange with Sir Redmond Barry [filmed at the Old Magistrates' Court, adjacent to the Gaol] ... Mick's performance ... was "very powerful"' (Jones 1969: 13).

Although some were coming to accept that Jagger might have the capacity to inhabit the role of Kelly, others were expressing an overall dissatisfaction with the overseas incursion, and the casting of an international star. The

Tribune (Sydney), for instance, wrote 'Ned Kelly was a gentleman compared to Woodville [sic] Films':

> English movie-maker Tony Richardson ... plans to begin shooting in a few days' time ... near Canberra, with British pop-star Mick Jagger ... Most Australian actors are by now resigned to the fact that Jagger ... will play the nation's most popular folk-hero. With an indigenous film industry virtually non-existent, it [the casting of overseas leads] seems to be the price we have to pay for the making of films by overseas companies who are seeking world-wide distribution of their product and who consequently consider they have to use some star of international fame ... in the main part. ('Ned Kelly Was a Gentleman' 1969: 6)

Admitting that Richardson had advanced an 'interesting theory' in justification of the choice of Jagger – namely, '[Jagger is] a rebel, the same as Kelly, and there's Irish blood in his veins' – and that the production would provide ample opportunity for local talent by way of another eighty-three speaking parts, the *Tribune* nonetheless noted that Actors Equity was not pleased with the 'wretched rates' offered by Woodfall for Australia's talent: '[our] actors [are] hopping mad and swearing that the bushranging era is not dead' ('Ned Kelly Was a Gentleman' 1969: 6). Acknowledging that Richardson's film was part of a worldwide pattern of major studios making films in countries where they could exploit local conditions and contract cast and crew at lower rates, the *Tribune* said Woodfall's attitude nonetheless represented 'a prime piece of cultural exploitation – in addition to treating Australians as if they were still colonial subjects' ('Ned Kelly Was a Gentleman' 1969: 7). Although these comments refer directly to the practices employed in the making of *Ned Kelly*, they also closely resemble some of the critical pronouncements that met the production of films such as *Kangaroo* (Lewis Milestone, 1952), *Summer of the Seventeenth Doll* (Leslie Norman, 1959) and *Walkabout* (Nicolas Roeg, 1971). As a result, *Ned Kelly* became caught up in the simmering debate around the need for a truly local film industry supported by government subsidisation and legislation.

Richardson, Jagger and other members of the cast – including Diane Craig, who had replaced Faithfull as Kelly's sister – flew into Canberra, and then on to company headquarters at Queanbeyan on Sunday, 13 July. Others connected to the film – including production designer Jocelyn Herbert, and construction and property people – were already at work preparing the principal township shooting locations at Braidwood, Bungendore and Captains Flat. Richardson had further antagonised the people of Glenrowan – arguing that the area was too settled and that the old buildings in the towns outside of Canberra could more readily stand in for the bank at Euroa and the hotels at Jerilderie and Glenrowan – but the townships in NSW playfully embraced the novelty of the location filming and the opportunity it provided for locals (Bosser 1970: 8–14). The previous month, when it was leaked that Richardson, Herbert and producer Neil Hartley were conducting a 'secret' survey of the environs by taking a motorised trolley along the Bungendore-Captains Flat railway line, locals from the largely derelict, former copper mining town of Captains Flat formed a 'Kelly gang' and rode out to intercept the railway party, telling Richardson to 'bail up' ('The "Kellys" at the Flat' 1969: 1). Tom 'Skunk' Kerr, who took the role of Ned in the raid, said 'if they want Mick Jagger to play the part of Ned Kelly [then] that's their business [but] the way we're planning things we'll get more out of that film company than they'll get out of us ... Old Captains Flat will get plenty of publicity out of it' (Newton 1969: 2). The same pragmatic attitude was taken up in the neighbouring towns of Bungendore and Braidwood. Frank Bryce, shire clerk at Tallaganda, reported that the people of Braidwood, whose main street would be prepared for filming by dumping hundreds of tons of dirt over the bitumen road, were not only 'excited' about the company using the town, but also by the casting of Jagger: 'we hope to start a tourist industry around here ... and this will be good publicity for the town' ('Braidwood is Laying it On' 1969: 3).

Local concerns over the suitability of an overseas production house telling the story of a national folk hero related not only to the casting of Jagger, but also as to whether Richardson, an outsider, was committed to historical accuracy – to the pursuit of the detail of a costume or the source of some obscure incident – in order to 'authentically' recreate the film's period setting. Like all dramatised versions of the Kelly story, there is in Richardson's telling some deviation with respect to actual persons and incidents, but from the outset Jones attested to the filmmaker's detailed knowledge of his subject and meticulous preplanning. Offering as evidence the production's reconstruction of the Kelly homestead (historically, a hut on Eleven Mile Creek, halfway between Greta and Glenrowan) about six miles out from Bungendore, Jones described the 'superb first impression [of] trudging up the well-churned track [of a small hill], topping the rise, and looking down to the small grey homestead beside the eroded creek':

> Your eye took in the smoke from the chimney, the dogs chained by their hollow-log kennels, the pigs, the chooks, the cabbage patch, the potato field, the rail fences. Closer, I was delighted by the detail of the building. The weathered, roughly adzed slabs, the bark roof with its jockey poles and riders, the worn stone work by the back door, the unself-conscious scatter of frontier Victoriana on the back porch. The total impression was almost staggeringly authentic. (Jones 1969: 11)

Entering the cottage, Jones admired the props and furniture and noticed that the walls were lined with smoked, worn and peeling newspapers. Upon closer inspection he read the masthead and dates of the papers – 'Benalla Ensign' and 'Melbourne Age' of 1873 – and came to the realisation that these had been 'specially printed by the art department, pasted on the rebuilt walls of the hut, then meticulously aged'. For Jones, the newspapers not only typified the passionate regard for detail shown by the art department – Herbert and art director, Andrew Sanders – but also that 'their attitude echoe[d] Tony Richardson's [careful] approach to the whole exciting project' (Jones 1969: 11).

Although accounts of the filming, in the middle of the Southern Hemisphere winter, reported fairly tough and demanding conditions (Thurston 1969: 7), at least one participant described the festive nature of the shoot: '[the location at Captains Flat was] like a huge circus encampment [with] large green and white striped tents and shining caravans litter[ing] the rough landscape' (Munson 1969: 12). In these accounts, the atmosphere appeared relaxed and Jagger charmed the locals, autographing pictures and posing for photographs. Overall antagonism towards the international production appeared to have eased even as residents of Glenrowan, led by Ned's nephew 'Jockey' Jack Griffiths, converged on Captains Flat for the 'challenge of the century': a battle of the Kelly towns, Glenrowan and Captains Flat, in the form of a beer drinking contest to be 'fought stoutly all day' at the Captains Flat Hotel, Workers Club, Returned Services League and Queanbeyan Leagues Club (Kelly 1969: 1). The carnival atmosphere spilled over to the following day, 24 August, for the 'Ned Kelly Gymkhana' held as a charitable event to raise funds for the local hospital. Although attended 'with fortitude and good humour [in icy conditions]' by such dignitaries as the Governor-General Sir Paul and Lady Alexandra Hasluck, the event failed to attract anyone from the film unit, disgruntled members of the Glenrowan mob once again avowing to 'get Mick Jagger' (Lynravn 1969: 3). The boisterous events of the 'Ned Kelly Gymkhana' found their reprise almost a year later (Tuesday, 28 July 1970) when the film's premiere at Glenrowan's Memorial Hall was interrupted by three homemade bombs, designed to make noise more than damage. The police believed Glenrowan residents still angry at the casting of Jagger had triggered the explosions ('Bombs, Police, and Ned' 1970: 1). The screening went ahead, with a predictable local verdict: 'Jagger as Ned was a washout' ('A Good Night Out' 1970: 22).

'Such is life': The Ballad of Ned Kelly

Ned Kelly begins with four opening titles – Woodfall presents/Mick Jagger in/A Tony Richardson film/*Ned Kelly*. These are followed by one more title-card – 'The End' – placed over a shot of a grubby prison-cell interior and the sound of a cell door clanging shut. The film's opening sequence, shot in sepia monochrome, depicts Kelly preparing for his execution at the Melbourne Gaol on 11 November 1880. The sequence – starkly rendered in just ten shots – is divided into five sub-segments, each one of which is separated by a horizontal wipe suggestive of Kelly's cell door being closed. The first (shot 1) shows Kelly taking his last ablutions, washing his hands and combing his hair in front of a grimy mirror, and muttering the words: 'This is how they shall remember me ... not broken, not bedraggled' and then (turning towards the camera) shouting: 'No prisoners.' In the next three 'segments' of this opening sequence, a photographer takes Kelly's portrait (shots 2–3), a priest secretly marries Kelly and his lover Caitlyn (shot 4) and Kelly is visited by his mother, Ellen, who instructs him: 'Mind you die like a Kelly, son' (shots 5–7). In the final segment, Kelly is silently marched along the prison gangway to the gallows where, upon having the noose placed around his neck, he calmly reflects and utters his legendary last words: 'such is life' (shots 8–10). The drop at the gallows abruptly cuts to the next sequence, and another titlecard – 'The Beginning' – heralds the narrative episodes that depict (now, in colour) the sequence of events that brought Kelly to the scaffold.

This prologue sets the tone for the rest of the film; namely, a number of loose, stylistic impressions with minimal dialogue, overlaid by a frame of realism and the careful recreation of historical events. In the film proper, these impressionistic episodes – some tragic, some romantic, some comic – are linked on the soundtrack by a succession of ballads (written by Shel Silverstein and mostly performed by 'outlaw' country music star, Waylon Jennings), which provide a commentary on or counterpoint to the events depicted. The first of these songs, 'Ned Kelly', accompanies lyrical shots of the titular character making his way by foot across both open pasture and heavily wooded land, the lyrics providing exposition: 'They turned him out of Beechworth Gaol in 1871 / He put in three long years behind those walls / For the stealing of a horse which he swore he never done / But now he sees the sun and turns his back upon it all.' As he gets nearer to home, the shots are intercut with scenes at the Kelly property: initially one of his mother Ellen (Clarissa Kaye) holding a naked infant aloft; a long shot of Ellen picking sprigs of wattle outside a modest cabin, turning (apparently) to see Ned approaching and running towards him; and a shot of Ellen, now inside the hut, pouring boiling water into a pot. Although not tied to any character's subjectivity, the three shots of Mrs Kelly – unmatched by anything similar until the end of the film when, in two flashes, Ned foresees his last stand at Glenrowan – appear to be Ned's memories (or anticipations) of home. The alternation of shots continues and when Ned reaches a crest and slows to a stop, a point-of-view shot shows Ned's sisters Maggie (Diane Craig) and Kate (Susan Lloyd) hanging out washing. There follows a close shot of Ellen inside the cabin – eyes framed between window and curtain – and, once she realises it is Ned, a sequence of shots leads through to their reunion and embrace. This evocative opening also introduces Ned's brother Dan (Allen Bickford) and Ellen's paramour (and father of the infant glimpsed earlier), the Californian, George King (Bruce Barry).

The prologue and opening sequences establish the film's principal relationship: that of Ned to his mother. Along with the next sequence – the boisterous indoor celebrations that accompany Ned's first evening back home – they also begin to demonstrate that Ned (and others in his circle) have been driven to crime by their circumstances: limited means and even poverty, as well as a corrupt police and judicial system that favours the landowners. A verse of the opening song, 'Ned Kelly', has already signalled this with respect to Ned's father, John 'Red' Kelly: 'In prison ship and shackles his father reached this land / He stole one pig and for that crime he paid / Inside a cold dark prison cell he died a broken man / And he left his wife to curse the Crown while his children dug his grave.' The evening's welcome depicts, then, not only the close-knit Kelly clan but also the solidarity of an Irish immigrant community set against the authorities of colonial northeastern Victoria. It additionally introduces – in one of the film's key diversions from the historical record – the character of Caitlyn (Janne Wesley), an amalgam of Kelly's various rumoured girlfriends and wives. Their relationship is underscored by the romanticism of 'She Moved Through the Fair' (sung in the film by Glen Tomasetti), which accompanies and bridges the transition from the welcome party to Ned's initially shy and idyllic meeting with Caitlyn early the following morning as she bathes at the creek. A traditional Irish folk song, popularised by Fairport Convention on their album *What We Did on Our Holidays* (released in January 1969), 'She Moved Thru' the Fair' was also recorded by Marianne Faithfull for her fourth studio album, *North Country Maid* (1966), and one can only suppose that – had Faithfull appeared as initially planned – she would have performed the song for the film.

The 'outlaw journey' begins when Ned becomes involved in a dispute over impounding, the process of incarcerating stray animals found on one's land until the rightful owner remits a fine to the landowner. Ned comes to the defence of some Irish farmers who are protesting the impoundment of their cattle by a wealthy English landowner named Mr Whitty (John Dease), and defiantly stares down Superintendent Nicholson (Ken Goodlet) who agrees to release the livestock, this one time, without penalty. Nicholson's words – 'I'll have no more of this brawling' – cut directly to Ned slugging it out with an opponent at the Greta Championships. The historical Kelly was known for his bare-knuckle fighting and the lyrics of the accompanying ballad, 'Pleasures of a Sunday Afternoon', provide an ironic counterpoint to the contest: 'The birds are in the coolabahs / I hear them sweetly sing / Of the pleasures of a Sunday afternoon.' Following his scrappy victory, Kelly is approached by Whitty with an offer of work. Ned scoffs, saying he does not steal the property of others in the 'name of English law', and finds instead an 'honest job' timber-getting at Joe Johnson's sawmill. There he wins the loyalty of two fellow ex-convicts, Aaron Sherritt (Ken Shorter) and Joe Byrne (Mark McManus), when he helps them land jobs.

The Wild Colonial Boy

During a quiet interlude, Ned sits reading a book in a forest of denuded, bleached-out trees where he encounters, and subsequently impounds, a ghostly stray white bull belonging to Whitty that has wandered onto Kelly land. Ned and his new-found cronies celebrate their small victory in the local pub where, even in the presence of a turncoat Irishman, Constable Fitzpatrick (Martyn Sanderson), Ned gives voice defiantly to the prohibited song, 'The Wild Colonial Boy'. While some objected to Richardson's 'ambling, folkloric approach to his hero's grim outlaw existence' (Dawson 1970: 158), the lyrics of this song nonetheless underline the film's social message and effectively (if indirectly) tell the story of Ned Kelly himself:

> [There was] a wild colonial boy, Jack Doolan was his name
> Of poor but honest parents, he was born in Castlemaine
> He was his father's only hope, his mother's pride and joy
> So dearly did his parents love their wild colonial boy
> When scarcely sixteen years of age, Jack left his father's home
> And found Australia's sunny clime, bushranging he would roam
> He robbed the lordly squatters, their flocks he would to destroy
> A terror to Australia, was the wild colonial boy
> In sixty one, this daring youth commenced his wild career
> With a heart that knew no danger, no stranger would he fear
> He bailed up the Beechworth royal mail coach up, and robbed Judge MacEvoy
> Who trembled and gave up his gold to the wild colonial boy
> He bade the judge good morning, and told him to be well
> He never robbed a poor man who whacked it on the square
> But a judge who robber a mother of her only pride and joy
> Well he was worse of an outlaw than the wild colonial boy
> One day while Jack was riding the mountain sides alone
> A listening to the kookaburras, pleasant laughing song
> Three mounted troopers came in sight, Kelly, Davis and Fitzroy
> Who thought that they would capture him, the wild colonial boy
> 'Surrender now, Jack Doolan, you see we're three to one
> Surrender in the Queen's name, you daring highwayman'
> Jack drew his pistol from his belt, and waved it like a toy
> 'I'll fight, but not surrender', cried the wild colonial boy.

When Ned awakens the next morning he finds himself in jail charged with disorderly conduct and, though beaten by the police, he is soon released with only a modest fine. Convinced by Fitzpatrick that his brother Dan, who is wanted for a minor indiscretion, will similarly be released after a fine, Ned persuades him to surrender. However, such is not the case and Dan receives a harsh three-month sentence of imprisonment. Further injustices follow, including the impounding of one of George King's horses by Whitty. Ned's rage at the favour shown towards the region's wealthy Protestants – judges, police chiefs, landowners – motivates him to mete out his own brand of justice. Recruiting Sherritt and Byrne, the gang retaliates by stealing Whitty's entire stockade of horses under the cover of night. The rustling is accompanied by the light humour of '[Daddy does his] Ranchin' in the Evenin'', the refrain of which carries over to the following morning, where the trio disguise the stolen animals with a crude coat of whitewash. Now wanted for the theft, and with a reward of 100 pounds offered, Kelly and his accomplices retreat into the cover of the bush for several months. In reprisal, the police intimidate the Kelly household, Fitzpatrick arriving one evening at the Kelly hut claiming to have a warrant to arrest Dan, only days earlier released from prison, for horse theft. When Fitzpatrick grabs at Ned's sister, Kate, a scuffle ensues and the constable is accidentally shot in the hand by his own pistol. It is a pivotal scene, for despite Fitzpatrick taking responsibility for his actions and promising to say nothing more of it, a dozen troopers descend upon the homestead the following day, arresting Ned's mother for aiding and abetting. Judge Redmond Barry (Frank Thring) subsequently sentences her, with babe in arms, to three years' imprisonment.

Given Ned's close relationship with his mother, the sentence imposed on Mrs Kelly dramatically shapes his response; later in the film, at the robbery of the National Bank at Euroa, Kelly addresses the townsfolk telling them, 'I was outlawed without cause while seeking justice for my mother.' In turn, the dispatch of a force of constables from Mansfield to search the bush for Ned and his gang leads to one of the most well-known episodes in the Kelly story: the 'massacre' at Stringybark Creek (the actual events of which took place on 26 October 1878). From the outset, Jagger had promised 'a very violent Ned Kelly' ('Braidwood is Laying it On' 1969: 3), and joined now by brother Dan and Steve Hart (Geoff Gilmour) the Kelly gang creeps upon the camp of the four troopers: Sergeant Kennedy and Constables Scanlan, Lonigan and McIntyre. Discovering that Kennedy and Scanlan are out scouting, the gang confronts the remaining two. Played out to the accompaniment of another ballad – 'Lonigan's Widow', which provides a close commentary on the events unfolding onscreen – Ned shoots down trooper Lonigan and instructs McIntrye to tell the others to surrender upon their return to camp. Instead, McIntrye calls out a warning, and Kelly shoots dead two more troopers. In a

NED KELLY (1970)

version of the Ned Kelly story that otherwise depicts him as a noble defender of the rights of the underprivileged against a 'justice' system that favours the wealthy, Kelly's actions – underscored by the lyrics of the song, which speak of the way in which the 'truth' is buried along with the dead – provide a sobering account of the legend.

Revolutionary Ned: The Jerilderie Letter

In the quiet bush interlude that follows the altercation at the creek, and with newspapers reporting parliament's approval of a massive bounty of 2,000 pounds on the outlaw's head, Kelly turns to the power of words in order to demonstrate the inequities of the society that has produced them. Kelly pens the famous Jerilderie Letter – an 8,000-word manifesto pleading the bushranger's version of the events that would lead to his downfall – with Caitlyn reading a portion of it aloud on the soundtrack:

> What would people say if they saw a strapping big lump of an Irishman shepherding sheep for fifteen bob a week or tailing turkeys in Tallarook Ranges for a smile from Julia. They'd say he ought to be ashamed of himself. That he'd be a king compared with a policeman who deserted the Shamrock, the emblem of wit true bravery to serve under the flag of a nation that has destroyed, massacred and murdered their forefathers by the greatest of torture as rolling transported its forefathers to Van Diemen's Land to pine away their young lives, their blood, their bone and beauty, in starvation and misery among tyrants worse than the promised hell itself.[1]

This excerpt from the letter hints at the way the Kellys are, as the film progresses, increasingly depicted and seen by the authorities as a threat not so much in terms of theft or assault, but as the leaders of a more general Irish rebellion. In this respect, their exploits are considered to be subversive rather than merely criminal, and it is for this anti-establishment attitude that Richardson cast Jagger and sought to connect his version of events to the upheavals and youth movement of the present day. It is, additionally, evidence of the 'ideological shading' that Richardson – as 'one of the key figures of the "angry young man" school of British stage and screen' (McFarlane 2005: 30) – brings to his version of the Kelly story.

Although the events at Stringybark Creek and the passage from the Jerilderie Letter seem to foreshadow a dark turn, the next episode shows the gang, now much emboldened by their growing reputation, undertake a series of daring, daylight exploits. Characterised by the lyrics of the song, 'Blame it on the Kellys' – which attribute all and sundry misdemeanours, from horse theft to poor weather, to the gang – the jocular tune accompanies a montage of scenes in which the gang takes possession of a station at Faithfull's Creek, holds up the National Bank at Euroa, and (wearing stolen police uniforms) robs the Bank of New South Wales at Jerilderie. The jokey mood – 'close [to] "baroque musical comedy"' (Dawson 1970: 158) – is further amplified through the use of sped-up footage of the gang who, during the raid at Faithfull's Creek, magically transform – mid-robbery – from rough bush kit to the fanciest of attire.

As the gang's wild escapades spread across the countryside, Ned's troubles with the law intensify. Sherritt turns police agent, not only informing on the gang but also advising the constabulary that no progress can be made until the police release those Kelly supporters who have been held without charge. As the mood of the film begins to turn, Ned addresses his followers in the film's clearest statement that the Kellys' rebellion is linked to the larger cause of a free Ireland:

> Fearless, free and bold: that's how we'll live. But first we have to fight. Take up our own colour; the green flag of Ireland . . . Declare war on the whole English world. Until this is our land, and our law. Friends, let's drink to it. To our own republic. To the republic of Victoria.

With Aboriginal trackers deployed in support of the police, Ned comes to realise the imminent threat, sending Caitlyn away from his hideout. As the film enters its final thirty minutes, the gloomy prognosis of the song 'Shadow of the Gallows' is heard over an almost dialogue-free sequence in which the setting changes from Ned's misty forest hideaway to the snow-covered high country. As the song continues, the sequence returns to the hideout where two impressionistic shots – flashforwards, very loosely tied to Ned's point of view – are shown: the first (recalling Nolan's paintings) is a shaky close-up of Ned's eyes seen through the slot in his helmet, accompanied by the sound of a bullet deflected by his armour; the second is a long shot of Ned, a grey figure in full armour silhouetted against the morning mist at Glenrowan.

The iconic amour finally materialises in the very next sequence, Ned telling his gang: 'the Bible says, "turn your armour into ploughshares". But I say unto you, "turn your ploughshares into armour."' Emboldened, Ned's thinking is that, protected from bullets by the armour, the gang can actively engage, rather than run from, the police. Ned devises a plan to draw an entire contingent of troopers from Benalla to Glenrowan, derail their train at the inn, attack and 'blow the hell out of them', and (then) joined by their supporters 'ride to Benalla and proclaim the Republic'. Gathering the townsfolk at the inn, Kelly is joined in a rousing reprise of 'The Wild Colonial Boy', unaware that a warning has been sent to the police. His plan in ruins, and surrounded by the 'bloody traps', Ned and the gang have to fight their way out, with all but Ned falling. Finally, with dawn breaking, Ned dons his helmet and body armour and with pistol raised makes his way – a ghostly apparition – towards the troopers assembled on the track. Shot from a low angle he strikes a towering and indomitable figure as he weaves towards them under the weight of the armour. In reverse shot, the handheld camera assumes his point of view: the police assembled on the track as seen through the roughly hewn slot in his helmet. The audience is allowed to momentarily see the world through Ned's eyes, in two distinct shots that 'resonate throughout Kelly's cinematic legacy' (Eisenberg 2011). Struggling gallantly against the many volleys of bullets, his wounded left arm dangling at his side, a well-directed shot finally takes out one of Ned's legs and he stumbles to the track. In the film's last moments, Ned faces Judge Barry, delivers the lines 'men are made mad by bad treatment', and defiantly states that he is not afraid of death. In the very last shot, Ned utters the words 'death, I'll meet you there'. He smiles and gestures downward – to hell – and the film ends in a freeze-frame.

'As strong looking as a kindling twig': Mick Jagger's Ned

Given the amount of pre-publicity that the *Ned Kelly* production received, it was likely that the film's success or failure would hinge very much on Jagger's performance, and its depiction of Kelly as a folk hero. In the UK, the *Monthly Film Bulletin* focused on the lead: 'Jagger delivers his lines with an almost catatonic lack of expression ... His flat delivery and diminutive stature undercut the Ned Kelly legend and without even evoking the Mick Jagger legend in its place' (Dawson 1970: 158). *Films and Filming* similarly noted: 'Jagger never seems quite big enough to dominate the film and carry it with him ... Even at his best in the heroic moments ... he seems a slightly wooden performer' (Tarratt 1970: 41). In Australia, some reviews conceded that Jagger did 'surprisingly well as an actor', but did not think he 'possessed the physical maturity' required for the role (Melton 1970: 7). Others, such as Dougal MacDonald, echoed the sentiments of the majority view: '[Mick Jagger] isn't the man, in a purely physical sense, for the part. He is little, weedy, lily-white and about as strong looking as a kindling twig' (1970: 16). Although giving Jagger 'credit for trying', MacDonald concluded that 'overall, [Jagger's] effect reminds me of a graffiti in an early edition of *Oz* [magazine]. "I dreamt I slept with Mick Jagger in my Maidenform bra and it was HORRIBLE!"' (1970: 16). Perhaps the most withering comment, though, came from a Glenrowan woman who attended the above-mentioned local premiere: 'I've got a son and I'd much rather he turned out like Ned Kelly than Mick Jagger' ('All Their Own Work' 1970: 22).

The criticisms of Jagger's performance were more broadly linked to commentary in reviews that questioned whether an outsider, Richardson, and his overseas production company had adequately and 'authentically' represented Kelly and the bushranger's legend. In Australia, the two loudest voices against the film – key commentators on the Australian film scene, Albie Thoms and Sylvia Lawson – cast their criticisms within the context of a call of support for a local film industry. In a hastily dismissive review (first published in *Revolution* in August 1970), Thoms wrote: '*Ned Kelly* has just opened in London, and it's a bummer ... It is shallow entertainment [that fails] to come to terms with the Australian myth' (1978: 99). Thoms was critical not only of the film's motivations – 'big hype aimed at the youth market' – but also its loose dramatic structure and a 'flat script' which '[throws] Jagger to the lions' (1978: 100). For Thoms, the film was ultimately 'neither raging pop nor analytic documentary', but 'half-cocked entertainment and half-arsed history ... Maybe the AFDC [Australian Film Development Corporation] will give someone else the bread to make a movie of the myth. An Australian perhaps' (1978: 101). Lawson's concerns and complaints were not dissimilar, if expressed with a little more restraint. Like Thoms, she found issue with the film's structure, citing 'Richardson's trendy indifference to old-fashioned narrative values' (1970: 19). And where Thoms complained that 'the pictorial style of the film is [like a] Rothmans [cigarette] Commercial', Lawson decried the lyricism of 'the static shots of landscape ... – some quite beautiful in themselves – [that] remain completely unassimilated' (1970: 19). Most telling, though, was Lawson's preference for the efforts of the Melbourne-based Eltham Film Productions which several years earlier had tried, unsuccessfully, to set up a Ned Kelly project. Defending her partiality for the promise of this unrealised local production, she insisted that her position was neither a case of 'militant cultural nationalism', nor an insistence on the deployment of Australian directors for films about Australian bushrangers, but rather an argument that '[indigenous] subjects become satisfactory entertainment only when handled by directors and writers hard-headed enough to grasp the *interaction* of place, character and community' (1970: 19, emphasis added). As in the case of roughly contemporaneous 'Australian international' films such as *Age of Consent* (Michael Powell, 1969), *Adam's Woman* (Philip Leacock, 1970) and *Walkabout* (Nicolas Roeg, 1971), *Ned Kelly* was caught within a growing debate around who should be able to tell such distinctly Australian stories. The varied and rarely successful 'Australian' films of this period – and by 1970 feature-film releases had built to a relatively healthy total of thirteen – speak to the schizophrenic character of these expectations.

National Hero and International Outlaw

The year 2003 saw the release of Gregor Jordan's *Ned Kelly*, a version of the story based on Robert Drewe's novel *Our Sunshine* (1991), starring Heath

Ledger and – like Richardson's film – intended for an international audience (see Bertrand 2003). The new film occasioned a retrospective of bushranger films at Melbourne's Australian Centre for the Moving Image, titled 'Iron Helmets, Smoking Guns: The Making of the Australian Bushranger Myth' (held from 30 January to 3 February 2003). Among the films screened were *The Glenrowan Affair* (Rupert Kathner, 1951), *Ned Kelly: Australian Paintings by Sidney Nolan* (Tim Burstall, 1960) and *The Stringybark Massacre* (Garry Shead, 1967). Also shown were Richardson's *Ned Kelly* and the 'experimental documentary', *A Stone in the Bush* (Michael Glasheen, Martyn Sanderson and John Allen, 1970), shot during the location filming near Bungendore. The programme was accompanied by a presentation by academic William D. Routt, 'Bush Westerns: The Lost Genre?', which examined the group of bushranger films that dominated the Australian film industry in the early 1900s. Elsewhere, Routt reviewed Jordan's new film, declaring it was the 'best feature film about Ned Kelly ... in the sense that it [was] the most "classical" ... [telling] an uncomplicated story smoothly ... [and] as a result of making Ned into such a perfect hero ... [had the effect] subtly to undermine his rebellion' (2003: 10, 16). Tellingly, Routt assigned the description of 'the most ambitious feature film about Ned Kelly' to Richardson's contribution. Routt did not elaborate but this can be understood to mean – that for all the criticism it attracted – Jagger's earnest, careful performance presented Kelly as a serious political figure: a national hero and an inter-national outlaw. Richardson's film may not have met with much success – either critically or commercially – but it continues to provide a fascinating case study of the ways in which 'Australian international pictures' often attempt to exploit the local *and* the global, unique stories *and* popular genres, historical detail *and* universal myth.

NOTE

1. The wording of the letter in the film differs slightly from that in the National Library of Australia transcript.

10. WALKABOUT (1971)

OUTBACK RELATIONS: *WALKABOUT* AND *WAKE IN FRIGHT*

'To think of this film purely as Australian would be a mistake', Grahame Jennings [*Walkabout*'s production manager] said later in Sydney. 'Nick [Roeg] meant the city to be any city; the desert is meant to be a desert anywhere. The characters of the three children could be any family unit group in the world. I don't think he meant the film to have a message, although perhaps it has one.' (Jennings interviewed in Strange 1971: 12)

1971 was a key year in the emergence of modern Australia cinema. Two seminal films, Nicolas Roeg's *Walkabout* and Ted Kotcheff's *Wake in Fright*, were screened in competition at the Cannes Film Festival in May and went on to become significant touchstones for the 1970s film 'revival', as well as the broader and ongoing iconography and thematic preoccupations of Australian cinema. These two films arose from the marginally more productive feature-film ecology that took root in the late 1960s and represented a way forward for the 'national' cinema in terms of style, theme, characterisation, filmmaking process and form, while also looking backwards, at times critically, to the largely international or 'locationist' productions of the 1940s, 1950s and 1960s. In *Walkabout*'s emphasis on the transcendental strangeness and mysticism of the Australian landscape, as well as its troubled but ground-breaking incorporation and representation of Aboriginal characters, their culture and agency, and *Wake in Fright*'s often grotesque, dark, dirty Gothic and deeply unsettling skewering of the foundational myths of Australian mateship and masculinity, it is also possible to see even deeper connections to key trends, forms and films of Australian cinema throughout the rest of the 1970s and into the 1980s.

Although both films are routinely listed as important works in various surveys of postwar Australian cinema – particularly after the rerelease of *Walkabout* in the late 1990s and *Wake in Fright*'s rediscovery in the late 2000s[1] – they also present a stout challenge to commentators proselytising for a national cinema that privileges, and even insists upon, key creative roles being filled by Australian practitioners and financing largely being sourced locally (see Lawson 1985: 175–83). *Walkabout* was of largely British provenance in terms of personnel, was funded and distributed by Twentieth Century-Fox in the US, and features only a small array of Australian talent onscreen – most memorably, in his film debut, Indigenous actor and dancer David Gulpilil, but also John Meillon and several others – and behind the production itself (including production manager Grahame Jennings).[2] As Michael Thornhill, a young critic, filmmaker and regular commentator on the push for a truly local cinema, claimed in the national broadsheet *The Australian* in March 1971, '[t]he only thing Australian about *Walkabout* is its setting; otherwise, apart from a couple of technicians, it is entirely British' (Nowra 2003: 64). *Walkabout* was also seen by some commentators as a pictorially beautiful travelogue that spoke very little to contemporary, cosmopolitan Australia: 'I can see any amount of the outback on screen in any BHP promotional film you care to name, and how many Australians relate to the outback?' (Kavanagh 1971:10).[3] As we will argue, *Walkabout*'s significant merits and legacies need to be disentangled, once and for all, from these once pertinent but now highly parochial and problematically essentialist debates about Australian national cinema.

This uncertainty in terms of national and cultural identity is reflected in the guarded, though often positive, response that met both films' local release in the early 1970s as well as the continued questioning of their provenance in subsequent accounts of Australian cinema by influential critics such as David Stratton and Neil Rattigan. In his seminal book *The Last New Wave*, Stratton praises Kotcheff's efforts to work attentively and carefully within Australia on *Wake in Fright*, but although he admires the craft and remarks positively on the 'cult' status of *Walkabout*, he dismisses Roeg's film as an American and not Australian or British film due to its financing (Stratton 1980: 8). Meanwhile, Rattigan's categorisation of *Walkabout* is even more cut and dried:

> *Walkabout* is not really an Australian film at all. It was funded with American money, written by a British writer, and directed by a British

director. It demonstrates so completely an outsider's response to Australia that its very shape and structure throw into relief the reflections, representations, and images of Australia offered by genuinely native productions. (Rattigan 1991: 308–9)

Although Rattigan's claims about the provenance of *Walkabout* are undeniable, he is significantly wide of the mark in separating Roeg and *Walkabout*'s admittedly singular, distinct and 'outsider's' vision from the 'genuinely native' films that would follow. Roeg himself has made claims for both *Walkabout*'s 'timeless' global relevance *and* its distinctively Australian qualities: 'It couldn't have been made anywhere else and it was an utterly Australian film ... But it did something, I think, and I like to hope that it touched emotional chords that were international. I think that helped in some ways to open doors for Australian movies' (Roeg quoted in White 1984: 25). We are also less convinced that Roeg's often ecstatic, romantic, mythic and downright peculiar vision of the Australian landscape is an outcome of his and the film's 'foreignness', or that *Walkabout*'s idiosyncratic approach to the Australian environment – both the outback *and* the city – and the national character can be neatly compartmentalised, and even dismissed, as a result of its deeply allegorical and universalised portrait of the modern city, the primordial desert and the eternal family, as partly suggested by Jennings in this chapter's opening quotation. The apparent dialectic *Walkabout* presents between modern and 'primitive' modes of being, Europe and Australia, the city and the outback, imported and Indigenous cultures is also destabilised by the oddness of many of the things actually found within the film.

'A BIG, EMPTY BACKCLOTH'

Of the two films, *Walkabout* has certainly been the more widely critiqued in terms of its international, even colonial mode of production and its largely pictorialist, impressionistic, universalised and clichéd response to the Australian environment, as well as its limited engagement with the traditional owners and custodians of the land: 'Roeg's film is not really concerned with Australia itself, as Kotcheff's is. Rather he has chosen it, it seems, as a vivid example of two opposed cultures living side by side' (Millar 1971–2: 48). On a more parochial note, *Walkabout* does engage with particular Australian pictorial and narrative traditions, betraying, for instance, the influence of postwar Australian modernist landscape painters such as Sidney Nolan, Russell Drysdale and Arthur Boyd. As Jenny Agutter – one of the film's three stars – has claimed, Roeg discussed Nolan with her in preparation for filming: 'He talked about Sidney Nolan's paintings and how a lot of artists have been fascinated by water, nakedness and the innocence of that' (Agutter 1999: 59).

Nevertheless, *Walkabout* offers, patently, an outsider's perspective that communicates little detailed knowledge of the geographical and experiential reality of the Australian landscape, beyond being immersed within it. As we will go on to discuss, this wilful (mis)representation and dazzling combination of incongruous landscapes and settings, flora and fauna – in contrast to the far more 'grounded' *Wake in Fright* – grants the film a peculiar, dream-like quality, while also closely following the lead of its source novel. It also resonates with common Western and colonial notions of the 'virgin' form of the Australian landscape and its perceived lack of prior representation and occupation: 'I liked the idea of a great landscape, like the Australian outback, which had hardly been surveyed and would be like a backcloth, a big, empty backcloth but visually very beautiful' (Roeg quoted in Combs 1999: 165). Like so many aspects of *Walkabout*, Roeg's bold if still poetic account of his intentions in making the film underlines the sympathetic *and* truly troubling elements of the production. *Walkabout* is responsive to this environment, and even to Indigenous experience, while being equally ignorant of the ancient, traditional and diverse practices of representing, narrativising, living within and connecting to the land.

Walkabout and *Wake in Fright* remain celebrated, transitional and deeply ambiguous works that have nevertheless been central to the conceptualisation of Australian cinema for half a century. Their status as transnational films made by overseas filmmakers and production companies that continue to provide defining moments of Australian national cinema was already being raised by Colin Bennett in his review of *Walkabout* on the occasion of its Australian (and specifically Melbourne) release in late October 1971:

> [O]ne way and another, Australians stand condemned. They suffer at the hands of two directors from overseas, descending on us armed with local tales of the outback.
>
> These men, with their disparate style – violent realism, poetic lyricism – have the guts to dare what we have never dare bring to the screen unaided. (Bennett 1971: n.p.)

This view of the bold, daring vision and contribution of these two films – and *Walkabout*, in particular – and how it reflects poorly on Australia and the other Australian movies of the period is reiterated by other writers: 'Nicholas [sic] Roeg's tragic bush idyll is a work of great beauty and, at the same time, a further indictment of ourselves' (*Melbourne Film Society Bulletin* 1975: 2). Meanwhile, the critic for *The Sydney Morning Herald*, Martha DuBose, exemplified the difficulties many Australian writers encountered when trying to account for the admixture of ambition, strangeness, Europeanness and cultural critique found in Roeg's film: 'Some will find *Walkabout* preachy and pretentious. I saw it as a filmic poem, a modern parable of loss and survival in cinematic blank verse. Not Homeric – but in that tradition' (1971b: 7).

Getting Lost: Making *Walkabout*

The elemental and troublingly Edenic nature of *Walkabout*'s plot is central to the tone, strategy and approach of these initial critical responses. A sixteen-year-old girl (Jenny Agutter) and her six-year-old brother (Roeg's son, Lucien John) are taken from Sydney into the desert by their father (John Meillon). After half-heartedly attempting to shoot them, the father commits suicide before leaving his children to fend for themselves. After struggling to survive for several days they encounter an Aboriginal adolescent (David Gulpilil) undertaking a 'walkabout' as part of his tribal initiation into manhood. He guides them through a magnificent and unfamiliar landscape where they encounter a range of flora and fauna as well as an unrealistically variegated environment. Despite the lack of a shared spoken language, the three children learn to communicate and form a clear bond, as sexual tension rises between the adolescent girl and boy. At the same time as these characters gradually start to stumble upon the grim outposts of white settlement, the Aboriginal adolescent enacts a night-long courtship dance that remains unacknowledged, misunderstood and unaccepted by the white girl. After they discover his corpse hanging from a tree the next morning – a mysteriously staged and unclearly motivated fate that is linked to his rejection by the girl as well as the fresh traumas of his encounters with settler-colonial inhabitants of 'his' land – the two white children travel on to a remote mining town before being transported back to Sydney. In the final moments, we see the girl – now a young woman ensconced in the kitchen of a modern home on the shore of Sydney Harbour – daydreaming of her outback idyll.

The production of *Walkabout* came about due to a diverse range of circumstances and events. By the late 1960s, Australia had started to emerge as one of a series of attractive if distant locations for international filmmaking. This is reflected in the production of a curious variety of international and transnational films between 1968 and 1971, including *Koya no toseinin* (*The Drifting Avenger*, Junya Sato, 1968), *Moeru tairiku* (*Blazing Continent*, Shogoro Nishimura, 1968), *The Age of Consent* (Michael Powell, 1969), *Squeeze a Flower* (Marc Daniels, 1970), *Color Me Dead* (Eddie Davis, 1970), *Adam's Woman* (Philip Leacock, 1970), *Ned Kelly* (Tony Richardson, 1970) and *Bello onesto emigrato Australia sposerebbe compaesana illibata* (*A Girl in Australia*, Luigi Zampa, 1971). The selected films included in this book reflect the importance of this brief period to the 'Australian international picture'. These films were made by a broad array of international studios (for example, Hollywood's Warner Bros. and Japan's Toei and Nikkatsu) and independent production companies. They range from genre hybrids and

TV-derived, low-budget, B-features to star-driven vehicles featuring a wide assortment of globally and regionally popular actors and entertainers such as James Mason, Mick Jagger, Ken Takakura, Beau Bridges, Alberto Sordi and Claudia Cardinale. They also sit alongside a small array of locally funded and distributed features – often completed on very small budgets – that hinted at a limited groundswell of activity in various parts of the country, including: *You Can't See 'Round Corners* (David Cahill, 1969), *Two Thousand Weeks* (Tim Burstall, 1969), *The Intruders* (Lee Robinson, 1969), *The Set* (Frank Brittain, 1970), *Jack and Jill: A Postscript* (Phillip Adams and Brian Robinson, 1970), *Nothing Like Experience* (Peter Carmody, 1970), *Homesdale* (Peter Weir, 1971), *Bonjour Balwyn* (Nigel Buesst, 1971) and *Stork* (Tim Burstall, 1971).

Roeg reportedly first encountered James Vance Marshall's popular, largely adolescent-oriented novel, *The Children* (retitled *Walkabout* when republished in 1961),[4] when it was brought to him by producer Jack Schwartzman after the completion of filming on *Petulia* (Richard Lester, 1968), shot by Roeg in San Francisco in 1967 (Combs 1999: 165).[5] It was originally slated to go into production in 1968 before filming was stalled. Roeg's earlier trip to Australia in late 1959 to shoot – as camera operator – Fred Zinnemann's *The Sundowners* (1960), gave him a taste of what might be required to make the film (see Gow 1972: 22). Although, in the late 1950s, Roeg was almost a decade away from moving onto his widely celebrated career as a feature-film director, his experience shooting in disparate locations across outback New South Wales and South Australia on the earlier film provided an essential 'backstory' for what was to become his first solo directorial effort after his collaboration with Donald Cammell on *Performance* (1970).[6]

This earlier experience would have alerted Roeg to the possibilities, difficulties and realities of making a film far away from the centres of movie production in Australia, as well as the logistics of working on a project that patched together disparate footage shot across a vast array of different locations and over an extended production schedule. The relatively arduous shoot on *The Sundowners* also prepared him for *Walkabout*'s itinerant shooting schedule that extended beyond four months from mid-August 1969 and that followed the equally peripatetic and only partly planned journey of the small cast and crew. Writing after production on the film was completed, Dorothy Strange called the shoot a '12,000-mile safari into the Australian outback' and appropriated the Aboriginal concept of 'walkabout' to describe the practice of the film crew itself (1971: 11). A number of the participants, such as Agutter, have also spoken of the highly reactive, improvisational and piecemeal processes that characterised the making of *Walkabout*:

> Mainly the experience of filming was about travelling, finding locations and getting immersed in the outback. I went out to Australia in August.

> I was there for four months. We started in Sydney then went to Adelaide. Then we went to a place called Quorn, and from there to an even smaller place. We slowly delved into the outback. After a while, we just started going off in trucks into the desert. (Agutter 1999: 58)

Many accounts of the making of *Walkabout* describe a gradual process of getting lost or overwhelmingly immersed; of the cast, crew and even the film itself losing their coordinates and a clear or locatable sense of time and place (see Agutter 1999: 58–9; Strange 1971: 8–15). This takes on a more pointed meaning in the various accounts of the difficulties David Gulpilil encountered adapting to life in the desert, an environment very far removed from his tropical home and culture (Yolngu) in North Arnhem Land in the Northern Territory:

> Used to the lush tropical country of his homeland the young teenager was profoundly distressed by the desiccated landscape in which he found himself. Even though he was accompanied by a close friend from his tribe who spoke his language, it didn't assuage his homesickness. (Nowra 2003: 21)

Louis Nowra, in his short monograph on *Walkabout*, claims that the decision to film across a vast and mismatched array of different locations not traversable by foot, and specifically the bewildering and instantaneous shift from the dry desert to the lush settings of Northern Australia thousands of kilometres away, was, in part, motivated by a concern for Gulpilil's well-being (Nowra 2003: 21). It was also made necessary by the unseasonal rain encountered in the normally bone-dry Lake Eyre.

But this unrealistic, fable-like movement through a shifting, largely allegorical and mythical landscape seems much more beholden to the novel than the above concerns would indicate. It is also reflective of Roeg's generally and increasingly accretive approach to filming: 'I shoot a lot. I always think that everything on the set, and everything around you, shapes your feeling . . . I like to shoot and cover the environment in a lot of ways because everything around us prompts our thought' (Roeg quoted in Kornits 1998: 14). In concert with this, Roeg was very keen to create a film that would maintain visual interest by exploiting the capacity of the cast and crew to travel across vast distances – by plane, Land Rover, etc. – as afforded by modern methods of international film production. The small cast and crew of between thirty to forty people, combined with the relatively large AU$1,000,000 or so budget, also enabled this cumulative, explorative, digressive and environmentally responsive approach to filmmaking (Pike and Cooper 1998: 258).[7] Although Roeg spent some time scouting locations with his production manager before filming commenced, as well as searching for Aboriginal actors to play the central role, during production the movement from one location to another was often haphazard and highly dependent on accrued local knowledge and advice. It is this combination of attentiveness to the detail of specific landscapes – often rendered blindingly majestic and consciously extreme by Roeg's extraordinary multi-scale camerawork – and a wilful obsession with changing focus and environment that underlies the tension between the specificity of place and its cinematic transformation. It also reflects Roeg's common tendency to explore and weave together 'extreme changes in scale and point of view' (Farber and Patterson 2009: 733). At heart, *Walkabout* betrays a responsiveness to the physical detail and experience of location that is truly remarkable within the Australian cinema of its time.

Writing and Adapting *Walkabout*

As hinted at earlier, Roeg initially intended to make *Walkabout* a year-and-a-half earlier and first cast Agutter as a fourteen-year-old. Due to delays in production caused by Roeg's work on *Performance* and changes in the film's financing – shifting from initial plans to work with the less experienced Apple Corps, the multimedia company founded by the Beatles, to a more conventional source of funding and production support offered by Fox (Nowra 2003: 13–14)[8] – the film didn't commence filming until August 1969. The delay further shifted the narrative emphasis towards the burgeoning sexuality of Agutter's character and her culturally incompatible relationship with the Aboriginal adolescent played by Gulpilil (he was also sixteen when filming commenced). It also led to another of Roeg's sons, Luke, being cast as Agutter's younger brother. Some concerns were also expressed about the paucity of Edward Bond's initial fourteen-page script – later fleshed out to around seventy – its preference for largely epigrammatic dialogue, and the gaps it left for Roeg to incorporate other elements and shots of the surroundings (such minimalist scripts became Roeg's preference across his subsequent work in the 1970s). At the time, Bond was a widely celebrated playwright, then most well-known for the censorship-busting *Saved* (1965), but he had little regard for screenwriting as a practice: 'I write films in order to live. I've never worked on a film script that interested me deeply – or if it did, imagined for one moment that one could be allowed to deal with the subject properly' (Bond quoted in Mangan 1998: 79). Bond's disregard for his own screenwriting and the sketched-out form of his initial screenplay for *Walkabout*, allowed copious opportunities for the film's various digressions. These ended up including a somewhat mysterious episode featuring Italian meteorologists, ultimately shot on Lake Torrens, and a late sequence dealing with the exploitative production of kitsch tourist giftware. These diverse moments act to both isolate the actions of the three central characters and suggest a set of parallel actions occurring within the landscape. This reinforces a sense of the loss of community, communication and connection between the various human figures scattered across the environment.

A number of authors have written about the relation of Roeg's film to its source material (see, for example, Nowra 2003: 7–11). These accounts have generally questioned the literary merit of Marshall's novel – for example, Anthony Boyle opens his comparison between novel and film by stating that Marshall's is 'an awkward and dishonest book' (Boyle 1979: 67) – praised the excisions and even simplifications made by Roeg and Bond, and placed most of the blame for the consciously incoherent rendering of landscape, flora and fauna at the hands of the author. Marshall's 1959 novel is indeed a curious artefact which provides a simplistic, fascinatingly muddled, anthropologically spurious but obviously still informed view of the Australian environment. The provenance of the novel itself is even open to debate. Some commentators have suggested that Marshall never even visited Australia and drew heavily on previously published, uncited material that helped furnish its pot-pourri of Australianised elements (see Byrnes). But other accounts claim that Marshall was indeed Australian and worked with other authors in the completion of the various novels that were ultimately published under his name. In a convoluted account of its provenance, Nowra suggests that *The Children* was largely written by British author Donald Gordon Payne, based on 'field' notes provided by Marshall (Nowra 2003: 7). Other sources suggest that Marshall was actually a pseudonym used by Payne.

This combination of authors and sources, as well as fiction and anthropology, may help account for the curious mixture of authenticity and fantasy that characterises the novel. It is marked by a number of passages that attempt to give a fuller context to Aboriginal culture through a largely racist and anthropological framework, while also providing a minimal backstory in terms of where the white children come from – they are North American survivors of a plane crash in the novel, while their accents are noticeably British in the film – their names, and other bits and pieces of information. The material that matter-of-factly recounts scientific experiments conducted on Aborigines is particularly disturbing and thankfully has no counterpart in Roeg's film. Its only partial equivalent appears in the easily excerpted scene mentioned earlier which shows a community of Aborigines working to produce kitsch tourist souvenirs for a grumpy and dissolute white boss. This scene was indeed excised from the film's original release but was restored for the 1998 rerelease.

But although the novel is weak in terms of character development, dialogue and situation, and is sometimes preposterous in its magic-realist cornucopia of animals ranging from lyrebirds and koalas to possums and various species of birds, it actually provides a more positive vision of Aboriginal life, as well as the shared concepts of home and community, than is ultimately found in Roeg's far chillier film. Although the Aboriginal adolescent still dies in the novel, his demise seems less determined by a mythic, Darwinian notion of racial fate, and the incompatibility of a traditional Indigenous life with modern existence, than his unconditioned exposure to the common cold. Whereas the film leaves us with the striking and depressing image of Gulpilil's character hanging from a tree – an abstractly motivated and staged act that is barely comprehensible to the white girl and boy or, indeed, to many in the audience – the novel moves onto a further encounter with an Aboriginal family who guide the two, somewhat transformed children back towards 'civilisation'. This encounter stages a very different act of communication. Roeg's *Walkabout* is ultimately about the impossibility of reconciliation and true communication across and even within cultures, despite the opportunities raised by the three children's shared journey. Marshall's novel presents a more utopian vision that ultimately relies upon the shared values of home and family – clumsily signposted by the cross-cultural recognition of a drawing of 'home' in its final passages – even if this seems to run counter to much else preceding it in the book. In some ways, the novel, for all its significant faults, datedness and underlying racism, seems more concerned with capturing, embracing and sharing Indigenous experience.

TABULA RASA: INTERPRETING *WALKABOUT*

Although Roeg's film does appear to have clear intentions in terms of its view of the relation of its human characters to nature and the built environment, it has also proved to be something of a tabula rasa for commentators and critics. This is largely a result of its allegorical form as well as its episodic and relatively unmotivated distribution of story events. It has been prey to auteurist, Freudian, Jungian, ethno-musicological, structuralist, ecological, sociological, postcolonial and anthropological interpretations, amongst others, all reflecting its rich openness as a text (see, for example, Held 1986: 21–46; Larkin 2014: 27–32).

Like many of Roeg's films, *Walkabout* is characterised by an audiovisual style that draws together and contrasts disparate events and times, relies heavily on contrapuntal editing, suggests the continuity or co-presence of past, present and future, and links together events difficult to situate spatially. It also utilises a vast array of cinematic devices including freeze-frames, zooms, disorientating combinations of the micro and macro, and a truly diverse soundtrack that ranges across John Barry's highly atmospheric score, snippets of radio broadcasts tuning into various languages, popular songs of the day such as Rod Stewart's 'Gasoline Alley' (1970), radio serials and various lessons in mathematics and haute cuisine, and other elements of score ranging from traditional Aboriginal music featuring didgeridoo to Karlheinz Stockhausen's 'Hymnen'. These last two are contrasted and combined in the film's early moments, swiftly, almost seamlessly moving from the outback to the city, and providing a science fiction-like view of the urban environment and its modulation of behaviour. This is particularly evident in the brief sequence showing a class of female schoolchildren taking part in breathing exercises, the sounds of which then merge into the experimental score. Although this is a work that may, at first, appear to offer an elemental and even simplistic set of contrasts between cultures, environments, races, genders, ways of living and modes of cinema, its view of these elements is far more complex than such a dichotomous framework may seem to initially suggest.

Inevitably and understandably, *Walkabout* has been most contentious with Aboriginal commentators who are torn between its dominant, majestic and even sympathetic representation of Aboriginality and its regressive vision of an impoverished Indigenous 'race' on the verge of extinction. Indigenous activist, academic and writer Marcia Langton critiques *Walkabout* for its exotic representation of Aboriginal life filtered through a 'quite shocking' 'English aesthetic', that falls back on Social Darwinist conceptions of the fate of Indigenous peoples under the onslaught of colonialism and modernity.[9] This damning view is reinforced by the strange and under-explained death of Gulpilil's character, as well as the absence of any other significant Indigenous characters. Although it is uncertain what motivates this 'suicide' – Gulpilil's character appears to be deeply affected by both the shockingly brutal practices of white buffalo hunters and the rejection of his 'love dance' by the white girl – the seeming inevitably of his demise speaks to the discourse of a 'dying race' that was foundational to the genocidal and assimilationist governmental policies of the first seventy years of the twentieth century. Indigenous activist, academic and actor Gary Foley remembers *Walkabout* in a very different light.[10] He praises it for foregrounding an Indigenous figure at a time when there were virtually 'no Aboriginal characters' in cinema and celebrates Gulpilil for giving him 'the first really positive and strong image of an Aboriginal person on a big screen'.[11] As Stratton has argued, we also need to remember that *Walkabout* was released only four years after *Journey Out of Darkness* (James Trainor, 1967), a locally made and financed feature that featured a 'black-faced' Ed Devereaux as an Aboriginal tracker and Sri Lankan singer Kamahl as an Arrernte prisoner.[12] *Walkabout* was also shot only a couple of years after the successful 1967 Referendum that enabled the Commonwealth to make laws for Aboriginal people and to include them in the census. It went on to be released a few months before the establishment of the Aboriginal Tent Embassy in Canberra, a potent symbol of the increasingly radicalised and direct action-based racial politics emerging at the time. In the context of this changing racial, cultural and political landscape, *Walkabout* is both an urgent, timely film and troublingly timeless.

Felicity Collins and Therese Davis provide a more nuanced analysis of the elements that position Gulpilil's character, and what he represents, within specific forms of colonial Australian storytelling and myth, while also critiquing the film's exclusion of Aboriginality from the representation of modern urban life (2004: 142–3). Referencing the work of Peter Pierce (1999) in his important monograph *The Country of Lost Children*, Collins and Davis examine the fate of Gulpilil's character in relation to the mythic figure of the lost white child subsumed by the Australian landscape littered across colonial and postcolonial culture. Drawing on a central trope of colonial literature and painting that is also referenced in seminal films like *The Back of Beyond* (John Heyer, 1954) and *Picnic at Hanging Rock* (Peter Weir, 1975),

> [h]is death is emblematic of the girl's refusal to submit to her primal urges, to stay lost in the bush . . . the Aboriginal boy is the true lost child of this film. For in the logic of this narrative, there is no place for Aboriginal people in modernity other than as the subject of a European romantic longing for an ideal primitive past. (Collins and Davis 2004: 143)

This 'longing for an ideal primitive past' re-emerges in the contrastive images and sounds that conclude the film. The girl's sun-kissed memory of her naked idyll with the Aboriginal adolescent is incongruously paired with lines from Alfred Edward Housman's nostalgic series of poems, *A Shropshire Lad*. There is a separateness and longing depicted here, of a figure emerging from another world or time, that is communicated from Gulpilil's very first appearance. As Collins claims in her provocative essay on the actor, '[i]n his very first appearance on screen in *Walkabout* (1971), Gulpilil seemed to emerge *ex nihilo* from the desert: cast as a tribal initiate and nomadic hunter, he entered the art cinema's field of vision as a "fresh" figure of the colonial imaginary' (2009: 189).

Anthropology in Eden: From Innocence to Experience

Although Collins and Davis' reading of *Walkabout*'s narrative is painfully accurate, the film still navigates an extraordinarily vivid odyssey from innocence to experience. The contradictions inherent in both the narrative and the mode of production are intimated from the first image that appears onscreen. An anthropological-style titlecard defines and explains the supposed derivation of the film's title:

> In Australia, when an Aborigine man-child reaches sixteen, he is sent out into the land. For months he must live from it. Sleep on it. Eat of its fruit

and flesh. Stay alive. Even if it means killing his fellow creatures. The Aborigines call it the WALKABOUT.
This is the story of a 'WALKABOUT'.

This written introduction – never sanctioned by Roeg, imposed by the studio and placed prior to the Fox fanfare logo – sets up a set of expectations that the movie will never fulfil. The concept of the 'walkabout' is taken up very liberally and is 'equally' applicable to all three central characters. This titlecard lays claims to the scientific or anthropological basis of the action, as well as its applicability across widely diverse Aboriginal cultures. Roeg also objected to the explanation as it diminished the deep mystery and ambiguous temporality of the story he was trying to tell and placed the film more firmly within a documentary reality to which it did not belong.

Roeg was aiming at a more transcendental and visionary view of the Australian landscape than such a prosaic titlecard could suggest. From its very first images and sounds, *Walkabout* plays with strange juxtapositions and connections between the natural and the built environment, a rock face and a brick wall, the orchestrations of atonal modernist music and the traditional rhythms of a didgeridoo. But rather than establish a set of clear contrasts, these movements across space, time, place and culture, often instigated by the lateral movement of the camera or the apparent retuning of a radio on the soundtrack, are profoundly disorientating and unsettling. *Walkabout* may overplay the alienating qualities of the modern city – showing us, for example, children swimming in a beautiful pool mere metres from the beckoning waters of Sydney Harbour – but this most iconic and familiar of environments is still rendered strange, forbidding, almost uncanny.[13] The brief scene showing a 'sea' of schoolgirls doing breathing and elocution exercises exemplifies this sense of uncertainty *and* anthropological distance. The girls' actions seem primal and incomprehensible, culturally familiar and radically decontextualised. Our interpretive response is partly conditioned by the anthropological explanations emphasised by the titlecard and the regimented compositions created by Roeg and his camera. What are we looking at here? A sense of dislocation is compounded by the lack of causal detail and motivation attached to narrative events as they unfold. For example, we are given little information about why the two children sound peculiarly British, how they are able to travel with their father on a seemingly short daytrip – in their school uniforms – from Sydney to somewhere north of Adelaide over 1,000 kilometres away, or what motivates the father's murderous and suicidal rampage when it quickly erupts. There is something profoundly disorientating and off kilter about the world we are introduced to here: a vision of an environment that is far removed from the documentary fidelity and interpretative framing of much anthropological filmmaking.

THE EDGE OF REALITY: SPACE, TIME AND *WALKABOUT*

Despite its influence, *Walkabout* sits in contrast to many other films that represent the Australian landscape. Although it is dazzled by the colours, aridity and peculiarity of this environment, it also celebrates its abundance and variegation. As we've established earlier, *Walkabout* is generally unconcerned with rendering an accurate vision of this environment in terms of its movement through space, place and time. While certainly grounded in the daily realities of living in the outback, it also has the sense of science fiction about it. This is reinforced by the film's approach to time. It is very difficult to get a clear hold on *Walkabout*'s temporal transitions, how they relate to the navigation of place, and how each of the varied elements meld together temporally, spatially and narratologically. This is most directly illustrated in the scene where the young white boy sees images of several early colonial explorers (most probably Burke and Wills) superimposed onto the landscape. This vision references Sidney Nolan's hallucinatory and discomfiting series on the doomed explorers and makes a link between the feral camels the children have just seen and the carcasses they pass by, the ancient history of the desert and the continuity of actions and cultures across time.[14] This combination of elongated and co-present time also helps account for *Walkabout*'s lack of narrative tension. The white children are plainly distressed by their abandonment in the desert, and struggle to stay hydrated from moment to moment, but there is little sense of a true drama of survival, even before Gulpilil's character comes to their rescue. The latter stages of their journey are also marked by a curious lack of any urgency. This is emphasised by their inattentiveness to a homestead they pass by, though, characteristically, it is difficult to clearly determine whether this is a vision generated by the Aboriginal adolescent or a more concrete reality.

This plainly visionary, allegorical, almost dreamlike journey also helps to justify the film's truly anachronistic elements. The journey the children take moves them across large tracts of Eastern, Central and Northern Australia, making a multi-thousand-kilometre expedition that extends far beyond the well-equipped capacities of the colonial explorers of the nineteenth century. Their encounter with a disorienting array of flora and fauna is also self-consciously staged in a manner that should make us question the documentary veracity of the journey we are watching. For example, as the brother and sister first set out into the desert they are hissed at by a lizard that sits within a few feet of them; a snake is artfully draped over the tree they sleep beneath; a very healthy looking wombat somehow wanders into frame to nuzzle the boy as he dozes; a virtual ornithology of bird species appears in the trees as they pass by; and compositions self-consciously isolate and stage objects within the environment. At various moments this appears to be more like the artfully directed and soundstage-shot childhood vision of a river journey in *The Night of the*

Hunter (Charles Laughton, 1955) than something that is grounded in actual locations or documentary reality (though the errant lyrebird of Marshall's novel is thankfully absent).

Although we are obviously watching these characters navigate an array of variegated Australian landscapes, there is also a sense that we are observing an 'unrepresented' environment that could equally be another planet. This reading is reinforced by the intermittent appearance of the portable radio. Incongruously, this device seems to be able to pick up a range of stations across most locations in the isolated desert and never runs out of batteries. The contrast between the content of these broadcasts and the environment they are received within further emphasises these dislocations in time, space, place, culture and human activity. The lessons that we often hear being broadcast also have no practical application in this vast amphitheatre. The obvious problem with such a reading of these elements is that it negates and de-prioritises Aboriginal relationships to and understanding of the land. This reading is a damning indictment of our general lack of engagement with the Australian environment on its own terms, but is also characteristic of the formal, conceptual and cultural limits of Roeg's film.

Walkabout is undoubtedly one of the most significant feature films produced in Australia between 1946 and 1975. As we have argued, it provides a fascinating and often schizophrenic vision of the Australia landscape while offering one of the richest and most critically contested, but influential representations of Aboriginal life to be found in the national cinema up to this moment in time. It provides an important instance of international and transnational film production in Australia during this era, and profiles the work of an emerging filmmaker who went on to become one of the defining figures of 1970s cinema with movies like *Don't Look Now* (1973) and *The Man Who Fell to Earth* (1976). It also introduces a great icon of Australian cinema: David Gulpilil. Like many of the other films discussed in this book, *Walkabout* vacillates between an outsider's perspective and a deeply immersive portrait of the Australian environment. A film both within and outside of time, *Walkabout* is an important touchstone for the last fifty years of Australian cinema, in both a positive and negative sense, as well as a truly singular aesthetic achievement.

NOTES

1. *Walkabout* was re-released in Australian cinemas in early April 1998. It has also been relatively widely available on DVD and Blu-ray internationally, including a 'prestige' release by the Criterion Collection on both formats. After core elements once thought lost were relocated, the restoration of *Wake in Fright* was screened at the Cannes and Sydney Film Festivals to significant acclaim in mid-2009.
2. Gulpilil went on to become one of the great icons of Australian cinema, memorably appearing in many significant films including *Mad Dog Morgan* (Philippe

Mora, 1976), *Storm Boy* (Henry Safran, 1976), *The Last Wave* (Peter Weir, 1977), *Crocodile Dundee* (Peter Faiman, 1986), *Rabbit-Proof Fence* (Phillip Noyce, 2002), *The Tracker* (Rolf de Heer, 2002), *Australia* (Baz Luhrmann, 2008) and *Charlie's Country* (Rolf de Heer, 2013).

3. This short review is paired with an even more dismissive response to *Walkabout* (combined with a glowing one for *Wake in Fright*) by Peter Timms (1971) in the same issue of *Lumiere*, an important, if short-lived, Melbourne-based industry and screen-culture journal. For a fuller discussion of *Wake in Fright* see Chapter 11.
4. Marshall (1971). This novel, originally released in 1959, was republished with production stills to coincide with the release of Roeg's film.
5. It was initially optioned by a company called American General. Strange – other sources suggest erroneously – claims that Roeg actually read the novel when visiting Australia in 1959 (1971: 8).
6. Roeg worked as director of photography on *Performance* but was granted a co-director credit by Cammell in recognition of his overwhelming influence on the look and form of the finished movie. *Walkabout* was initially planned to be Roeg's first feature as director and was to be completed prior to commencing production on his collaboration with Cammell. *Performance* was banned in Australia until 1973, so *Walkabout* was the first of his films to gain an Australian release.
7. Roeg later recalled the cost as being around AU$750,000 (Combs 1999: 167).
8. Founded in January 1968, Apple quickly started to suffer from financial mismanagement and many projects it was working on at this time were either stillborn or passed on to other producers and production companies.
9. See the interview with Langton in Darlene Johnson's documentary *Gulpilil: One Red Blood* (2003).
10. Foley is the co-star of one of the most significant short features made in the 1970s, Phillip Noyce's *Backroads* (1977). This is also an important film in terms of Indigenous representation and collaboration.
11. Interview with Foley in *Gulpilil: One Red Blood*.
12. Interview with Stratton in *Gulpilil: One Red Blood*.
13. The understandable choice to swim in a pool rather than a polluted harbour is also a less ideological decision than such a stark visual contrast suggests.
14. Nolan returned to the doomed subject of Burke and Wills at various points in his career from the 1940s to the 1980s. This sense of a vast, layered, interconnected history of place is also suggested in passages of *The Back of Beyond*. Nolan was friendly with director John Heyer and visited him on location, producing a series of photographs and sketches that are strongly echoed by passages of the film.

11. WAKE IN FRIGHT (1971)

Dreaming of the Devil

Based on Kenneth Cook's 1961 novel, *Wake in Fright* (Ted Kotcheff, 1971) takes its title from 'an old curse': 'May you dream of the Devil and wake in fright' (Cook 1971 [1961]: 3). These words appear as an epigraph on the book's title page, but the book could just as readily have drawn its inspiration from the first words of Hunter S. Thompson's contemporaneous *Fear and Loathing in Las Vegas*: 'He who makes a beast of himself gets rid of the pain of being a man' (2005 [1971]: n.p.). Kotcheff's film tells the story of a city-educated schoolteacher, John Grant, who becomes stranded in the outback town of Bundanyabba (the 'Yabba') on his way home to Sydney for the Christmas holidays. What follows is a lost weekend of drinking, cruelty and violence during which time Grant is confronted with beastly aspects of his own character, hitherto concealed from him. Now recognised as a film that 'prepared the way for [the] mix of hyperrealism, excessive masculinity, ambiguous sexuality, and misogyny [that is] so insistently present in subsequent Australian cinema' (O'Regan 1996: 57), *Wake in Fright* achieved some critical recognition but little commercial success upon its original release. Writing in industry-centred Melbourne-based magazine *Lumiere*, Barry Lowe observed: '*Wake in Fright* [has] caused the biggest furore (if you discount the carry-on which surrounded Mick Jagger as the choice to play Ned Kelly) ... by portraying Australians as an ugly, boozing lot' (Lowe 1974: 4–5). As

Scott Murray noted decades later (at the time of film's 2009 restoration and re-release), this type of response needs to be contextualised as part of the 'cultural war' that surrounded international companies and filmmakers who used Australia as an 'exotic' location but failed, in their often pastoral visions of the continent, to adequately engage with nationalist themes and the local industry: 'in this atmosphere of resignation and despair, it was not surprising that Tony Richardson's *Ned Kelly* (1970) was eviscerated ... Canadian Ted Kotcheff's *Wake in Fright* ... was written off as a brutal and dishonest picture of outback Australia, while Brit Nicolas Roeg's *Walkabout* was cruelly undervalued and dismissed as an aimless travelogue' (Murray 2009: A23).

As Murray's comments indicate, it is only in hindsight that these films – particularly *Walkabout* and *Wake in Fright* – have been fully embraced for their ground-breaking portrayals of the Australian character, identity and landscape, and as important instigators of the 'revival'. For many commentators in the early 1970s, their status as international productions exploiting Australian stories and locations was anathema to the needs of a truly local film industry then just starting to gain some momentum through the piecemeal completion of films like *Three to Go* (Peter Weir, Brian Hannant and Oliver Howes, 1970) – a portmanteau feature most commonly shown as three separate short films – the very down-at-heel *Bonjour Balwyn* (Nigel Buesst, 1971) and, most significantly in terms of impact, *Stork* (Tim Burstall, 1971).

Wake in Fright was co-produced by NLT Productions – an Australian television company, established by Jack Neary, Bobby Limb and Les Tinker – and Group W Films, a subsidiary of American Westinghouse. It was the second film produced as part of this collaboration, and followed *Squeeze a Flower* (Marc Daniels, 1970), a wildly unsuccessful 'Australian international' undertaking starring Walter Chiari and released early the previous year. Prominent British actor Dirk Bogarde had optioned the rights to Cook's *Wake in Fright* shortly after it was published, with the intention that Joseph Losey should direct from a script prepared by London-based screenwriter, Evan Jones. The production did not go ahead, and the film rights (along with Jones' initial script) were purchased by Australian writer Morris West, who in turn sold the package to NLT. When Group W began searching for a director, Jones recommended the book to recent collaborator Ted Kotcheff, a Canadian who had been working, mostly in television, in London since the late 1950s. Impressed by the intense atmosphere, central character and distinctive outback setting of the work, Kotcheff approached Group W and secured the opportunity to direct the project. The film was financed on the condition that it should feature an established international star in a leading role. Accordingly, British actor Donald Pleasence was selected to play 'Doc' Tydon, with the lesser-known theatre and television actor Gary Bond taking the central role of John Grant. Principal cast and crew – including British cinematographer Brian West and producer George Willoughby – arrived in Australia in the summer of 1969–70. The filming began with around four weeks of studio (and other) interior work in Sydney, commencing on Monday, 12 January 1970, before moving on to eight weeks of location work in and around the mining town of Broken Hill in western New South Wales (see Caputo 2009; Buckley 2009: 137–51; Kaufman 2010: 11–34).

Heat and Dust: *Wake in Fright*, Ted Kotcheff and Australian Masculinity

Given the high level of international participation, Kotcheff thought local communities might be affronted by a team of non-Australians – specifically, a Canadian director – making a film in Australia, about Australians. Kotcheff expressed some trepidation, but following his location scouting around Broken Hill (the town upon which Cook had modelled Bundanyabba) he came to the realisation that, as former British colonies, there was a degree of similarity between Australia and Canada: the two countries had the same settler-colonial background, the same lack of self-confidence, similar relationships to much larger close cultural and political allies, and the same vast, open spaces that were, paradoxically, not liberating but confining to many non-Indigenous inhabitants: 'one of the fascinating things about Australia is this sense of claustrophobia in the midst of such an infinity of space' (Moorehead quoted in Jennings 2009: 41). In addition, Kotcheff noted the same kind of intensely masculine ethos – particularly the rituals of mateship – that had evolved in response to the extreme isolation, inhospitable environment and gender imbalance in remote locations of both countries (Caputo 2009; Jennings 2009). Kotcheff embraced these commonalities, taking them as a baseline from which to build a solid foundation for his 'non-judgmental' understanding of the attitudes and values of these rough men: 'their camaraderie, their support of each other and their generosity' (Caputo 2009). To this end, upon arrival in Broken Hill, Kotcheff devoted much of his first month there to simply observing the behaviour of the locals: 'I met with people, drank with the guys, watched them, listened to them and tried to understand them, and obviously tried to make the film with verisimilitude and authenticity' (Caputo 2009; Jennings 2009: 42–4). Peter Timms understood this when, at the time of the film's release, he remarked that Kotcheff's film (in a departure from the attitude expressed in Cook's novel) did *not* set out to criticise: '[*Wake in Fright*] is not . . . an indictment, for all its stark realism . . . Kotcheff doesn't use his camera to moralise or to create visual symbols, but *merely to observe*' (1971: 10, emphasis added).

Kotcheff's sympathetic undertaking to 'observe and empathise' (Caputo 2009) contrasts not only with Cook's approach, but also markedly with Tony Richardson's account of his time in Australia, in which he describes his visit to an outback community while shooting *Ned Kelly* the previous year. To Richardson 'Australia seemed a mysterious and unsympathetic land', and his imperious account of the outback might have been written in John Grant's own words:

> I wanted desperately to see the 'bush' in the raw [and] one weekend we hired a plane and flew to the ranch of a friend . . . deep in Queensland and about 100 miles from an opal-mining town . . . It was announced that we would visit the opal town that afternoon, in time for the opening of the bar at four o'clock . . . The drive took about an hour and a half on the straight red-dirt roads. The opal town consisted of two or three dirt streets lined with shacks . . . Social activity for the whole district, an area of probably 1,000 square miles, was centred in this one bar . . . The girls were all to one side. It was one of the more unpleasant features of Australia at the time that there was complete sexual segregation . . . Here the only contact was that one of the louts would stagger over to the group of local nurses and teachers, grab one of them and drag her off to have her outside . . . The hours blurred on, stale with beer and dirty ditties . . . There was nothing to do except drink . . . Our host had disappeared, but finally I found the two sheep-farming brothers [to drive us back] . . . They hurtled off at about 120 mph. Big kangaroos leaped across the road in front of us, startled by the headlights. Each time they saw one, the brothers whooped and gunned forward, trying to hit the animal . . . *Drunkenness was endemic in Australia; one or two beers were enough to set anyone off in a violent and destructive way.* (1993: 222–3, emphasis added)

In contrast, Kotcheff's genuinely ethnographic attitude – of the men of Broken Hill, he said: 'I wanted to get inside their heads and see what drives them. It was the heat and dust and lack of women that was contributing to their behaviour' (Caputo 2009) – contributes to the 'authenticity' and detail found in *Wake in Fright*, but the film is informed, too, by the 'universal' questions it asks. Kotcheff was attracted to the 'heat and dust' of Cook's novel, but he described the 'whole theme' of the picture as the story of 'a man who discovers he is basically in the same existential boat as everyone else, and [this] discovery liberates and humanises him' (Caputo 2009). Something similar is stated in the Preface to the screenplay:

> This is a film about prisons, for its characters are all imprisoned in an immense space. The outback of Australia at Christmas time is a limitless oven . . . The exits are illusory. The slim lines of railroads and highways lead only to another part of the oven, exactly like the first [. . .]
> The film is about an introvert imprisoned in a world of extroverts, for the cruelties of the place produce an aggressive hospitality, a kind of

virile togetherness which has elevated the phrase 'Have a drink, mate' to the status of the first commandment.

The film is about a man imprisoned within himself, separated from society by his hatred of his surroundings and his scorn of his associates, by his sense of intellectual superiority . . . and most of all by his nagging, unrealized fear of his own inadequacy.

The outback cages him, strips him bare, and tortures him, but in exchange it gives him, on this brief, destructive holiday in hell, a new understanding of his own humanity.

The film is about a moth, imprisoned in a world of light. (Reprinted in Jennings 2009: 43, emphasis added)

Wake in Fright's 'unflinching portrait of mordant masculinity' is shaped by an outsider's view – both that of the central character and director Kotcheff – but Gabrielle O'Brien cautions that a singular focus upon the specificity of the film's representation of outback life is undertaken at the expense of an interrogation of its universality *and* its distinctive style:

'Much writing about [*Wake in Fright*] seems to take it up as a kind of socio-historical artefact [sic] rather than a potent work of cinematic fiction. In sidelining [its] uniquely filmic qualities . . . there is a tendency to approach it as a static text rather than a film that uncomfortably immerses us in a mobile, kinetic, full sensory experience' (O'Brien 2017: 94).

For O'Brien, the 'enduring hypnotic power' of *Wake in Fright* resides not so much in the particularity, or veracity, of its commentary on the Australian outback but rather in its exaggerated, transnational rendering of place: '[Kotcheff's] outsider's gaze offers an irrational space that takes up cultural imagery – the XXXX beer can, the cajoling Aussie mate, the blazing sun, Anzac remembrance rituals, the boxing kangaroo – and *distorts* their signification' (2017: 96, emphasis added). That is, if *Wake in Fright* is an outsider's encounter with the 'menacing strangeness' of the Australian interior then this is (at least in part) due to the fact that its cultural ethnography is mediated by a 'lyrical expressivity' (Rooney 2011: 7). Pointing to the overall structure of the film's form, O'Brien argues that *Wake in Fright* conveys its sense of *dis*-location – its hesitation between actuality and dream, physicality and phantasm – right from its very first shot: a panoramic view of a pseudo-mystical landscape in which the 'claustrophobia of endless space creates an oppressive keynote [for all that follows]' (2017: 96). It is this movement between the specific and the universal, the insider and the outsider, the claustrophobic and a vast openness, that speaks to the lasting strangeness, continuing resonance and uncanniness of *Wake in Fright* for both international and Australian audiences.

The First Circle of Hell: Leaving Tiboonda

The opening shot of *Wake in Fright* strikes a plaintive note: the camera making a steady 360-degree pan around the tiny town of Tiboonda situated in the middle of a plain: flat, bare and red. The shot begins on the railway line, the small siding visible in the middle ground, moves clockwise past the town pub, over the other end of the track, and then to the schoolhouse, showing that the two buildings – the town's *only* two buildings – are situated opposite one another, either side of the railway track. Timms writes that 'by taking the longest route between two points [the shot] sets the scene and subtly suggests something of the hero's attitude' (1971: 11). The circuitous route also anticipates both Grant's roundabout journey – Tiboonda and back, via Bundanyabba – and the concentric circles of 'hell' that he is about to encounter in the outback town. In the next group of shots, a slow dolly moves in on the town name of Tiboonda displayed on the elevated railway platform, the schoolhouse visible in the background, before cutting to its interior where a ticking clock marks out the final minutes of the school term that both teacher (Grant) and pupils silently endure. The opening credits roll as Grant locks up the schoolhouse and crosses the track to the pub where he lives in a rented room in the back. The lodging immediately tells us something of his character: one wall is lined with shelves holding geological specimens, and against another is a portable record player from which Grant returns the album 'Blind Faith' (1969) to its sleeve. The title of the record gestures towards Grant's unshakable belief in his intellectual superiority, and track A2, 'Can't Find My Way Home', anticipates his thwarted journey to the coast. A third wall reveals Grant's pencil sketches of the local environment, and finally – illustrating that he is a middle-class, coastal Australian – a calendar photograph of Sydney Harbour, and framed portraits of his suburban family home, his parents and, most prominently, his girlfriend (Robyn) in graduation gown and cap. As he picks up his two suitcases and leaves the room, the camera pans back to the record player to settle upon the 'Blind Faith' album cover as the final credit – 'Directed by Ted Kotcheff' – appears onscreen.

The music that accompanies the credits is abruptly cut short by a cry of 'shut up' and a cut to a surly publican, Charlie (John Meillon), as he moves past a hand-painted sign, 'Tiboonda Picnic Races, Boxing Day', to the bar where Grant is seated. In the first of the film's many drinking sessions, the two share a beer. Grant hurries out to meet the approaching train and Charlie's words – 'see you in six weeks' – and wry smile will resonate at the end of the film when Grant returns full circle to his humble lodgings. As he boards the 'Friday train' that will take him to Bundanyabba for a connecting flight to Sydney, Grant is greeted by the singing of the stockmen and miners congregated at the front of the carriage and who invite him to 'come and have a beer'. He moves instead to the rear of the cabin, seating himself alongside the other 'outsider' on the train: a middle-aged Aboriginal stockman. As the train grinds its way across the open plain, Grant opens his wallet to look at a small black-and-white snapshot of his girlfriend in a swimsuit, holding a surfboard. He puts on his sunglasses – a level of protection not only from the glare of the sun, but also from the intrusions of the too familiar passengers – and leans back into his seat. The 'screen' of the sunglasses occasions a series of shots, projections from Grant's point of view: a shot of rolling waves, two shots of his girlfriend Robyn in red swimsuit emerging from the breaking waves, and three shots of Robyn on the sand, standing over Grant in a sexually provocative manner. As she drops to her knees and leans in towards him, Grant rubs a stubby bottle of beer between her breasts. Despite the matching snapshot of Robyn in his wallet, it is unclear whether the sequence consists of recollected memories or Grant's anticipations (fantasies) of home. The sequence is significant not only for being the first to deliberately blur the distinction between reality and imagination, but also for bringing together 'the two central elements' (Caputo 2009) – sex and alcohol – that will challenge Grant's sense of identity and secure knowledge of self.

'Everybody likes the Yabba'

Arriving in Bundanyabba, Grant takes a taxi from the station, whereupon the outsider is greeted by a question that will resound on a number of occasions: 'new to the Yabba?' The cab driver proceeds to tell him that the Yabba is 'the best place in Australia. Everybody likes the Yabba [...] It's a friendly place. Nobody worries who you are, or where you come from. If you're a good bloke, you're all right. You know what I mean?' It is evident from Grant's expression (and the fact that he rides in the back of the cab) that he finds the friendly habits of the locals crude, embarrassing and somewhat unsettling. Things move to another level when, after checking into his accommodation, he goes to the Imperial Hotel for a drink. Entering through a doorway over which there is a clock that reads 8.20 p.m. and a sign that says 'This Bar Closes 6.30 p.m. By Order', the camera follows Grant as he weaves his way between the patrons, craning his head slightly to take in the island bar, with a tinsel Christmas tree at its centre, surrounded by dense crowds of working-class men.

Filmed in early January 1970 around the long bar in the Sheridan Stand of the Sydney Cricket Ground and with 220 male extras – 'the largest crowd assembled for a made-in-Australia movie' (O'Brien 1970a: 23) – the sequence (along with the two-up game episode that follows) contributes to Pauline Kael's assessment that the 'semi-documentary aspects of the film are ... vivid and authentic and original' (1972: 90). The miner's bar is where Grant first experiences the Yabba's extreme hospitality when he meets the town's uniformed police officer Jock Crawford (Chips Rafferty). Introduced by his 'flamethrower' lighter – the long arm of the law reaches into the frame to ignite Grant's cigarette – and the question: 'new to the Yabba?', Jock is at once benevolent and menacing. His watchful determination that Grant quickly drink up so that he can down another beer is the harbinger of Grant's inevitable downfall. Although affable, Crawford is astute enough to recognise Grant's haughtiness: in response to the schoolteacher's explanation that he is a 'bonded slave of the Education Department' – a practice that saw new teachers post a bond of $1,000 to guarantee that they serve out their contract, no matter where they were posted – Crawford nods his approval: 'I suppose they know what they're doing. You clever blokes never like to stop in the one spot long.' The choice of Rafferty to play this role is particularly telling. By this time a true icon of Australian cinema, Rafferty appeared in many of the key films made by international companies in Australia during the postwar era – including important, often central roles (as a stockman, law officer, miner, shearer, pioneer or builder) in *The Overlanders* (Harry Watt, 1946), *Eureka Stockade* (Harry Watt, 1949), *Bitter Springs* (Ralph Smart, 1950), *Smiley* (Anthony Kimmins, 1956), *The Sundowners* (Fred Zinnemann, 1960) and *They're a Weird Mob* (Michael Powell, 1966) – and was also born in Broken Hill. In his last film performance – Rafferty would die before *Wake in Fright*'s release – the actor's big-framed, avuncular but tight-lipped 'everyman' persona is deployed to draw Grant's character *and* the audience into the dull but insidious menace lurking behind the lure of mateship and masculinity.

Crawford becomes the guide to Grant's journey through the netherworld of the Yabba, conveniently appearing at critical moments. The huge flame of Crawford's lighter, along with the lurid red light that bathes the one-minute of silence of the Remembrance ceremony that briefly interrupts the revelry at the Imperial, are among the overt signs of Grant's descent. Of even greater significance in the allegory of the arrogant schoolteacher's fall is the light shone in Grant's face – Crawford reassures the doorman, 'this is a mate of mine' – when he takes Grant for a meal at the local RSL (Returned and Services League) club that fronts 'the biggest two-up game in Australia'. This use of light – which recalls the (above-mentioned) description that '[*Wake in Fright*] is about a moth, imprisoned in a world of light' – is but one of several instances in which 'the symbolism of the light [is used] to suggest the idea of it shining into [and illuminating] the dark side of human nature' (Kotcheff in Caputo 2009). The most deliberate comment on Grant's situation and character comes, however, just minutes later when he sits down to his one-dollar plate of steak, eggs and chips. In response to Crawford's estimation that the meal will be the 'best dollar's worth you've had in your life', 'Doc' Tydon (already seated at the table) volunteers: 'all the little devils are proud of hell'. Grant is momentarily stunned by Doc's candid assessment of the Yabba, but the educated Doc – a self-described 'doctor of medicine . . . a tramp by temperament, and an alcoholic'

– takes no time to assess Grant's attitude: 'Discontent is a luxury of the well to do. You gotta live here, you may as well like it.' Grant's impatient reply – 'I'm just bored with the aggressive hospitality. The arrogance of stupid people who insist that you should be as stupid as they are' – immediately rebounds when Doc quietly provides an explanation well beyond the schoolteacher's intolerant view of the situation in the Yabba: 'It's death to farm out here. It's worse than death in the mines. You want them to sing opera as well?'

A close-up of Grant's open wallet, the photo of Robyn clearly visible in its clear plastic pocket, announces Grant's entry into the two-up game. Like the earlier sequence, the actual interior used for this episode was a location in Sydney, 'up a back alley somewhere in Paddington [where] the men running the game were the real thing, while many of the extras turned out to be from the underworld' (McDonald 2010: 111). The veracity of the segment is balanced, however, by its deliberate stylisation: in particular, the rhythm established through the alternation between the 'raucous chatter' of the gamblers placing bets and the 'bated silence' of the coin toss (Hoskin 2009: 153). Grant plays two successful rounds and exits straight after his big win, running back to his hotel room where he places the windfall on the floor. His exuberance gives rise to the thought that just one more successful spin will yield enough money to buy himself out of his government teaching contract and allow him to never have to return to Tiboonda. As he leaves his room, a lingering close-up of his sunglasses suggests that he has left behind a screen that has shielded him to this point in his outback sojourn. Assuming the role of spinner, Grant now stands in the centre of the two-up ring, a single overhead light underlining his extreme vulnerability as the camera scribes – in imitation of the cyclical ritual of the game – a dizzying 360-degree circle around him. Instructed to toss the coins above his head, an overhead shot captures the throw. As Grant's eyeline follows the trajectory of the pennies, the sequence alternates between close-ups of the blinding light and shots of Grant as he flinches under its glare. The toss goes against Grant, and in one last desperate move he cashes his holiday pay and returns to the game. This time it is Doc, Grant's dark shadow, who has assumed the role of spinner. Grant's desperation is rendered in a series of subjective shots of the gamblers seemingly directing their harsh, distorted laughter towards him. Once again, Grant's eyeline follows the toss, the coins slowly and silently spinning in the darkness. Sound withheld, the segment cuts from a close-up of Grant to an elevated shot of him, now face down and naked on his hotel room bed. Moving to the window to draw the tattered blind, he is immediately struck by the glaring light of the morning after, and the realisation that he is now almost penniless and trapped in the Yabba.

RITUALS OF MATESHIP: THE SECOND CIRCLE OF HELL

Dave Hoskin writes that the two-up sequence is a 'key plot development [in] that it unifies the film's themes [and] demonstrates that Grant carries the seeds of his own destruction within himself' (2009: 153). A victim of his own sense of superiority, Grant has earlier dismissed the contest as 'a nice simple-minded game'. The hubris Grant displays in thinking he can dominate the game marks the point at which he forfeits the ability to control his fate and must increasingly rely upon the 'aggressive hospitality' of the locals. Leaving his accommodations, Grant wanders into one of the Yabba's many hotel bars (in actuality, the Palace Hotel in Sydney) where he is befriended by Tim Hynes (Al Thomas), a small man sporting a bow tie and Panama hat: 'New to the Yabba?' he asks. Hynes insists that Grant accept his hospitality, first shouting him to several rounds of beer and then taking him back to his house where he introduces him to two hard-drinking miners, Dick (Jack Thompson) and Joe (Peter Whittle), and Hynes' daughter, Janette (Sylvia Kay). After lunch, Grant finds the antics of the miners – teasing and bragging, but mostly just drinking – boorish and turns his attention to Janette, only to have Dick ask: 'What's the matter with him? Rather talk to a woman than drink?' Finding a sympathetic listener, Grant gives voice to his frustration, telling Janette that he longs to leave Australia to pursue a career as a journalist in London. Janette leads Grant outdoors. They stop at the gate where, still ignorant of his own boorish behaviour, he recites a couple of hackneyed lines from Omar Khayyam, before Janette takes him along to a secluded spot. She lies back while Grant, half drunk, fumbles with her dress and then vomits. No stranger to this scenario, Janette silently wipes his mouth with her handkerchief. When they return to the house the men are gathered around Hynes' dog, wondering when it will give birth and who the sire of the pups might be. Karen Jennings writes that Janette's reply – 'She's a skag, this little mutt. She'd try anything', delivered while pointedly looking at Doc – demonstrates that 'like Doc Tydon, Janette has self-knowledge in contrast to Grant's obliviousness' (2009: 45). Embarrassed, Grant proceeds to get even drunker. A dizzying sequence of whip pans and rapid edits (underscored by abrasive notes on the soundtrack) recalls, as O'Brien describes it, 'the mental confusion of an alcoholic blackout' and ends the sequence 'suddenly without the [objective] logic of continuity' (2017: 96).

Grant awakens the following afternoon to find himself in Doc's shack, a spot of light playing on his face from a hole in the tin roof. Recoiling from Doc's hospitality – an open bottle of flat beer, a plate of kangaroo meat, and an aria from *La Traviata* – he tries to excuse himself, only to be told that arrangements have been made to go kangaroo hunting with Dick and Joe. The hunt commences in the afternoon – like Richardson's farmers, Dick and Joe run down a kangaroo with their Ford – and resumes after sunset, following a pause for more drinking at an outback pub which boasts a giant inflatable beer bottle on its roof. By this point, Grant is a more willing participant in the carnage. Half drunk and feeling the effects of a drug (most likely Benzedrine) administered by Doc, he gleefully takes part in the savage cull, including the tearing open of the throat of a wounded kangaroo. More drinking and drunken brawling follows the hunt, before Grant and Doc are returned to the shack. The 'notorious' kangaroo hunt – consisting of perfectly matched footage of the actors intercut with a professional shoot arranged for the film – which nonetheless seems to spiral out of control, has been much commented upon. To this point, Grant (and the viewer alike) has been worn down by the relentless sensation of heat and dust and flies, augmented by a deliberately restricted palette of 'hot colours': reds, oranges and burnt sienna (Kotcheff in Caputo 2009). But it is the nightmarish nocturnal shoot – the Ford bumping and shuddering across the desert corrugations, the hapless animals dazzled by the vehicle's hypnotic spotlight, Joe's taunting wrestle with a wounded kangaroo – that makes the film such an uneasy – visceral, violent and kinetic – experience. As Martha DuBose concluded in an early review, *Wake in Fright* is 'a physically demanding film [,] like a nightmare from which one awakens limp, drained and vaguely queasy' (1971a: 7).

The nocturnal kangaroo hunt might be seen as the culmination of the film's rituals of mateship and violent masculinity, the point at which *Wake in Fright* 'gets under the coat [of civilization] to the animal hides that live inside' (DuBose 1971a: 7). But the jostling for domination continues back at Doc's shack: Grant douses Doc in beer, Doc discharges his rifle, and then Doc re-enacts the killing of a kangaroo by shining the overhead light in Grant's face and grabbing him around the neck from behind. The light swings wildly across the ceiling, Doc wrestles Grant to the floor, and finally – as Grant comes face to face with his own dark shadow – the blinding white light fills the entire frame. The film cuts to a close-up of the light fitting, now stationary, and tilts down to show Grant awakening, naked on the floor, with Doc's legs strewn across the lower part of his body. Jennings writes 'we don't see Doc Tydon buggering Grant' but we know what has happened. The sexual encounter has been foreshadowed by Doc's unconventional views on sexuality ('sex is like eating. It's a thing you do because you have to, or because you want to'), shared with Grant when he first comes to Doc's shack. And most tellingly (in Jennings' account) by 'a small shoulder movement' during that same conversation when Grant goes outside to relieve himself against a wrecked car and Tydon follows him, trying to get a look at his junk. As in the book, Grant's realisation – his disavowal, justification and acceptance – of what has happened is jumbled and oblique: 'the light was bright and this could not be ... It was all to do with being drunk because this could not, did not happen ... It should not have happened. It could not have happened. It had happened twice' (Cook 1971 [1961]: 95). With few words, Grant dresses, and casts one last look at Doc. Upon leaving the shack, he takes his sunglasses from his breast pocket, only to find that this last protection from his dark inner reality – his beastiality – has been shattered.

RETURN TO SENDER: FROM BUNDANYABBA TO TIBOONDA

In the film's final sections, Grant makes his way back to town, where he staggers down the main street, unshaven and dirty, clothes fouled and stiff with blood and clutching his rifle, a gift from Dick and Joe. Underscoring the allegorical nature of the tale, Grant again encounters Crawford, but this time he is sincere, genuinely grateful and accepting of the police officer's hospitality: the shout of a beer, and a darting flame to light his cigarette. Somewhat revived, Grant makes one last attempt to get to Sydney, hitching a ride out east as far as the Silverton Hotel where in response to the driver's confusion when he refuses 'to come get a drink', he lets loose his most sustained tirade against the outback culture: 'What's wrong with you people? You sponge on you. You burn your house down. Murder your wife. Rape your child. That's alright . . . Don't have a flaming bloody drink with you. That's a criminal offence. That's the end of the bloody world.' In town Grant finds a transport that he thinks will take him right through to Sydney, only to be thwarted – brought full circle – when the lorry driver misunderstands his plea for a ride to 'the city' and returns him to Bundanyabba. In a final moment of delirium and rage, Grant makes his way back towards Doc's hut, suitcase in one hand, rifle in the other. His movement is intercut with a series of subjective images, initially a mid-shot of Doc as spinner at the two-up game, laughing mockingly, and next of Robyn emerging from the surf. The tempo quickens, and as Grant drops his suitcase and begins to run, the images we see combine real and imagined events: Janette unbuttoning her dress, Doc sodomising Janette, Doc defiling Robyn. These are intercut with shots of Doc's and Grant's tryst at the shack, and the sequence culminates in a reprise of the exaggerated chorus of laughter Grant imagines upon placing his final disastrous bet at the two-up game. The sequence ends with an iconic image: a zoom in to a close-up of Doc as the two-up pennies magically flip upwards to cover his eyes with the crosses that mark the 'tails' side of the coins. By the time Grant reaches the shack it is clear that he is intent upon killing Doc; but finding no one there he breaks down. Earlier in the film, Crawford has admitted that, as good as life is in the Yabba, it does have its share of suicides. Grant's response – 'that's one way of getting out of town' – is acted upon now as he turns the gun upon himself in a (failed) attempt to end the nightmare of it all.

At the very end of the film, Grant boards the train at Bundanyabba for his return trip to Tiboonda. It is evident that has spent the reminder of his vacation in the Yabba recovering from his 'accident' (Crawford and Janette visit him in hospital; Doc sees him off at the station) and his small steps towards acceptance and self-enlightenment are indicated by his gracious receipt of a can of beer from a fellow passenger on the train. In the very last segment, Grant makes his full circle return to the Tiboonda siding. Watched by the dishevelled Charlie, who sits drinking beer from a bottle on the pub's porch, they exchange a few words. Asked 'Did you have a good holiday?' Grant dryly answers, 'The best.' The next-to-final shot is of Charlie, who smiles and chuckles in response to the reply. Charlie may (or may not) have heard about what had come to pass in the Yabba, but it is as though he takes some pleasure in the knowledge of this 'smart bloke's' degradation. More evidently, Grant's reply suggests – as described in the Preface to the screenplay (see above) – that his 'brief, destructive holiday in hell' has delivered to him 'a new understanding of his own humanity'. Closing out the circular form of the film, the very last shot mirrors the opening: a wide, craning view of the open plain, with the town's two buildings facing one another from opposite sides of the railway track.

Outback: Projecting Australia to the World

Wake in Fright opened commercially in Australia in October 1971. Ahead of this, it had its first public screening in competition at the Cannes Film Festival in May before it opened to a very successful five-month run in Paris in July (Pike and Cooper 1998: 259). It was rolled out to other territories over the following months, including London on 29 October. Describing the 9 October Australian premiere at the Embassy Theatre in Sydney, the *Australian Women's Weekly* reported that the 'new Australian film ... followed the usual [city] premiere pattern': 'guests arrived at the theatre in chauffeur-driven cars while a pipe band played loudly on the footpath ... Most men guests wore dinner jackets ... [and] guest-of-honour [the Prime Minister's wife] Mrs. William McMahon, in a gold lame gown, stole the fashion show' (Lyons 1971: 1).

When it came to *Wake in Fright*'s general release it was difficult to reconcile the glittering Sydney premiere (in aid of the NSW Society for Crippled Children) with the 'epic horror' (Kael 1972: 90) of the story displayed onscreen. Kotcheff attributed the film's very limited theatrical run in Australia to its 'ugly portrayal of Australian men, including the notorious six o'clock swill and the violence of [the] kangaroo hunt' (Maddox 2009: 3), while others have thought it likely that 'John Grant's imperiousness and [seemingly] British bearing' had alienated Australian audiences (Stewart 2014: 38). Either way, the film's commercial failure was not reflected in its local critical reception that was, in the main, positive. Sandra Hall wrote that it was 'the first film in a long time to tell Australians something worth knowing about themselves[;]

it is very much a landmark [work]' (1971: 16). At least two critics announced that *Wake in Fright* was the best film made in Australia since *The Sundowners* (Bryning 1971: 10; Stratton 1972: 53), and another declared that 'although *Wake in Fright* cannot be described as 100 per cent made-in-Australia, it certainly qualifies for the accolade of being the most "Australian" film of the post-war era' (MacDonald 1971: 11). In these reviews, and others, the focus was resolutely on the veracity of the picture's representations: 'the film is a palpably honest attempt to define the Australian character' (MacDonald 1971: 11); and 'the film is an achievement for characterising a border-less condition in particularly Australian terms' (DuBose 1971a: 11).

In its major international English-language markets, *Wake in Fright* was distributed by United Artists under the less evocative title, *Outback*. The United Artists press sheets dishearteningly headlined the film as an 'Outback drama of Despair, Filmed Down-Under': 'It has the sound, look and feel of authenticity, because most of it was filmed in the "outback" section of Australia – a tropically hot, violent, gambling, drinking area. This controversial film was the official 1971 Australian entry at the Cannes Film Festival' (*Wake in Fright*, United Artists Press Sheet, 1971). The film's one-sheet poster similarly promoted it through a narrative image focused on violence and discomfort:

> 'Outback;
> Have a drink, mate?
> Have a fight, mate?
> Have a taste of dust and sweat, mate?
> There's nothing else out here.' (*Wake in Fright*, United Artists Press Sheet, 1971)

Kotcheff ascribed the film's underperformance in North America to the ill-advised change of title and a poor promotional strategy by United Artists (Canfield 2012), but – as in Australia – the critical response was mainly favourable. Making note of the fact that an Australian film at Cannes was 'something of a novelty' – though *Walkabout* also appeared in competition in 1971 as Britain's official entry – *Variety* predicted that the 'forceful glimpse of little-known territory in which the emphasis is on booze and violence, with a touch of sex for good measure ... should generate average b.o. [box office]' (Myro 1971: 3). *Monthly Film Bulletin* was a little less convinced, writing that *Wake in Fright* suffered from a 'loosely-knit and over-melodramatic storyline which never achieves thematic coherence', but admitted that 'Kotcheff has captured the mindless brutality of life in the outback with extraordinary felicity' (Hanson 1971: 244). More considered, though, was Pauline Kael's review in *The New Yorker* in which she describes Evans and Kotcheff as 'cultural anthropologists':

> [The film has as its subject] the crude comradeship among the white men in the vast desert areas [of Australia], and their erratic destructiveness ... The men in this sterile, parched back country are crazily hospitable ... They no sooner see a stranger than they toss him a can of beer and invite him to join them. They guzzle all day and all night; they garland themselves with the pull tabs from beer cans ... They smash things for excitement, or brawl, or shoot anything that moves. (1972: 89–90)

Most telling, though, is Kael's understanding that the film's greatest strength is not the '[unconvincing] melodrama that requires that [Grant] come to a new understanding of himself', but its *observational* attitude that leaves the audience wanting to 'learn more [of] the rough white men out there in the wilderness ... *They [are] beasts but not villains*; they're "decent" and unaware of wrongdoing – and that suggests that they are unreachable' (1972: 90, emphasis added).

Too Australian or not Australian Enough: *Wake in Fright*'s Legacy

Despite the many favourable reviews, and its ongoing importance and value as an unvarnished portrait of Australian masculinity, the commercial failure of *Wake in Fright*, combined with its overseas provenance, led to its neglect and virtual disappearance from cinema and television screens. In 1996 an enquiry into the whereabouts of the film's negative and soundtrack prompted its editor, Anthony Buckley, to undertake an extended decade-long search to locate the original materials (Buckley 2009: 150–1). This mostly took place outside of Australia. These original materials were eventually uncovered in a Pittsburgh film depot in a bin marked 'for destruction'. The film was subsequently restored and re-released in 2009, reaching a wider audience and attracting belated recognition as a key forbearer of both the Australian New Wave (see for example, Fenton 2009: 5; Maddox 2009: 3; Molitorisz 2009: 5) and what has subsequently been coined 'Ozploitation' (see Ryan 2010). The locationist strategies of *Wake in Fright* – along with its focus on a distinctively Australian iconography, and its myths of masculinity and mateship – situate the film as a lynchpin between the international pictures of the 1950s and 1960s, the 'ocker' genre of the early 1970s, and the nationalist preoccupations of the 'revival'. It is characteristic of the power and resonance of Kotcheff's film that it can forge these connections while continuing to trouble and unsettle critics and audiences for over fifty years. In one of many accounts of this rediscovery, American critic Michael Atkinson wrote: '[while] the Australian New Wave was still in its squawking, colicky infancy ... [the] hyperventilating bad dream [of *Wake in Fright*] emerged from the dust, sticky with sweat, cheap beer, kangaroo guts and frontier vertigo' (2013: 118). For Atkinson, *Wake in Fright* presented, along with other 'peak' achievements in the New Wave – *Stork*, *The Cars That Ate Paris* (Peter Weir, 1974), *The Chant of Jimmie Blacksmith* (Fred Schepisi, 1978) – the 'most scalding' example of a national cinema that had arrived 'seething with queasy ambivalence, post-colonial guilt and a remarkable dose of self-loathing' (2013: 118). As Atkinson concluded: 'Australians had decent reason to shun [*Wake in Fright*] ... The film's [long] exile from cultural consciousness [arguably fitting] its grotty persona far better than its [glossy restoration and subsequent] coronation at international festivals' (2013: 118). *Wake in Fright* remains a truly unsettling and uncomfortably 'close' experience, one not dimmed by the more benign portrait of out-sized Australian masculinity found in more tourist- and audience-friendly films like *Crocodile Dundee* (Peter Faiman, 1986). Like *Walkabout*, it is a provocative, intense, unsettling and unresolved foundation stone of the 'revival' that washes up in its wake.

12. THE MAN FROM HONG KONG (1975)

Kung Fu on Uluru: Asian-Australian Cinema

From its outrageous, pre-credit sequence – an absurdly situated drug deal at Uluru (referred to in the film as Ayers Rock) that culminates in an extended kung fu fight and car chase (also involving a helicopter) on and around the 'rock' – through to its literally explosive finale atop a Sydney high-rise, Brian Trenchard-Smith's international co-production, *The Man from Hong Kong* (1975), is a ground-breaking work of transnational Asian-Australian cinema and a prime example of 1970s 'Ozploitation' (a term that connects a diverse group of Australian genre films to international and transnational exploitation movie-making). *The Man from Hong Kong* also provides a significant point of connection to the 'Australian international pictures' of the 1950s and 1960s, the 1970s feature-film 'revival' – it was released in the key year of 1975 – and the boom in exploitation and genre-based commercial filmmaking in Australia in the late 1970s and into the 1980s enabled by changing funding mechanisms and ideologies. Like many co-productions and internationally financed features made in Australia, *The Man from Hong Kong* is a vanguard work that has been largely written out of nationalist and even postcolonial accounts of Australian cinema. As we will demonstrate in this final chapter, along with films such as *The Overlanders* (Harry Watt, 1946), *The Sundowners* (Fred Zinnemann, 1960), *Walkabout* (Nicolas Roeg, 1971) and even *Koya no toseinin* (*The Drifting Avenger*, Shogoro Nishimura, 1968), *The Man from Hong Kong* needs to be included in any discussion of what constitutes Australian cinema under the transformations wrought by globalisation, postcolonialism, transnationalism and the fracturing of national identity. As the final film discussed in this book, it provides a bridge between the 'Australian international pictures' of the postwar era and the relative boom in transnational co-productions and globally-focused features that follow the 'revival'. It is also an important, if contested, work within what Olivia Khoo, Belinda Smaill and Audrey Yue categorise as 'Asian-Australian cinema' (2013).

ENTER THE DRAGON: BRIAN-TRENCHARD SMITH, OZPLOITATION AND HONG KONG GENRE FILMMAKING

Writer-director Trenchard-Smith began his career in the UK before moving to Sydney, where he initially edited news footage and film trailers at Channel TEN-10 before moving to Channel 9 as promotions director. In the early 1970s, he formed his own production house, The Movie Company, to make a one-hour colour television special for Channel 9, *The Stuntmen* (1973), which featured the work of Bob Woodham and introduced Trenchard-Smith to an important later collaborator in stuntman Grant Page. Trenchard-Smith would go on to expand the idea into the 1987 compilation documentary *Dangerfreaks*, but his interest in stunt work and martial-arts cinema led more immediately to two television specials: *The World of Kung Fu* (1973) and *Kung Fu Killers* (1974). The first of these was intended to be a documentary about martial arts sensation Bruce Lee, but the actor's sudden death in July 1973 forced Trenchard-Smith – who had fully committed to the project – to rethink the film as a posthumous tribute (see Brennan 1979–80: 598–603, 674; Hartley 1996: 10–11).

The World of Kung Fu brought the director into contact with producer Raymond Chow of Golden Harvest, the major Hong Kong production company behind such seminal films as Lee's *Fist of Fury* (aka *The Chinese Connection*, Wei Lo, 1972) and *Enter the Dragon* (Robert Clouse, 1973). As the latter was the first major co-production between a Hong Kong and a Hollywood studio (Warner Bros.), it spearheaded the concerted effort by Hong Kong's two most powerful studios – Golden Harvest and Shaw Brothers – to advance the wider appeal of the genre through a strategy of international co-production and genre hybridisation (for details see Desser 2006: 143–55; Fore 1994: 40–58; Fu 2000: 43–51). In this context, Trenchard-Smith was able to negotiate a deal for his later film, *The Man from Hong Kong*, to be co-produced by Chow at Golden Harvest alongside an Australian consortium headed by John Fraser at Greater Union (Golden Harvest's distributor in Australia) and Trenchard-Smith's own The Movie Company. Like *Enter the Dragon*, the division of labour would feature a Western writer-director (Trenchard-Smith) and a Chinese choreographer (credited as Hung Kam Po but more commonly known as Hung Kam-bo or Sammo Hung) and star (Jimmy Wang Yu). Initially budgeted at AU$450,000, the negative cost for *The Man from Hong Kong* came to around AU$550,000 after the Hong Kong partners requested additional stunts be filmed for the film's extended car-chase sequences as well as a hit song for the opening credits, which was negotiated with Leeds Music in London (Brennan 1979–80: 600). With the largest budget of any Australian-produced feature of the time – though toppled from that position by the ruinously expensive *Eliza Fraser* (Tim Burstall, 1976) the following year – *The Man from Hong Kong* featured two main units (one for each partner country) with a shooting schedule extending between September and December 1974, comprising approximately five weeks in Sydney, a week around Uluru and another six weeks in Hong Kong ('*The Man from Hong Kong*' 1996: 24).

The Man from Hong Kong belongs to what has been called 'late transnationalism' by Asian cinema scholar Stephen Teo (2005: 195), specifically referring to the 1973–5 period of international co-production designed to launch Hong Kong stars in the West (and elsewhere) and to replicate the massive success of *Enter the Dragon* (Hunt 2002: 99). Other co-productions of the time included Shaw Brothers collaborations with Hammer Film Productions (*The Legend of the 7 Golden Vampires*, Roy Ward Baker, 1974; and *Shatter*, Michael Carreras, 1974) and with Warner Bros. (the blaxploitation film *Cleopatra Jones and the Casino of Gold*, Charles Bail, 1975) (Hunt 2002: 100). This represents a significant recalibration of co-production opportunities – for Australian filmmakers – beyond the traditional centres of film capital in Europe and the US. Further momentum was added to the global promotion of the kung fu cycle by the success of Warner Bros.' made-for-TV movie *Kung Fu* (first aired in August 1972) and the subsequent weekly television series, also titled *Kung Fu* (Desser 2000: 24; see also Hunt 2011: 141–9).

Late Transnationalism: Taking Hong Kong Cinema to the World

Across these examples, kung fu action demonstrated its strong affinity with other established genres and cycles – western, horror, blaxploitation – but, like *Enter the Dragon*, *The Man from Hong Kong* positioned its kung fu within the conventions and international geopolitics of the spy and police thriller, which provided 'obvious motivation for action, violence, stunts, and good guy/bad guy pairings' (Desser 2000: 26). As David Desser points out, *Enter the Dragon* had clear connections to the James Bond films, which employed martial arts (especially judo) and often cast Asian actors in the roles of both villains and heroes (2000: 26). *The Man from Hong Kong* would likewise exploit but also invert this connection, 'falling back on the James Bond formula' (Rayns 1975: 201) and casting an actual former Bond – Australian George Lazenby from *On*

THE MAN FROM HONG KONG (1975)

Her Majesty's Secret Service (Peter R. Hunt, 1969) – in the role of arch-villain Jack Wilton. The film would also be released the year after *The Man with the Golden Gun* (Guy Hamilton, 1974), Roger Moore's second Bond movie, which highlighted its Southeast and East Asian settings and was mostly filmed in Thailand, Hong Kong and Macau. More importantly, *The Man from Hong Kong* uniquely combines martial arts combat with the type of (Australian) stunt-filled action already evident in *Stone* (Sandy Harbutt, 1974) and popularised a few years later in *Mad Max* (George Miller, 1979) and its immediate sequels, *Mad Max 2: The Road Warrior* (George Miller, 1981) and *Mad Max: Beyond Thunderdome* (George Miller and George Ogilvie, 1985). Such stunt-driven action would also become a signature of Trenchard-Smith's subsequent work such as *Deathcheaters* (1976), *Stunt Rock* (1978) and *Turkey Shoot* (1982) and would come to define a particular subgenre and significant area of expertise of Australian cinema.

The casting of Jimmy Wang Yu in *The Man from Hong Kong*'s lead role, which was originally written with Bruce Lee in mind, was a response to 'both the loss of, and challenge posed by, [the death of] Bruce Lee' (Hunt 2002: 99). Although *Enter the Dragon* has often been identified as *the* single event that opened up a new transnational channel of martial arts film culture in the West and beyond, it is predated by several other Chinese-language and Hong Kong-made movies that were widely exported to the rest of the world (Rayns 1984: 26). These films included not only Golden Harvest's previous Lee films – *The Big Boss* (Wei Lo, 1971), *Fist of Fury* and *The Way of the Dragon* (Bruce Lee, 1972) – but also various Shaw Brothers' productions, including *King Boxer* (aka *Five Fingers of Death*, Chang Ho Cheng, 1972) and Wang's own influential directorial debut, *The Chinese Boxer* (1970), the film that is widely credited with 'launching' the modern kung fu movie. Although overshadowed by Lee's success, Wang was a veteran of martial arts films, having signed with Shaw Brothers in the mid-1960s before subsequently starring in such important wuxia films as *Tiger Boy* (Chang Cheh, 1966), *One-Armed Swordsman* (Chang Cheh, 1967) and *Golden Swallow* (Chang Cheh, 1968). In the early 1970s, Wang moved to Golden Harvest, and even though his films there – *One-Armed Boxer* (Wang Yu, 1972) and *Beach of the War Gods* (Wang Yu, 1973) – are similar in style to those he made at Shaw Brothers, his new studio gave him a higher international profile (Hunt 2002: 92). By the time of his arrival in Sydney in September 1974 for the shooting of *The Man from Hong Kong*, Wang had been relaunched as 'Jimmy' Wang Yu, headlined as 'Asia's Steve McQueen' (Forsyth 1974) and crowned the 'Kung-fu king' ('Kung-fu King to Make Aust Film' 1974: 10).[1]

Meaghan Morris describes *The Man from Hong Kong* as a 'kangaroo-kung fu cross-over film' and 'an unusual experiment, combining forces from two cinemas marginal to both the British and American industries, each hoping to use the other as a conduit to wider international success' (Morris 2004:

250). Both of these industries also had strong colonial and postcolonial links to Britain and the US, and each represented significant exhibition and distribution markets for both countries. A few years after its release, Trenchard-Smith sought to defend *The Man from Hong Kong*'s uneven style, explaining that he had worked to accommodate the co-producers' different – sometimes competing – interests by constructing a film that would be

> 'viewed as a serious action drama in Asia, and elsewhere [in Australia, and the rest of the world] as a spoof of the indestructible "hero" of the James Bond, Charles Bronson, or Bruce Lee type [. . . the] pseudo-fascist superhero who causes an appalling amount of destruction in the course of propagating the cause of justice' (Brennan 1979–80: 600).

This type of characterisation – which also coincides with Clint Eastwood's contemporaneous police inspector, Harry Callahan – imagines Wang's Inspector Fang as a type of Chinese Dirty Harry: 'Wang is a rogue cop given an Orientalist makeover, manifesting the brutal "East", but at the same time [like Callahan] cleaning up the corrupt Western city' (Hunt 2011: 144). In a later interview, Trenchard-Smith added that he had 'tried to pack [*The Man from Hong Kong*] with the stuff audiences want in that particular genre' and wrote the film 'to a formula: one action scene, one dialogue scene, one action scene, one dialogue scene', but always with the secondary intention of sending up the whole genre of the martial arts film (Palathingal 2008: 7). But this constant movement across genres, tones, styles and audience expectations also speaks to the film's transnationalism, a 'signature' style that is even evident in the contrastive modes of performance and dialogue found within individual scenes. This process of hybridisation is self-consciously highlighted on many occasions, including in the incongruous juxtaposition of the Uluru setting with an explosive car chase and kung fu fight sequence in the carefully staged but breathless opening moments. Although spectacular and highly photogenic, Uluru – in the centre of the vast continent of Australia and widely popular with the highly visible tourists – would have to be one of the most unlikely places on Earth to effectively stage an international drug deal. In another example from later in the film, Wang's character responds to a lover's disappointment in the lack of novelty and innovation in their intercultural pairing by asking, 'What'd you expect, acupuncture?'

Sky High: From the Red Centre to Downtown Kowloon

As introduced above, *The Man from Hong Kong* begins at the foot of Uluru, where an Australian drug courier (played by stuntman Ian Jamieson) is seen waiting in his sedan with a Connair travel bag full of cash. Approaching Uluru on a dirt road is a Pioneer Express tourist coach transporting scar-faced Hong

THE MAN FROM HONG KONG (1975)

Kong drug courier, Win Chan (Hung Kam Po), who is toting an identical bag, but for the fact that this one is full of heroin. Unbeknown to Chan, the bus also carries Bob Taylor (Roger Ward) of the Federal Bureau of Narcotics, a hard-nosed cop disguised as a tourist who snaps photos of the two couriers as they make contact and exchange bags. When the pair becomes aware of Taylor's surveillance, the presence of law enforcement is emphatically announced by the arrival of a police helicopter, a second cop who leaps from the bus and a radical cranking up of the film's moog-synthesised score. The movie then bursts into action: Taylor chases after Chan, who makes his way up the face of the rock; the Australian courier takes off in his car with the police helicopter in close pursuit.

Except for the words of the coach driver – 'The next stop on our tour is Ayres Rock, the most famous rock formation in Australia, if not the world' – the extended opening segment is dialogue free, put into *action* through a series of matching eyeline and reaction shots. Additionally, as described by Morris, this early scene centres on two parallel 'lines' of action. The primary chase – the (Hong Kong) martial arts line – follows Chan and Taylor as they scramble up the rock, throwing kung fu kicks and punches until Taylor saves Chan from a deadly fall at the summit. The secondary chase – the (Australian) stunt-filled line – involves the courier knocking out the second cop and speeding down the dirt road, only to have his swerving vehicle corralled by the low-flying chopper, whereupon the sedan hits a dirt bank, rolls, and explodes into flames (Morris 2004: 252–4). In each case, the pursuit and capture exploit the outback location: the hand-to-hand combat on the side of Uluru offers panoramic views of the surrounding terrain (flushed green by recent rains), while the exploding vehicle is perfectly framed in a long shot of the massive rock. Additionally, each of the chases is almost an inversion of the other: the vertical chase up the rock features a (white) cop in pursuit of a (Chinese) villain; the horizontal one along the dirt track displays a (Chinese) pilot in pursuit of a (white) villain. To Morris, the two lines of action serve not only to unsettle a common 'white law/Chinese crime dichotomy' but also to prepare viewers for the struggle between 'Chinese heroism' (as embodied by Inspector Fang Sing Leng, played by Jimmy Wang Yu) and 'white villainy' (Jack Wilton, played by George Lazenby) that underpins the main narrative (Morris 2004: 254). This juxtaposition also prepares and 'trains' the audience for the combination of Australian and Chinese elements that characterises the rest of the film that follows.

The Man from Hong Kong's extended (almost eight-minute-long) opening gives way to the title sequence and the introduction of Inspector Fang of Hong Kong's Special Branch. Accompanied by the movie's signature tune – UK pop outfit Jigsaw's 'Sky High', which was commissioned specifically for the film and became a worldwide hit, reaching number three on the pop charts in Australia and the US – the credit sequence demonstrates Fang's deadly accuracy with a pistol and equally devastating proficiency in martial arts. It also, in part, mirrors the film's opening segment by combining an identifiably Chinese character and location (the cityscape and surrounding mountains of Hong Kong) with a Western soundtrack (the song by Jigsaw). His training routine for the troops is interrupted, however, when a journalist from Sydney, Caroline Thorne (Ros Spiers), hang-glides onto the police training grounds. Confiscating her kite, Fang tells Caroline he will escort her back to her hotel, but first drives them in his Mercedes 350SL convertible to the city's panoramic Victoria Peak. Asked what she thinks of Hong Kong, Caroline replies (in one of the film's first openly self-conscious moments), 'Ah, beautiful ... squalid, exhilarating and frightening. All the traditional contradictions of the East in one city', before clarifying: 'At least, that's what I'll write in my column.' In return, she asks Fang, 'What's so special about the Special Branch?' His immediate response is to quickly take her to bed: 'you're my first Chinese', Caroline tells him. In another of the film's inversions (this one relating to the Caucasian male-Asian female coupling common in the Bond films), this interracial afternoon tryst was likely designed as a deliberate provocation (at least to the white male audience of the time).

As well as marking Fang's first sexual conquest in the film, the no-nonsense Caroline – after bedding down with Fang, she asks, 'Can I have my kite back now?' – later uses her professional connections to facilitate Fang's introduction to Wilton at a high-society function. More urgently, the spectacular aerial shots of Caroline's hang-glider swooping over Hong Kong's skyline not only provide a complement and counterpoint to the outback scenery at Uluru, but also mirror – in a model of classical Hollywood closure – the end of the film, when Fang himself pilots the hang-glider to penetrate Wilton's seventeenth-floor apartment-fortress in a Sydney high-rise.

THE YELLOW PERIL: CULTURAL STEREOTYPES AND POSTCOLONIALISM

Travelling to Sydney to extradite Chan, Fang is met at Kingsford Smith Airport by Taylor (now conventionally dressed in suit and tie) and his partner, the scruffy long-haired undercover narcotics cop Morrie Grosse (Hugh Keays-Byrne). Together the two make up a 'comic cop double-act' (Hartley 1996: 10), their comments often undercutting or providing ironic counterpoint to the film's acts of violence and mayhem. Asked whether he would 'fancy a cup of tea', Fang is taken to an outdoor café, located at the base of the towering precast concrete shells of the Sydney Opera House (then only recently opened in October 1973) – the film highlighting 'modern' Sydney in a way that resonates with both *Moeru tairiku* (*Blazing Continent*, Shogoro Nishimura, 1968) and *Color Me Dead* (Eddie Davis, 1970). Proceeding to the jail where Chan is held, Grosse cautions Fang, telling him right from the outset, 'No torture, no thumbscrews – this is Australia, mate', but the inspector wastes no time in forcefully extracting the name of the drug baron for whom Chan works. The 'interrogation' takes place in the cell while the two Australian cops enjoy a drink and game of pool at a local bar, the beating that is administered by Fang making for an inspired cross-cut when a groin kick is matched by a rack of balls being broken on a pool table. Fang continues to brutalise the suspect, immersing Chan's head in the cell's toilet bowl and eventually procuring the name of his boss: Wilton. Upon their return, Taylor and Grosse warn Fang against interfering in the case they have been building against Wilton over a period of two years. But when Chan is shot dead on the way to his court hearing by one of Wilton's assassins (Grantly, played by Grant Page), Fang becomes an unstoppable force, causing incredible damage and complications for the Australian police.

The two local cops, whose dialogue scenes give pause to Fang's action sequences, play an important twofold role in the film: they 'at once [explain] Australian police procedures to the foreign hero' and also act as 'a buffer between the Australian audience and the foreign protagonist by inducting the audience into accepting foreign heroes in Australian movies' (Teo 2006: 188). They also help frame and explain Fang's actions to the audience more generally. Additionally, Taylor and Grosse's commentary on Fang's unorthodox and forceful methods of pursuing and (often) violently eliminating criminals – 'they've got a million subtle methods of torture, these Chinese', Grosse tells Taylor – gives voice to 'certain racialised pejoratives' (Teo 2006: 188). For instance, observing the destruction that (later in the film) Fang wreaks on the open road, Grosse exclaims, 'Talk about the bloody yellow peril!' Nevertheless, Fang's true adversary is Wilton, the sleazy kingpin who, on their first encounter, taunts Fang with the film's most straightforwardly racist line: 'I never met a Chinese yet that didn't have a yellow streak.'

Fang's pursuit of Wilton and his gang begins in earnest when, following Chan's assassination outside the federal courthouse, Fang sights the gunman on an adjacent rooftop and gives chase (with Taylor and Grosse trailing behind, slowed up by having been cuffed to Chan). The foot race through the narrow back streets of inner Sydney features a unique moment of intimately combined kung fu action and (Australian) stunt work: a flying kick from Wang (captured in a single shot) that unseats the assassin from a speeding motorcycle that he has commandeered. Police cars join in the pursuit and the chase leads to one of the film's most elaborate set pieces, a deadly kung fu fight in a local Chinese restaurant, where Fang dispatches the gunman, later identified as Grantly, one of Wilton's bouncers. Using Sydney exteriors to establish its location, the fight sequence was actually shot over four consecutive days (after-hours) in a Hong Kong restaurant. Repurposing any number of kitchen implements and utensils as deadly weapons, the combatants slash and bash one another: Grantly slashes with a chef's knife and wields a meat hook, Fang hurls a wok of boiling oil, Grantly strangles Fang with a telephone cord, Fang releases the deadly choke by mercilessly squeezing the assassin's testicles. Moving from the restaurant kitchen to dining room, the combatants scatter patrons and overturn tables until Fang ends it all by breaking a bottle over Grantly's head and slamming him into the restaurant's fish tank. In the aftermath, Fang declares that the assassin was a worthy opponent and tells Taylor and Grosse that he wants to meet the man who employed the killer. The request (which comes a little over thirty minutes into the film) makes for Wilton's first appearance. Seen at his martial arts academy, Lazenby's Wilton is in the process of trialling a replacement assassin, wherein he demonstrates, in a punishing display that sends his opponents flying through the air in slow motion, that he is a formidable opponent: another villainous master of kung fu.

'THIS IS AUSTRALIA, MATE, NOT 55 DAYS AT PEKING'

Fang and Taylor's visit to Wilton's high-rise office building and penthouse at Millers Point is met with obstinate resistance from his minder, Willard (played by Frank Thring). And Fang's attempt to strong-arm his way through to Wilton only further frustrates Grosse who erupts in anger, warning him: 'Enough's enough ... This is Australia, mate, not 55 Days at Peking.'[2] To Taylor's amusement, Fang stares down Grosse, telling him, 'don't give me any shit'. Wilton's response is to send two assassins to Fang's hotel room (they are quickly dispatched) and the following day Fang thinks to contact Caroline. Fang's inspiration comes from a dawn training routine, shot against the backdrop of Sydney's northern beachside suburb of Narrabeen, during which the sight of a pigeon taking wing calls up a memory of Caroline's kite from earlier in the film. The segment also provides an excuse, according to Trenchard-Smith, to use more of the spectacular footage shot over Hong Kong: a graphic match cuts directly from the pigeon in flight to the hang-glider. Fang subsequently meets Caroline in the beachside town of Stanwell Park, 59 kilometres south of Sydney. Gesturing past a windsock – yellow, tumescent and bobbing in the stiff breeze – to her boyfriend on a hang-glider, Caroline provides an evener for some members of the audience: 'He's very good at it. He can stay up for hours.' On a more sober note, Fang tells Caroline that he wants to meet Wilton socially, explaining (in a passage that anticipates and describes his final duel with the crime boss): 'In my country [...] we have a sport. We take a giant praying mantis and put him in a wooden cage and make him fight for his life with his own kind. I thought you would enjoy such a sport.'

A sound bridge carries Caroline's words – 'You and Jack Wilton in a wooden cage. He's a very dangerous man' – over to a close-up of Wilton, raising a crossbow in direct aim at the viewer. A reverse shot shows that Wilton is taking aim (William Tell-style) at an apple seated atop the head of a young woman, while guests gathered at the harbour-side, high-society party look on in awed anticipation. When Fang and Caroline arrive, the colonial playboy Wilton immediately recognises and provokes Fang, telling him that he travels regularly to the East and finds that 'Chinese make the best servants'. Wilton invites Fang to demonstrate his kung fu skills to the socialite crowd, whereupon the two briefly spar before – in a one-against-many confrontation typical of the genre – Fang dispatches four of Wilton's armed henchmen. Later that evening, Fang goes looking for evidence at Wilton's martial arts centre building, daringly scaling its walls to get to the tenth floor and engaging several more of Wilton's thugs, including one played by Trenchard-Smith himself. Seriously injured in the ensuing fight where he faces multiple armed assailants, Fang narrowly escapes death, throwing himself through a glass door and onto the street, where he is rescued by a passing vehicle, a Commer FC.

The two young women responsible for saving Fang – Angelica (Rebecca Gilling) and her friend Mei Ling (Elaine Wong) – realise the danger of taking him to a hospital and retreat instead to the safety of a country homestead. There, with the help of her bush veterinarian father (Deryck Barnes), Angelica tends to Fang's wounds and nurses him back to health, while (back in Sydney) Taylor and Grosse inspect the carnage at the martial arts centre and wonder over the inspector's whereabouts. In a manner characteristic of the genre, Fang's recovery is played out as a country idyll, with a montage of horse riding, swimming and picnicking depicting his physical recuperation in the bush and developing relationship with Angelica. Replete with star filters and overlaid with a saccharine pop song ('A Man is a Man is a Man', sung by Deena Greene), the sequence leads to the film's second sex scene. A barely disguised (or perhaps, unintended) parody of the romantic interlude found in many contemporaneous television commercials and films such as *Play Misty for Me* (Clint Eastwood, 1971), the sex scene is also a marker of the film's curious hybridity. As Teo points out, at one level Fang's sexual appetite is another (subversive) inversion of the 'super-sexed [white] male hero as represented by James Bond'; at another, his willingness to mix pleasure with business is at odds with the persona of the virtuous kung fu hero, who is typically 'more celibate than the Western action hero' (Teo 2006: 190). Fully recovered from his injuries, Fang asks Angelica to return him to Sydney, but their van is intercepted and run off the country road by Wilton's heavies. Angelica is killed instantly, but Fang – goaded now into fully using his faculties for revenge and destruction – flags down a passing car (conveniently it is an iconic Australian muscle car, a Valiant Charger) and takes off in pursuit along the winding mountain road, mercilessly dispatching each of the three offending vehicles and their drivers.

The multi-car chase sequence – which includes (in anticipation of the high-octane opening of *Mad Max*, in which the police interceptor bursts through a caravan mobile home) a Ford Falcon XT that spectacularly explodes through a frame house before bursting into flames – ends with Fang driving his now beaten and rattling wreck of a car to a final confrontation with Wilton. Hearing of Fang's escape, Wilton locks down his penthouse apartment, securing the entrance with a steel shutter and arming himself with an automatic weapon. Fang now asks one last favour of Caroline: borrowing her kite, he is hoisted by speedboat high above Sydney's Circular Quay, which enables him to hang-glide to and land on the roof of Wilton's high-rise building. Crashing in through a window, Fang – now in a 'wooden cage' with his own kind – engages Wilton in an extended bout of hand-to-hand combat. After overpowering the criminal, Fang extracts a full written confession by fiendishly inserting a hand grenade into Wilton's mouth, securing it with tape and threatening to set off its 90-second timing device. When the pin to the grenade is accidentally pulled during a struggle, Fang pushes Wilton into his explosives-packed armoury and sails down the side of the building to safety. The hapless Taylor and Grosse arrive late on the scene – as they have throughout the entire film. Fang presents them with the signed confession as well as evidence in the form of a packet of heroin. Their lame response – 'You're a hard act to follow. What do you do for an encore?' – perfectly coincides with the explosion at Wilton's armoury which blows the top of the building 'sky high'.

'WHAT'D YOU EXPECT, ACUPUNCTURE?': RELEASING *THE MAN FROM HONG KONG*

The Man from Hong Kong premiered to a packed media audience in four Australian capitals – Sydney, Melbourne, Adelaide and Brisbane – on 3 and 4 September 1975, where its 'exciting blend of comedy, spectacle and almost non-stop action' earned it 'spontaneous laughs, applause and gasps' ('*The Man From Hong Kong* Away to Sky-high Start' 1975: 1). The Sydney premiere at Greater Union's Rapallo Theatre was hosted by co-producer (and general manager of British Empire Films) John Fraser, but at the centre of attention were the film's stars George Lazenby, Hugh Keays-Byrne and Rebecca Gilling, stunt coordinator and actor Grant Page and writer-director Brian Trenchard-Smith.[3] After the screening, the director observed: 'This audience reaction is as good as we ever hoped for [. . .] While the big action scenes are working on one level, the underlying comedy accent is being picked up and greatly appreciated ('*MFHK* Away to Sky-high Start' 1975: 1). Among the industry personalities who attended the theatre, and the champagne reception that followed at the Grand Ballroom of Sydney's Hilton Hotel, was renowned veteran Australian director Ken G. Hall, who endorsed the film, saying: 'Brian Trenchard-Smith comes up as the best possibility among the new breed of Australian action directors to date. *The Man from Hong Kong* looks to me like a sure-fire box-office attraction' ('*MFHK* Away to Sky-high Start' 1975: 1). Hall's praise clearly aligns Trenchard-Smith's contemporary approach with much of the work he himself completed for Cinesound Productions in the 1930s and 1940s – such as *Lovers and Luggers* (1937) and *Dad and Dave Come to Town* (1938) – and that carefully melded together overtly Australian elements with imported or international forms and innovations (for a discussion of Hall's work in this regard, see Danks 2018: 19–39). Hall's films for Cinesound and *The Man from Hong Kong* also shared patronage from the exhibitor, Greater Union.

The positive industry and media reaction to the premiere – enhanced by advance media cross-promotion – continued into *The Man from Hong Kong*'s national theatrical release. Strongest of these promotional strategies was the awareness campaign, spearheaded by EMI's advance local release of [British] Jigsaw's single 'Sky High', which received significant airplay in New South Wales (on such stations as 2UE, 2SM and 2UW) and charted very well nationally ('*MFHK* Away to Sky-high Start' 1975: 4). On television, a thirty-minute documentary film – *The Making of 'The Man from Hong Kong'* (written and directed by the film's associate producer, Michael Falloon) – highlighted the film's action sequences and was aired nationally on Channel 9 to coincide with the premiere ('*MFHK* Away to Sky-high Start' 1975: 4). Further promotional high points – typical of junkets of the day – included 'previews to travel and music people, national magazine coverage, local press support, street posters, leaflets at football grounds, [and] record store displays' ('*MFHK* Away to Sky-high Start' 1975: 4). The various awareness and maintenance strategies buoyed the film through the lucrative Christmas vacation and summer period (December 1975 to January 1976) that followed its release, with some cinemas requesting extensions on print hire to meet demand. The film's drive-in debut at the end of January 1976 fared equally well ('BEF Money Makers' 1976: 12).

Prior to its Australian release in September 1975, *The Man from Hong Kong* screened at the Cannes Film Festival market, where expectations for international sales were high, especially in light of releases guaranteed in the UK, Germany, Belgium, the Netherlands, Israel, Lebanon, Spain, Italy, Switzerland, France, South America and throughout Southeast Asia ('Date for *Man From Hong Kong*' 1975: 11). In North America, *The Man from Hong Kong* was sold to Twentieth Century-Fox, which changed the film's title to *The Dragon Flies* and excised some dialogue scenes that were deemed too parochial. Its initial US box-office performance was disappointing, with the two-week premiere at the Cine Theatre in New York only taking US$14,000. But by early September 1975, interest had picked up, and *The Dragon Flies* grossed US$175,000 across fifteen US theatres before going into wider general release ('Australian

Films on Release' 1975: 200). In the UK (where it was distributed by Rank), *The Man from Hong Kong* opened more strongly, its October 1975 premiere at the London Pavilion earning more in its first week than any film since John Schlesinger's Oscar-winning *Midnight Cowboy* in 1969 (White 1975). The film's first runs in other European markets were similarly strong: it opened simultaneously in twelve Paris cinemas, where it played for two weeks, and in Copenhagen's World Cinema, where it grossed three times that of Roger Moore's roughly contemporaneous Bond film, *The Man with the Golden Gun* ('Australian Film Opens in Paris' 1976: 3). Perhaps most impressive was *The Man from Hong Kong*'s box-office performance in Karachi, where it was imported by the National Film Development Corporation and, in just seven weeks, out-grossed such 1960s blockbusters as *The Guns of Navarone* (J. Lee Thompson, 1961), *Cleopatra* (Joseph L. Mankiewicz, 1963) and *Where Eagles Dare* (Brian G. Hutton, 1968) to become the highest-grossing foreign film since the inception of Pakistan ('*Man from Hong Kong* Ding Dong in Karachi' 1976: 33).

Leon Hunt writes that even though *The Man from Hong Kong*'s mixture of martial arts and stunt-filled action paved the way for the likes of Jackie Chan's *Police Story* series (1985–2013), the movie is 'usually judged a [critical] failure' (Hunt 2002: 100). Reviews of the time, however, suggest that its critical reception was (in the main) quite favourable both locally and internationally. For instance, writing for *The Australian*, Mike Harris declared that *The Man from Hong Kong* is 'an action film and pretends to be nothing else: it is deliberately (if not cynically) aimed at the kung-fu fanciers [...] and is destined for as big a commercial success here as any Australian film has had – if not bigger' (Harris 1975). In *Cinema Papers*, Jim Murphy similarly described *The Man from Hong Kong* as 'tongue in cheek, knee in groin action' and 'the sort of bread-and-butter [genre] film that has always been the backbone of film industries' (1975: 261–2). One of the most enthusiastic and prescient local reviews appeared in the *Australasian Cinema*, which – speaking from a commercial perspective – described *The Man from Hong Kong* as 'undoubtedly the most significant Australian motion picture to date'. The review asserted that, as a 'brilliant send-up [and] colossal spoof of James Bond, Kung Fu, [etc.]', the film has 'all the ingredients that go into a box-office hit. Top team work, spectacular photography, action galore, good story line, and it's humorous.' The reviewer's principal point of concern was that *The Man from Hong Kong* had been dealt 'a deadly blow' locally by way of its unjustifiably severe R-rating that admitted patrons only eighteen years old and over ('*The Man from Hong Kong* Export Quality' 1975: 3).

Internationally, the *Hollywood Reporter* had no issue with the film's classification, writing: '*The Dragon Flies* [...] is an extremely violent, bloody attempt to keep the kung fu genre films alive, but its extensive fight sequences seem tired and trite' ('*The Man from Hong Kong*' 1975: 3). More positive were reports from *Screen International*, which rated *The Man from Hong Kong* 'a popular choice for all addicts of busy-busy action' (Bilbow 1975: 17), and *Variety*, which announced that the movie had 'all the necessary ingredients for good b.o. [box-office . . . including] comedy, crisp dialog, and lovely damsels to be conquered by the yellow peril, Inspector Fang' (Tobias 1975: 19). In the UK, *Films and Filming*'s Eric Braun – who had attended a local press screening that featured an introduction by Trenchard-Smith – wrote that *The Man from Hong Kong* had achieved its director's goal for 'constant action and, at the same time [. . .] succeed[ed] in its satirical intent, delivered during brief moments when hero Jimmy Wang Yu desists from sprinting, swirling, climbing, high-kicking, chopping' (Braun 1976: 36).

No *Picnic*: *The Man from Hong Kong* and Australian (Inter)national Cinema

The positive press that *The Man from Hong Kong* attracted at the time of its theatrical release did not, however, prevent the film from subsequently being marginalised by more 'respectable' works, especially those later canonised as part of the 1970s 'revival' such as *Picnic at Hanging Rock* (Peter Weir, 1975) and *Sunday Too Far Away* (Ken Hannam, 1975), both released in the same year. Some thirty years later, Trenchard-Smith observed that *The Man from Hong Kong*, along with other Australian exploitation films from the period, had been 'swept under the carpet by the [. . .] professional arts bureaucrats and the [cultural] critics who wanted [. . .] high-minded films or great social documents of Australia's past and present' (Palathingal 2008: 7). Prioritising national interests over commercial imperatives, these cultural tastemakers had largely rejected genre films and failed to appreciate that *The Man from Hong Kong* was, as Trenchard-Smith described, a 'Tom and Jerry [cartoon], Chinese style, with a bit of red paint!' (Bren 2000: 77). Its reputation also suffered as an outwardly commercial co-production seeking to attract the Australian and wide international audience for action cinema. In respect to its international and transnational credentials, it provides a link back to several of the 'Australian international' films of the 1950s and 1960s and forward to many of the exploitation movies that would follow in its wake. In the 2000s, *The Man from Hong Kong* was re-evaluated along with other contemporaneous Ozploitation films – such as *Alvin Purple* (Tim Burstall, 1973), *The Cars That Ate Paris* (Peter Weir, 1974) and *Patrick* (Richard Franklin, 1978) – and featured in Mark Hartley's widely-seen and much-discussed documentary, *Not Quite Hollywood: The Wild, Untold Story of Ozploitation!* (2008). Discovered by a new generation of cinemagoers, *The Man from Hong Kong* is now recognised as a pioneering work of Australian transnational cinema: 'the first Australian-Hong Kong co-production and the first local example of the now-cool "chop socky" genre' (Cockington 2001: 7).

The Man from Hong Kong is also an appropriate and illustrative film to consider as we bring the discussion in this book to a close. It foregrounds and self-consciously performs ideas of Australianness – as Grosse declaims to Fang at one point, 'this is Australia. We're not allowed to get into that sort of thing, mate' – and the relation of Australia to the rest of the world (particularly Asia), and it provides a formative example of a strong transnational co-production model that draws equally on local and international elements. It links back to the 'Australian international pictures' of the 1940s, 1950s and 1960s, but also belongs to the 'revival' – it was released in the seminal year of 1975 – and the commercial modes of genre and exploitation filmmaking that took flight in the 1970s and 1980s. Unlike films such as *Kangaroo* (Lewis Milestone, 1952), *On the Beach* (Stanley Kramer, 1959), *The Sundowners*, *The Drifting Avenger* and *Walkabout*, many of its key creative participants were Australian. It provides a model and example that informs many of the 'Australian international' films that would follow including the work of George Miller and Baz Luhrmann and some of the large-budget films made across the studio complexes on the east coast of Australia over the last thirty years. *The Man from Hong Hong* also recognises the geographic, cultural and economic significance of Australia's place in the Pacific and its relation to Asia. In some ways, this book charts a partial shift from Britain to the US and Asia in the 'Australian' cinema of this thirty-year period. Although part of a relatively minor strand of international production in Australia until the twenty-first century, *The Man from Hong Kong* establishes a path for the incursions of other Asian film industries into Australia including Bollywood, along with overseas filmmakers like Jackie Chan who made two films 'down under' in the 1990s: *First Strike* (Stanley Tong, 1996) and *Mr. Nice Guy* (Sammo Hung, 1997).

The story of *The Man from Hong Kong* further deepens and expands our understanding of the practices of international and transnational filmmaking in Australia during this transformative era. As has been argued throughout, a re-examination of *The Man from Hong Kong*, along with many of the other works discussed in this book, makes us reconsider the points of connection, influence and difference between the films of the 'interval' and those of the 'revival' and beyond. This is a tale which details the tenacity of filmmaking and filmmakers in Australia across the thirty years after World War II, but which also recognises a continuity of practices and perspectives between the movies made during this era and the more robust feature-film ecology that would emerge. It is time to recognise and embrace the continuity between this sparse era of feature-film production and the richer vein of filmmaking that followed. The essential arguments and narratives put forward for government assistance to the film industry in the 1960s and 1970s – and how these approaches commonly claimed a 'void' or 'interval' of true Australian feature-film production in the postwar era – need to be adjusted once and for all.

NOTES

1. See also the headline 'Asia's Steve McQueen joins our James Bond' (Forsyth 1974: n.p.).
2. The reference is to the film *55 Days at Peking* (Nicholas Ray, 1963) set during the Boxer Rebellion. With its dramatisation of the rebellion through the point of view of characters representing the colonial powers occupying China, this seems to be a very inexact, even ironic point of reference.
3. Andrew Pike and Ross Cooper write that the film's Australian distributor, British Empire Films (BEF), opened *The Man from Hong Kong* simultaneously in two Sydney cinemas: the Rapallo and the Metro Kings Cross (1998: 288).

REFERENCES

A. C. (1960), 'On the Beach', Age (Melbourne), 4 May, 6.
'A Good Night Out' (1970), Bulletin, 8 August, 22–3.
'Actors Upset at Ned Kelly Offers for Parts in Movie' (1969), Canberra Times, 3 July, 9.
'Age of Consent', TCM: Turner Classic Movies, http://www.tcm.com/tcmdb/title/3772/Age-of-Consent/misc-notes.html
Agutter, Jenny (1999), 'Going Walkabout', Sight and Sound, 9: 3, March, 58–9.
'Albright Home – and Off to "Zanuckville"' (1950), Film Weekly, 7 December, 1.
'All Their Own Work' (1970), Bulletin, 8 August, 22.
Allen, John (1969), 'Non-events and Others', Masque, August–September, 6–9.
Anderson, Joseph L. and Donald Richie (1982), The Japanese Film: Art and Industry, Princeton, NJ: Princeton University Press.
'Another Film Here by Japs' (1968), Sydney Morning Herald, 28 July, 33.
Armitage, Mary (1952), 'Adelaide – 20th-Fox and Hoyts "did" Magnificently by Red Cross, MPI Status', Film Weekly, 12 June, 40.
Atkinson, Michael (2013), 'Waking Nightmare', Sight and Sound, 23: 5, May, 118.
'Australian Adventure Story' (1951), Australian Women's Weekly, 17 October, 43.
'Australian Film Opens in Paris' (1976), Filmnews, 6: 9, September, 3.
'Australian Films on Release Overseas' (1975), Cinema Papers, 7, November–December, 200.
'Australia's Gary Cooper' (1946), Australian Women's Weekly, 30 March, 29.
Barr, Charles (1977), Ealing Studios, London: Cameron and Tayleur.
'Bass Strait Oil Hunt Inspires a Japanese Film' (1968), Sydney Morning Herald, 13 February, 6.
Baxter, John (2014), Paris at the End of The World: The City of Light During the Great War, 1914–1918, New York: Harper Perennial.
Bazin, André (1971), What is Cinema? Vol. 2, trans. Hugh Gray, Berkeley: University of California Press.

Beattie, Max (1969), 'Ned Kelly Swings Again', *Age (Melbourne)*, 12 July, 1.
'BEF Money Makers' (1976), *Australasian Cinema*, 4: 1, 22 January, 12.
Bennett, Colin (1959a), 'On the Beach: Great Impact of New Film', *Age (Melbourne)*, 18 December, 2.
Bennett, Colin (1959b). 'Last Days of Melbourne: Hollywood's Pacifist Film', *Age (Melbourne)*, 26 December, 11.
Bennett, Colin (1961), 'Films in 1961: A Vintage Year for Melbourne', *Age (Melbourne)*, 30 December, 11.
Bennett, Colin (1966), 'The Man Who Made the Mob', *Age (Melbourne)*, 20 August, 23.
Bennett, Colin (1969), 'Warm, Likeable, but Unambitious', *Age (Melbourne)*, 9 May, 2.
Bennett, Colin (1971), '*Walkabout*', *Age (Melbourne)*, 30 October, n.p.
Bertrand, Ina (2003), 'New Histories of the Kelly Gang: Gregor Jordan's *Ned Kelly*', *Senses of Cinema*, 26, May, http://www.sensesofcinema.com/2003/australian-contemporary-cinema-26/ned_kelly/
Bilbow, Marjorie (1975), '*The Man from Hong Kong*', *Screen International*, 6, 11 October, 17.
Birtles, Dora (1987 [1946]), *The Overlanders*, London: Virago.
'*Blazing Continent*' (1969), *UniJapan Film Quarterly*, 12: 2, 14.
'Bombs, Police, and Ned' (1970), *Canberra Times*, 29 July, 1.
Bosser, A. W. (1970), 'The Kelly's Rode Again with the Shire Council's Help!', *Australian Municipal Journal*, July, 8–14.
Boyle, Anthony (1979), 'Two Images of the Aboriginal: *Walkabout*, the Novel and Film', *Literature/Film Quarterly*, 7: 1, 67–76.
'Braidwood is Laying it on' (1969), *Canberra Times*, 9 July, 3.
Brand, Harry (1951), '*Kangaroo: The Australian Story*', 20th Century-Fox Studios, 27 December.
Braun, Eric (1976), '*The Man from Hong Kong*', *Films and Filming*, 22: 4, January, 36.
Braun, Eric (1977), *Deborah Kerr*, London: W. H. Allen.
Bren, Frank (2000), 'Notes on Australasia', in Law Kar (ed.), *Hong Kong Cinema Retrospective: Border Crossings in Hong Kong Cinema*, Hong Kong: The 24th Hong Kong International Film Festival, pp. 71–81.
Brennan, Richard (1979–80), 'Brian Trenchard-Smith: Interview', *Cinema Papers*, 24, December–January, 598–603, 674.
'Brilliant Scene at Opening of *Kangaroo*' (1952), *Advertiser (Adelaide)*, 5 June, 1.
Broderick, Mick (2013), 'Fallout *On the Beach*', *Screening the Past*, 36, June, http://www.screeningthepast.com/issue-36-first-release/fallout-on-the-beach/
Brog (1952), '*Kangaroo*', *Variety*, 21 May, 6.
Brown, Geoff (1984), 'A Knight and His Castle', in Jane Fluegel (ed.), *Michael Balcon: The Pursuit of British Cinema*, New York: The Museum of Modern Art, pp. 17–41.
Brown, Max (1951a), 'The Film Natives are all Smiles', *Mail (Adelaide)*, 27 January, Sunday Magazine, 2.
Brown, Max (1951b), 'Australia Makes Debut in T.V. Films', *Sunday Herald (Sydney)*, 8 April, Features, 1.
Brown, Max (1958), *Wild Turkey*, Melbourne: Georgian House.
Bruno, Giuliana (2001), 'Driven', *2wice*, 5: 2, 56–64.
Bryning, Mal (1971), '*Wake in Fright*', *Lumiere* 12, November–December, 10.
Buckley, Anthony (2009), *Behind a Velvet Light Trap: A Filmmaker's Journey from Cinesound to Cannes*, Prahran, VIC: Hardie Grant Books.
Byrnes, Paul, '*Walkabout*: Curator's Notes', *Australian Screen: An NFSA Website*, https://aso.gov.au/titles/features/walkabout/notes/

Canfield, Kevin (2012), 'Director Ted Kotcheff on *Wake in Fright*', *Filmmaker*, 1 October, https://filmmakermagazine.com/52805-ted-kotcheff-on-wake-in-fright/#.YhGXF5NBxp8
Capua, Michelangelo (2010), *Deborah Kerr: A Biography*, Jefferson, NC and London: McFarland.
Caputo, Raffaele (2009), '*Wake in Fright*: An Interview with Ted Kotcheff', *Senses of Cinema*, 51, http://www.sensesofcinema.com/2019/20-years-of-senses/wake-in-fright-an-interview-with-ted-kotcheff-issue-51-july-2009/
Clarke, Charles (1952), 'We Filmed *Kangaroo* Entirely in Australia', *American Cinematographer*, 33: 7, 292–3, 315–17.
Cleary, Jon (2013 [1952]), *The Sundowners*, Sydney: HarperCollins.
Cockington, James (2001), 'Kung-fu in Flares', *Sydney Morning Herald*, 3 August, 7.
Collins, Felicity (2009), 'Resisting the Ethical Violence of Coercive Aboriginality: David Gulpilil', in Robert Clarke (ed.), *Celebrity Colonialism: Fame, Power and Representation in Colonial and Postcolonial Cultures*, Newcastle Upon Tyne: Cambridge Scholars, pp. 189–207.
Collins, Felicity and Therese Davis (2004), *Australian Cinema After Mabo*, Cambridge: Cambridge University Press.
Collins, Felicity, Jane Landman and Susan Bye (eds) (2019), *A Companion to Australian Cinema*, Hoboken, NJ: Wiley-Blackwell.
Combs, Richard (1969), '*Age of Consent*', *Monthly Film Bulletin*, 36: 431, December, 256.
Combs, Richard (1999), 'Not God's Sunflowers: Nicolas Roeg on *Walkabout*', in Raffaele Caputo and Geoff Burton (eds), *Second Take: Australian Film-Makers Talk*, St Leonards, NSW: Allen & Unwin, pp. 165–73.
Cook, Kenneth (1971 [1961]), *Wake in Fright*, Harmondsworth: Penguin.
Corfield, Justin (2003), *The Ned Kelly Encyclopaedia*, Melbourne: Lothian.
Craven, Allison (2016), *Finding Queensland in Australian Cinema: Poetics and Screen Geographies*, London: Anthem Press.
'Crisis Over for Miss Faithfull' (1969), *Age (Melbourne)*, 11 July, 1.
Crowther, Bosley (1959), 'Screen: *On the Beach*', *New York Times*, 18 December, 34.
Cunningham, Stuart (1989), 'The Decades of Survival: Australian Film 1930–1970', in Albert Moran and Tom O'Regan (eds), *The Australian Screen*, Melbourne: Penguin, pp. 53–74.
Cunningham, Stuart (1991), *Featuring Australia: The Cinema of Charles Chauvel*, Sydney: Allen & Unwin.
Danks, Adrian (2011), 'Don't Rain on Ava Gardner Parade', *Senses of Cinema*, 59, June, https://www.sensesofcinema.com/2011/melbourne-on-film/dont-rain-on-ava-gardner-parade/
Danks, Adrian (2018), 'Rudimentary Modernism: Ken G. Hall, Rear-Projection and 1930s Hollywood', in Adrian Danks, Stephen Gaunson and Peter C. Kunze (eds), *American-Australian Cinema: Transnational Connections*, Cham: Palgrave Macmillan, pp. 19–39.
Danks, Adrian and Constantine Verevis (eds) (2010), 'Australian International Pictures', Special Issue, *Studies in Australasian Cinema*, 4: 3, 195–8.
Danks, Adrian, Stephen Gaunson and Peter C. Kunze (eds) (2018), *American-Australian Cinema: Transnational Connections*, Cham: Palgrave Macmillan.
'Date for *Man from Hong Kong*' (1975), *Sydney Morning Herald*, 24 July, 11.
Davey, Philip R. (2005), *When Hollywood Came to Melbourne: The Story of the Making of Stanley Kramer's On the Beach*, Melbourne: Philip R. Davey.
Dawson, Jan (1970), '*Ned Kelly*', *Monthly Film Bulletin*, 37: 432, August, 158.
'Deborah Kerr in Australian Film' (1957), *Sydney Morning Herald*, 20 April, 3.

Dermody, Susan and Elizabeth Jacka (1987), *The Screening of Australia, Vol. 1: Anatomy of an Industry*, Sydney: Currency Press.
Dermody, Susan and Elizabeth Jacka (1988), *The Screening of Australia, Vol. 2: Anatomy of a National Cinema*, Sydney: Currency Press.
Desser, David (2000), 'The Kung Fu Craze: Hong Kong Cinema's First American Reception', in Poshek Fu and David Desser (eds), *The Cinema of Hong Kong: History, Arts, Identity*, Cambridge: Cambridge University Press, pp. 19–43.
Desser, David (2006), 'Diaspora and National Identity: Exporting "China" Through the Hong Kong Cinema', in Elizabeth Ezra and Terry Rowden (eds), *Transnational Cinema: The Film Reader*, London: Routledge, pp. 143–55.
'Disney Gesture to Red Cross' (1952), *Film Weekly*, 29 May, 1.
Dolgopolov, Greg (2021), 'New Australian Crime Drama', in Kelly McWilliam and Mark David Ryan (eds), *Australian Genre Film*, New York and London: Routledge, pp. 74–89.
Drewe, Robert (1969), '"Ned" in Disorder as Marianne Lies Ill' (1969), *Age (Melbourne)*, 10 July, 1.
'Drifting Avenger' (1968), *UniJapan Film Quarterly*, 11: 4, 24.
DuBose, Martha (1971a), 'Nightmare Visit to the Dark Side of Human Behaviour', *Sydney Morning Herald*, 11 October, 7.
DuBose, Martha (1971b), 'A Visual Odyssey', *Sydney Morning Herald*, 20 December, 7.
Duguid, Mark (2012), 'The Dark Side of Ealing', *Sight and Sound*, 22: 11, November, 54–61.
Eells, George (1984), *Robert Mitchum*, New York and Toronto: Franklin Watts.
Eisenberg, Daniel (2011), 'The Camera in the Iron Helmet: *Ned Kelly* (Gregor Jordan, 2003)', *Senses of Cinema*, 58, March, http://www.sensesofcinema.com/2011/key-moments-in-australian-cinema-issue-70-march-2014/the-camera-in-the-iron-helmet-ned-kelly-gregor-jordan-2003/
Ellis, John (1975), 'Made in Ealing', *Screen*, 16: 1, Spring, 78–127.
Erickson, Todd (1996), 'Kill Me Again: Movement Becomes Genre', in Alain Silver and James Ursini (eds), *Film Noir Reader*, New York: Limelight, pp. 307–29.
Farber, Manny and Patricia Patterson (2009), 'Nicolas Roeg', in Robert Polito (ed.), *Farber on Film: The Complete Film Writings of Manny Farber*, New York: Library of America, pp. 731–8.
'February Start on *Kangaroo Kid*' (1950), *Adelaide Mail*, 14 January, 5.
Fenton, Andrew (2009), 'A Big Awakening', *Daily Telegraph (Sydney)*, 27 June, 5.
'1500 See Filming at Frankston' (1960), *Age (Melbourne)*, 2 March, 3.
'Film Reviews' (1946), *Australian Women's Weekly*, 5 October, 36.
'Film Seen as Bad Publicity for Australia' (1952), *West Australian*, 21 June, 5.
'Film Star Had Looked Us Up' (1950), *Sydney Morning Herald*, 25 November, 4.
'Filming on an Island' (1968), *Bulletin*, 90: 4601, 11 May, 57–8.
'First *Kangaroo* Scenes Filmed in Sydney' (1950), *Advertiser (Adelaide)*, 12 November, 3.
'First S.A. Color Drama will Help Red Cross' (1952), *Advertiser (Adelaide)*, 4 June, 8–9.
'First Scenes Shot for *Kangaroo*' (1950), *Advertiser (Adelaide)*, 22 December, 3.
Fitzpatrick, John (1983), 'Fred Zinnemann (1907)', in Jean-Pierre Coursodon and Pierre Sauvage (eds), *American Directors, Vol. II*, New York: McGraw-Hill, pp. 378–86.
'5000 Watch Filming in City Streets' (1959), *Age (Melbourne)*, 23 February, 3.
Fore, Steve (1994), 'Golden Harvest Films and the Hong Kong Industry in the Realm of Globalization', *Velvet Light Trap*, 34, Fall, 40–58.

Forsyth, Malcolm (1974), '$450,000 Budget for Aussie Film', *Daily Telegraph (Sydney)*, 19 September, n.p.
'Four Aussie Films Release in Sydney' (1970), *Film Weekly*, 19 March, 1.
Frizell, Helen (1959), 'Mr. Mitchum is Full of Surprises', *Australian Women's Weekly*, 14 October, 5.
Frizell, Helen (1968a), '*Blazing Continent* is Real Hot Stuff', *Sydney Morning Herald*, 16 September, 6.
Frizell, Helen (1968b), 'Beaten to the Draw', *Sydney Morning Herald*, 21 June, 6.
Frizell, Helen (1969), 'Almost as Game as Ned Kelly', *Sydney Morning Herald*, 10 July, 6.
Fu, Poshek (2000), 'Going Global: A Cultural History of the Shaw Brothers Studio, 1960–1970', in Law Kar (ed.), *Hong Kong Cinema Retrospective: Border Crossings in Hong Kong Cinema*, Hong Kong: The 24th Hong Kong International Film Festival, pp. 43–51.
'Gala Atmosphere for *Kangaroo* Preview' (1952), *Age (Melbourne)*, 5 June, 2.
Gaunson, Stephen (2010), '"International Outlaws": Tony Richardson, Mick Jagger and Ned Kelly', *Studies in Australasian Cinema*, 4: 3, 255–65.
Gaunson, Stephen (2013), *The Ned Kelly Films: A Cultural History of Kelly History*, Bristol: Intellect.
Gibson, Mark (2014), 'Tchk, Tchk, Tchk: *Skippy the Bush Kangaroo* and the Question of Australian Seriousness', *Continuum*, 28: 5, 574–82.
Goldsmith, Ben (2010), 'Outward-looking Australian Cinema', *Studies in Australasian Cinema*, 4: 3, 199–214.
Goldsmith, Ben, Susan Ward and Tom O'Regan (2010), *Local Hollywood: Global Film Production and the Gold Coast*, St Lucia: University of Queensland Press.
'Governor at *On the Beach* Premiere Last Night' (1959), *Age (Melbourne)*, 18 December, 10.
Gow, Gordon (1972), 'Identity: An Interview with Nicolas Roeg', *Films and Filming*, 18: 4, 208, January, 18–24.
Grace, Helen (2001), 'The Persistence of Culture: Recovering *On the Beach*', *Continuum*, 15: 3, 289–301.
'Graham Compares *Bible* with *On the Beach*' (1959), *Sydney Morning Herald*, 2 March, 9.
Grant, Bruce (1952), 'Kangaroo Tripe', *Meanjin*, 11: 4, 411–13.
Griffen-Foley, J. (1950a), 'From Pins to Elephants', *Film Monthly*, November, 18–19.
Griffen-Foley, J. (1950b), 'Trouble-shooter in a Headache Job', *Film Weekly*, 26 October, 3.
Guinness, Daphne (1968), 'A Crowd Scene that Wasn't in the Script', *Bulletin*, 90: 4602, 18 May, 9–10.
Haigh, Gideon (2007), 'Shute the Messenger', *Monthly*, June, https://www.themonthly.com.au/issue/2007/june/1268876839/gideon-haigh/shute-messenger#mtr
Hall, Sandra (1971), 'Sinister Banality', *Bulletin*, 16 October, 39.
Hanson, Gillian (1971), '*Outback*', *Monthly Film Bulletin*, 38: 445, December, 244.
Harper, Sue and Vincent Porter (2003), *British Cinema of the 1950s: The Decline of Deference*, Oxford: Oxford University Press.
Harris, Mark (2008), *Scenes from a Revolution: The Birth of the New Hollywood*, Edinburgh: Canongate.
Harris, Max (1960), 'Prophet of Doom', *Nation*, 2 January, 8–10.
Harris, Mike (1975), 'Fast, Funny – and Shallow', *Australian*, 13 September, n.p.
Hartley, Mark (1996), 'Man of Action: Part One – The 70s', *Screenprint*, 3, November, 10–11.

Held, Leonard (1986), 'Myth and Archetypes in Nicolas Roeg's *Walkabout*', *Post Script*, 5: 3, Spring–Summer, 21–46.
'Herald TV Guide' (1977), *Sydney Morning Herald*, 2 October, 73.
Higham, Charles (1969), 'Painter's Eye on *Age of Consent*', *Sydney Morning Herald*, 28 July, 8.
Holmes, Cecil (1954), 'The Film in Australia', *Meanjin*, 13: 2, 189–98.
Hoorn, Jeanette (2005), 'Comedy and Eros: Powell's Australian Films *They're a Weird Mob* and *Age of Consent*', *Screen*, 46: 1, Spring, 73–84.
Horton, Robert (1997), 'Day of the Craftsman: Fred Zinnemann', *Film Comment*, 33: 5, September, 60–7.
Hoskin, Dave (2009), 'Aggressive Hospitality: *Wake in Fright*', *Metro*, 162, 152–4.
Houston, Penelope (1959–60), '*On the Beach*', *Sight and Sound*, 29: 1, Winter, 37–8.
Houston, Penelope (1960–1), '*The Sundowners*', *Sight and Sound*, 30: 1, Winter, 36–7.
Hunt, Leon (2002), 'One-Armed and Extremely Dangerous: Wang Yu's Mutilated Masters', in Xavier Mendik (ed.), *Shocking Cinema of the Seventies*, Hereford: Noir Publishing, pp. 91–105.
Hunt, Leon (2011), 'Dragons Forever: Chinese Martial Arts Stars', in Song Hwee Lim and Julian Ward (eds), *The Chinese Cinema Book*, London: BFI and Palgrave Macmillan, pp. 141–9.
'I'm a Lux Girl' (1951), *Australian Women's Weekly*, 12 December, 26.
Irving, Freda (1959), 'The Day Ava Walked the Planks', *Australian Women's Weekly*, 25 February, 4–5.
'Jagger's Girlfriend Still Unconscious' (1969), *Papua New Guinea Post-Courier*, 11 July, 7.
'Jagger's Locks Gone' (1969), *Canberra Times*, 12 July, 3.
'Jagger's Role in Film Confirmed' (1969), *Canberra Times*, 6 June, 6.
'Jap Western Dead on Schedule' (1968), *Sydney Morning Herald*, 26 May, 45.
'Japan Rolling Oater on Aussie Location' (1968), *Variety*, 1 May, 30.
'Japanese Oater Ready to Roll on NSW Locations' (1968), *Film Weekly*, 2 May, 3.
Jennings, Karen (2009), 'Home Truths: Revisiting *Wake in Fright*', *Monthly*, July, 36–49.
Jones, Ian (1968), 'A New View of Ned Kelly', in Colin F. Cave (ed.), *Ned Kelly: Man and Myth*, Melbourne: Cassell, pp. 154–89.
Jones, Ian (1969), 'Impressions of "Ned Kelly"', *Script, Screen & Art*, October–November, 11–13.
Jones, Kent (2009), 'Audio-commentary', *The Films of Michael Powell*, DVD, Sony Pictures.
Jones, Lon (1950a), '*Kangaroo* Story Again Changed', *Advertiser (Adelaide)*, 21 October, 7.
Jones, Lon (1950b), 'Hollywood Insists on Kangaroos', *Advertiser (Adelaide)*, 28 November, 7.
Kael, Pauline (1972), 'Literary Echoes – Muffled', *New Yorker*, March 4, 88–93.
Kael, Pauline (1987), *Kiss Kiss Bang Bang*, London: Arena.
'*Kangaroo*' (1952a), *Newsweek*, 2 June, 87.
'*Kangaroo*' (1952b), *Sunday Herald (Sydney)*, 22 June, 10.
'*Kangaroo*: An Intriguing Australian Sagebrusher' (1952), *Hollywood Reporter*, 19 May, 3.
'*Kangaroo* Big Boost for Australia – SA Premier' (1950), *Film Weekly*, 14 December, 12.
'*Kangaroo* Film, N. York Premiere' (1952), *Central Queensland Herald*, 15 May, 21.
'*Kangaroo* Going Well – Producer' (1951), *Film Weekly*, 11 January, 1.
'*Kangaroo* May Aid Film-making Here' (1950), *Argus (Melbourne)*, 23 August, 5.

'*Kangaroo* Plans Altered; Accommodation Trouble' (1950), *Film Weekly*, 19 October, n.p.
Kangaroo Print Advertisement (1952), *Mercury (Hobart)*, 24 June, 12.
'*Kangaroo* Release Set on Giant Scale' (1952), *Film Weekly*, 5 June, 1.
'*Kangaroo* Shooting Ending; Unit Leaving' (1951), *Film Weekly*, 22 February, 1.
Kangaroo Special Report (1952a), *Film Weekly*, 12 June, 17–42.
Kangaroo Special Report (1952b), *Film Weekly*, 26 June, 15–32.
'*Kangaroo* Stars Arrive' (1950), *Advertiser (Adelaide)*, 1 December, 3.
'*Kangaroo* Stars to Have Short Stay Here' (1950), *Advertiser (Adelaide)*, 27 November, 3.
Kaufman, Tina (2010), *Wake in Fright*, Sydney: Currency Press.
Kavanagh, Brian (1971), '*Walkabout*', *Lumiere*, 12, November–December, 10.
Keavney, Kay (1968), 'The Film Could be a Winner', *Australian Women's Weekly*, 17 April, 8–9.
Kehr, Dave (2009), 'New DVDs: Michael Powell', *New York Times*, 5 January, https://www.nytimes.com/2009/01/06/movies/homevideo/06dvds.html
Kelly, Frances (1969), 'The Kelly Country War', *Canberra Times*, 23 August, 1.
'Kelly Roles' (1969), *Canberra Times*, 21 May, 3.
Kemp, Philip (1999), 'On the Slide: Harry Watt and Ealing's Australian Venture', in Raffaele Caputo and Geoff Burton (eds), *Second Take: Australian Film-makers Talk*, Sydney: Allen & Unwin, pp. 145–64.
Khoo, Olivia (2010), 'Tokyo Drifting: Toei Corporation's *The Drifting Avenger* and the Internationalization of the Australian Western', *Studies in Australasian Cinema*, 4: 3, 231–41.
Khoo, Olivia, Belinda Smaill and Audrey Yue (2013), *Transnational Australian Cinema: Ethics in the Asian Diasporas*, Lanham, MD: Lexington Books.
King, Noel, Constantine Verevis and Deane Williams (2014), *Australian Film Theory and Criticism, Vol. 1: Critical Positions*, Bristol: Intellect.
Kitamura, Hiroshi (2020), 'Frontiers of Nostalgia: The Japanese Western in the Postwar Era', in Hideaki Fujiki and Alastair Phillips (eds), *The Japanese Cinema Book*, London and New York: BFI and Bloomsbury, pp. 518–29.
Kornits, Dov (1998), 'A Roeg's Tale', *Filmink*, 2: 7, April, 12–14.
Kramer, Stanley (1999), 'Directing Doomsday', *Herald Sun (Melbourne)*, 30 May, 14.
'Kung-fu King to Make Aust Film' (1974), *Sydney Morning Herald*, 20 September, 10.
Lacourbe, Roland and Danièle Grivel (2003), 'Rediscovering Michael Powell', in David Lazar (ed.), *Michael Powell: Interviews*, Jackson: University Press of Mississippi, pp. 44–66.
'Lady Norrie Given Toy Kangaroo at Red Cross Film' (1952), *Advertiser (Adelaide)*, 5 June, 10.
Larkin, Ryan (2014), 'Exploring Archetypal Images in Roeg's *Walkabout*', *Film Matters*, Spring, 27–32.
Lawson, Sylvia (1961), 'The Sight of Green Galahs', *Nation*, 84, 16 December, 22.
Lawson, Sylvia (1965), 'Not for the Likes of Us', *Quadrant*, May–June, 27–31.
Lawson, Sylvia (1966), 'They're a Dull Mob', *Nation*, 203, 17 September, 17–18.
Lawson, Sylvia (1968), 'Co-productions', *Nation*, 236, 3 February, 18.
Lawson, Sylvia (1969), 'Australian Film', *Quadrant*, November–December, 20–4.
Lawson, Sylvia (1970), 'Kelly Kelly, Bang Bang', *Nation*, 19 September, 19.
Lawson, Sylvia (1982), 'Towards Decolonisation: Film History in Australia', in Susan Dermody, John Docker and Drusilla Modjeska (eds), *Nellie Melba, Ginger Meggs and Friends*, Malmsbury: Kibble, pp. 19–32.
Lawson, Sylvia (1985), 'Australian Film, 1969', in Albert Moran and Tom O'Regan (eds), *An Australian Film Reader*, Sydney: Currency Press, pp. 175–83.

L. B. (1959), 'Premiere of Film Version of Shute's *On the Beach*', *Sydney Morning Herald*, 18 December, 7.
Leitch, Thomas (2002), *Crime Films*, Cambridge: Cambridge University Press.
Lev, Peter (2003), *Transforming the Screen: 1950–1959*, Berkeley: University of California Press.
Limbrick, Peter (2007), 'The Australian Western, or a Settler Colonial Cinema *par excellence*', *Cinema Journal*, 46: 4, 68–95.
Limbrick, Peter (2010), *Making Settler Cinemas: Film and Colonial Encounters in the United States, Australia and New Zealand*, New York: Palgrave Macmillan.
Lindsay, Norman (1962 [1938]), *Age of Consent*, Sydney: Ure Smith.
'London Views *The Overlanders* as Truly Epic Film' (1946), *Advertiser* (Adelaide), 19 September, 8.
Lowe, Barry (1974), 'Australian Film Esthetics', *Lumiere*, March, 4–7.
Lynravn, Joan (1969), 'The Weather was the Only "Robber"', *Canberra Times*, 25 August, 3.
Lyons, Mollie (1971), 'Premiere of New Film', *Australian Women's Weekly*, 27 October, 1, 3.
MacDonald, Dougal (1970), 'A Weedy Ned Kelly', *Canberra Times*, 22 August, 16.
MacDonald, Dougal (1971), 'Australian Ethos Captured', *Canberra Times*, 5 November, 11.
McDonald, Neil (2010), 'Inside *Wake in Fright*', *Quadrant*, January–February, 110–12.
McFarlane, Brian (2005), 'Ned Kelly Rides Again ... and Again and Again', *Screen Education*, 41, 24–32.
McIntyre, Angus (1982), 'Ned Kelly, a Folk Hero', in John Carroll (ed.), *Intruders in the Bush: The Australian Quest for Identity*, Melbourne: Oxford University Press, pp. 38–53.
McLachlan, Noel (1968), 'What's on at the Flicks? Past and Present Attractions', *Meanjin*, 25: 4, 505–9.
McWilliam, Kelly and Mark David Ryan (eds) (2021), *Australian Genre Film*, New York and London: Routledge.
Madden, E. S. (1959), 'The Australian Film Industry', *Twentieth Century*, 13, Winter, 317–27.
Maddox, Garry (2009), 'Dream Run Awaits *Wake in Fright*', *Sydney Morning Herald*, 11 June, 3.
'*Man from Hong Kong* Ding Dong in Karachi' (1976), *Variety*, 12 May, 33.
Mangan, Michael (1998), *Edward Bond*, Plymouth: Northcote House.
Manzie, Keith (1952), 'Melbourne – No Effort Spared; "Great Interest" in Best-yet Australian Film', *Film Weekly*, 12 June, 38.
Marshall, James Vance (1971), *Walkabout*, rev. edn, New York: Belmont Books.
'Maureen O'Hara's Big Sydney Welcome' (1950), *Film Weekly*, November 30, 5.
'Maureen O'Hara to Star in Australian Film' (1950), *Mercury (Hobart)*, August 31, 2.
Meares, Norman (1950a), 'Film Stars Welcomed in North', *Advertiser (Adelaide)*, 8 December, 3.
Meares, Norman (1950b), 'Film Work Delayed on *Kangaroo*', *Advertiser (Adelaide)*, 11 December, 3.
Meares, Norman (1950c), '*Kangaroo* Shooting Postponed', *Advertiser (Adelaide)*, 20 December, 4.
Melbourne Film Society Bulletin (1975), 30 November, 2.
Melton, Robert (1970), '*Ned Kelly*: A Near Miss at the Iron Outlaw', *Tribune* (Sydney), 25 November, 7.
'Mick Jagger "Ned Kelly"' (1969), *Canberra Times*, 20 May, 3.
Millar, Gavin (1971–2), '*Walkabout*', *Sight and Sound*, 41: 1, Winter, 48.

Millard, Kathryn (2019), 'Indigenous Colour: The Quest to Make Australia's First Natural Colour Feature Film', *Screening the Past*, 44 (April), http://www.screeningthepast.com/issue-44-first-release/indigenous-colour-the-quest-to-make-australias-first-natural-colour-feature-film/
Mills, Jane (2014), 'Sojourner Cinema: Seeking and Researching a New Cinematic Category', *Framework: The Journal of Cinema and Media*, 55: 1, Spring, 140–64.
'Miss Kangaroo Here with Pal Joey' (1952), *Pittsburg Press*, 25 January, 2.
'"Miss Kangaroo" Visits Washington' (1952), *Daily Advertiser*, 10 January, 1.
Molitorisz, Sacha (2009), 'Keeping it Reel', *Sun-Herald (Sydney)*, 21 June, 5.
Molloy, Bruce (1990), *Before the Interval: Australian Mythology and Feature Films, 1930–1960*, Brisbane: University of Queensland Press.
Moran, Albert and Tom O'Regan (eds) (1985), *An Australian Film Reader*, Sydney: Currency Press.
Moran, Albert and Tom O'Regan (eds) (1989), *The Australian Screen*, Melbourne: Penguin.
Morgan, Stephen (2012), 'Ealing's Australian Adventure', in Mark Duguid, Lee Freeman, Keith M. Johnson and Melanie Williams (eds), *Ealing Revisited*, London: BFI, pp. 165–74.
Morris, Meaghan (2004), '*The Man from Hong Kong* in Sydney, 1975', in Judith Ryan and Chris Wallace-Crabbe (eds), *Imagining Australia: Literature and Culture in the New New World*, Cambridge, MA and London: Harvard University Press, pp. 235–66.
Morrison, Peter (1952), 'Sydney – Dignity, Splendor; The Film a Solid, Stock-type Box Office Proposition', *Film Weekly*, 12 June, 37, 40.
Mosby, Aline (1952), 'Kangaroo Makes Monkey of his Glamour-girl Chaperone', *Brooklyn Daily Eagle*, 16 May, 9.
'MP Acts to Keep Jagger Out' (1969), *Canberra Times*, 25 June, 3.
Munson, Christobel (1969), 'No Lush Life at the Flat', *Canberra Times*, 8 September, 12.
Murphy, Jim (1975), '*The Man from Hong Kong*', *Cinema Papers*, 7, November–December, 261–2.
Murray, Scott (ed.) (1980), *The New Australian Cinema*, Melbourne: Nelson/Cinema Papers.
Murray, Scott (2009), 'The Federal Government and Unions Became the Arbitrators of What Constituted Australian-ness on Screen', *Age (Melbourne)*, 18 June, A23.
Musgrove, Nan (1968), 'Dodge City, Goonoo Goonoo-Style', *Australian Women's Weekly*, 15 May, 4.
Musgrove, Nan (1969), '*Color Me Dead*: The Film that Proves Australian Knowhow', *Australian Women's Weekly*, 22 January, 8–10.
Myro (1971), '*Outback*', *Variety*, 21 May, 3.
Naremore, James (1998), *More Than Night: Film Noir in its Contexts*, Berkeley: University of California Press.
'Ned Kelly was a Gentleman' (1969), *Tribune* (Sydney), 9 July, 6–7.
'New Films Reviewed' (1946), *Sydney Morning Herald*, 30 September, 10.
Newton, Gloria (1969), 'Three Old Towns are Livening up', *Australian Women's Weekly*, 6 August, 2.
Nolletti, Jr, Arthur (1994), 'Conversation with Fred Zinnemann', *Film Criticism*, 18: 3/19: 1, Spring–Fall, 7–29.
Nowra, Louis (2003), *Walkabout*, Sydney: Currency Press.
O'Brien, Denis (1968), 'Communicating', *Bulletin*, 1 June, 56.
O'Brien, Denis (1970a), 'Back to Work, Thirstily, on the Film Set', *Bulletin*, January 24, 23–4.

O'Brien, Denis (1970b), 'Suddenly... An Australian Film Industry?', *Bulletin*, August 1, 35–8.
O'Brien, Gabrielle (2017), 'Dreaming of the Devil: Revisiting Ted Kotcheff's *Wake in Fright*', *Metro*, 193, 93–7.
'Officials Fear Film on Australia Misleading' (1952), *Sydney Morning Herald*, 27 May, 3.
'*On the Beach* Premiere in Melbourne' (1959), *Age (Melbourne)*, 18 December, 1.
'*On the Beach* Spurs May 15 Peace Rally' (1960), *Tribune*, 4 May, 2.
O'Regan, Tom (1983), 'Australian Film Making: Its Public Circulation', *Framework*, 22–3, Autumn, 31–6.
O'Regan, Tom (1987), 'Australian Film in the 1950s', *Continuum*, 1: 1, 1–25.
O'Regan, Tom (1996), *Australian National Cinema*, London and New York: Routledge.
O'Regan, Tom, Ben Goldsmith and Susan Ward (2010), *Local Hollywood: Global Film Production and the Gold Coast*, Brisbane: University of Queensland Press.
'Outdoor Shooting for *Kangaroo* Begins' (1950), *Adelaide Mail*, 30 December, 3.
Palathingal, George (2008), 'The Wizards of Ozploitation', *Sydney Morning Herald*, 29 August, 7.
Palmer, R. Barton (1994), *Hollywood's Dark Cinema: The American Film Noir*, New York: Twayne.
Passi, Federico (2017), *The City Unseen: Iconography, Specificity and Mise-en-scène in the Cinematic Representation of Melbourne's Urban Space, 1896–1966*, unpublished PhD thesis, Melbourne: RMIT University.
Perkin, Graham (1959), '*On the Beach* Winds Up: The End of the World is an Anti-Climax', *Age (Melbourne)*, 31 March, 2.
Perry, George (1981), *Forever Ealing: A Celebration of the Great British Film Studio*, London: Pavilion.
Petty, Homer B. (2016), 'Introduction: The Noir Impulse', in Homer B. Petty and R. Barton Palmer (eds), *International Noir*, Edinburgh: Edinburgh University Press, pp. 1–13.
Pierce, Peter (1999), *The Country of Lost Children: An Australian Anxiety*, Cambridge: Cambridge University Press.
Pike, Andrew (1969), 'Diary of Sex', *Canberra Times*, 7 October, 13.
Pike, Andrew (1971), 'Japanese "Westerns" and More', *Hemisphere*, 15: 8, August, 10–15.
Pike, Andrew (1980), 'The Past: Boom and Bust', in Scott Murray (ed.), *The New Australian Cinema*, Melbourne: Nelson/Cinema Papers, pp. 11–25.
Pike, Andrew and Ross Cooper (1998), *Australian Film, 1900–1977: A Guide to Feature Film Production*, rev. edn, Melbourne: Oxford University Press.
P. J. D. (1961), '*The Sundowners*', *Monthly Film Bulletin*, 28: 325, February, 21.
'Plans for Film Here' (1950), *Sunday Herald (Sydney)*, 30 July, 4.
'Plans Set for *Kangaroo* Charity Shows' (1952), *Film Weekly*, 29 May, 1.
'Playford Wins in Film Race' (1950), *Argus (Melbourne)*, 11 September, 6.
Poe, G. Tom (2001), 'Historical Spectatorship on and Around Stanley Kramer's *On the Beach*', in Melvyn Stokes and Richard Maltby (eds), *Hollywood Spectatorship: Changing Perceptions of Cinema Audiences*, London: BFI, pp. 91–102.
Pomerance, Murray (2008), *The Horse Who Drank the Sky: Film Experience Beyond Narrative and Theory*, New Brunswick, NJ: Rutgers University Press.
'Port Augusta Plans to Help in *Kangaroo*' (1950), *Advertiser (Adelaide)*, 25 August, 3.
Powe (1959), '*On the Beach*', *Variety*, 27, 2 December, 6.
Powell, Michael (1992), *Million-Dollar Movie*, London: Mandarin.
'Praise for *Kangaroo*' (1951), *Brisbane Worker*, 2 July, 8.

'Preparing for Ned's End' (1969), *Canberra Times*, 8 July, 3.
'Rain-making Ritual Shown in *Kangaroo*' (1951), *Australian Women's Weekly*, 24 March, 61.
Raine, Michael (2019), 'The Cold War as Media Environment in 1960s Japanese Cinema', in Poshek Fu and Man-Fung Yip (eds), *The Cold War and Asian Cinemas*, New York: Routledge, pp. 120–38.
Rattigan, Neil (1991), *Images of Australia: 100 Films of the New Australian Cinema*, Dallas: Southern Methodist University Press.
Rawlins, Adrian (1969), 'Ned Kelly in Two Dimensions', *Go-Set*, 4: 31, 2 August, 9.
Rayner, Jonathan (2021), 'Sun-Lit Noir: Australian Thrillers', in Kelly McWilliam and Mark David Ryan (eds), *Australian Genre Film*, New York and London: Routledge, pp. 186–201.
Rayns, Tony (1975), '*The Man from Hong Kong*', *Monthly Film Bulletin*, 42: 500, September, 201.
Rayns, Tony (1984), 'Bruce Lee and Other Stories', in Li Cheuk-to (ed.), *A Study of Hong Kong Cinema in the Seventies*, Hong Kong: The 8th Hong Kong International Film Festival and Hong Kong Urban Council, pp. 26–9.
Richardson, Tony (1993), *Long Distance Runner: A Memoir*, London: Faber and Faber.
Rooney, Monique (2011), '"A Heart that Could be Strong and True": Kenneth Cook's *Wake in Fright* as Queer Interior', *JASAL: Journal of the Association for the Study of Australian Literature*, 11: 1, 1–15.
Routt, William D. (2001), 'More Australian than Aristotelian: The Australian Bushranger Film, 1904–1914', *Senses of Cinema*, 18, http://www.sensesofcinema.com/2001/feature-articles/oz_western/
Routt, William D. (2003), 'Red Ned', *Metro*, 136, 10–16.
Ryan, Mark David (2010), 'Towards an Understanding of Australian Genre Cinema and Entertainment: Beyond the Limits of "Ozploitation" Discourse', *Continuum*, 24: 6, 843–54.
Ryan, Mark David and Ben Goldsmith (eds) (2017), *Australian Screen in the 2000s*, Cham: Palgrave Macmillan.
Salwolke, Scott (1997), *The Films of Michael Powell and the Archers*, Lanham, MD: Scarecrow Press.
Sandars, Steven M. (2008), 'An Introduction to the Philosophy of TV Noir', in Steven M. Sandars and Aeon J. Skoble (eds), *The Philosophy of TV Noir*, Lexington: University Press of Kentucky, pp. 1–31.
Sarris, Andrew (1996), *The American Cinema: Directors and Directions, 1929–1968*, rev. edn, New York: Da Capo Press.
Schilling, Mark (2007), *No Borders No Limits: Nikkatsu Action Cinema*, Godalming: FAB Press.
Scorsese, Martin (1994), 'Foreword', in Ian Christie, *Arrows of Desire: The Films of Michael Powell and Emeric Pressburger*, London and Boston, MA: Faber and Faber, pp. xv–xx.
Server, Lee (2001), *Robert Mitchum: 'Baby, I Don't Care'*, London: Faber and Faber.
Shail, Robert (2012), *Tony Richardson*, Manchester: Manchester University Press.
'She's Still Ned's Sister' (1969), *Age (Melbourne)*, 11 July, 2.
Sherington, Geoffrey (1980), *Australia's Immigrants, 1788–1978*, Sydney: Allen & Unwin.
Shirley, Graham and Brian Adams (1989), *Australian Cinema: The First Eighty Years*, rev. edn, Sydney: Currency Press.
Shute, Nevil (1957), *On the Beach*, Melbourne: Heinemann.

Silke, James R. (2005), 'Zinnemann Talks Back', in Gabriel Miller (ed.), *Fred Zinnemann: Interviews*, Jackson: University Press of Mississippi, pp. 9–26.
'Site for Film Homestead "Pin-pointed"' (1950), *Advertiser (Adelaide)*, 30 August, 3.
'Six Shearers Get Film Trip to U. K.' (1960), *Australian Women's Weekly*, 13 January, 7.
'$65,000 for *Kangaroo*' (1952), *Motion Picture Herald*, 20 May, 3.
'*Smiley*' (1956), *Monthly Film Bulletin*, 23: 264, 100.
Smyth, J. E. (2014), *Fred Zinnemann and the Cinema of Resistance*, Jackson: University Press of Mississippi.
Solomon, Eric (1952), 'Canberra Premiere – Brilliant Spectacle; Entire Series as a Magnificent P. R. Gesture', *Film Weekly*, 12 June, 36.
Spicer, Andrew (ed.) (2007), *European Film Noir*, Manchester: Manchester University Press.
Spil (1970), '*Color Me Dead*', *Variety*, 14 January, 38.
S. S. (1950), 'Hollywood Man to Direct Here', *Argus (Melbourne)*, 26 July, 5.
Stanley, Raymond (1969), '*Age of Consent*': *Variety*, 14 May, 32.
Stanton, Geoff (2019), 'Like A Rolling Stone: The Making of 1970's *Ned Kelly*', *Filmink*, 24 July, https://www.filmink.com.au/like-rolling-stone-making-1970s-ned-kelly/
Stewart, Clare (2014), 'Intruder in the Dust', *Sight and Sound*, 24: 3, March, 36–8.
Strange, Dorothy (1971), '*Walkabout* ... A 16-Week Safari Through the Modern Dreamtime', *Walkabout*, 37: 8, August, 8–15.
Stratton, David (1972), '*Outback*', *International Film Guide*, 9, 53.
Stratton, David (1980), *The Last New Wave: The Australian Film Revival*, Sydney: Angus and Robertson.
'Studio for Indoor Filming of *Kangaroo*' (1950), *Barrier Miner*, 11 September, 4.
'Sydney Sees How Hollywood Makes a Movie – First Hand' (1950), *Film Weekly*, 16 November, 5.
Tarratt, Margaret (1970), '*Ned Kelly*', *Films and Filming*, August, 41–2.
Tennant, Kylie (1962), 'Fiction Chronicle', *Meanjin*, 21: 3, September, 377–80.
Teo, Stephen (2005), '*Wuxia* Redux: *Crouching Tiger, Hidden Dragon* as a Model of Late Transnational Production', in Meaghan Morris, Siu Leung Li and Stephen Chan Ching-kiu (eds), *Hong Kong Connections: Transnational Imagination in Action Cinema*, Durham, NC: Duke University Press, pp. 191–204.
Teo, Stephen (2006), '*The Man from Hong Kong*', *Metro*, 149, 188–90.
Teo, Stephen (2017), *Eastern Westerns: Film and Genre Outside and Inside Hollywood*, London and New York: Routledge.
Te Pana (1946), '*The Overlanders* is Our Best Yet', *Courier–Mail (Brisbane)*, 21 October, 1.
'The Flickering Flame' (1969), *Bulletin*, 91: 4649, 19 April, 42.
'The Hollywood Touch is Here: Glamour on The Rocks' (1950), *Sunday Herald (Sydney)*, 12 November, 6.
'*The Kangaroo Kid*' (1952), *Monthly Film Bulletin*, 19: 216, 21.
'The "Kellys" at the Flat' (1969), *Canberra Times*, 11 June, 1.
'*The Man from Hong Kong*' (1975), *Hollywood Reporter*, 237: 18, 21 July, 3.
'*The Man from Hong Kong*' (1996), *Cinema Papers*, 111, August, 25.
'*The Man from Hong Kong* Away to Sky-high Start in Glamour Premieres' (1975), *Australasian Cinema*, 3: 18, 11 September, 1, 4–5.
'*The Man from Hong Kong* Export Quality' (1975), *Australasian Cinema*, 3: 18, 11 September, 3.
Thompson, Hunter S. (2005 [1971]), *Fear and Loathing in Las Vegas*, London: Harper Perennial.

Thoms, Albie (1978), *Polemics for a New Cinema*, Sydney: Wild and Woolley.
Thomson, David (2002), *The New Biographical Dictionary of Film*, 4th edn, London: Little, Brown.
Thornhill, Michael (1985), 'Strategies for an Industry – Government Intervention', in Albert Moran and Tom O'Regan (eds), *An Australian Film Reader*, Sydney: Currency Press, pp. 166–70.
Thurston, John (1969), '*Ned Kelly*', *Cinema Papers*, 1: 2, December, 7.
Timms, Peter (1971), '*Wake in Fright* & *Walkabout*', *Lumiere*, 12, November–December, 10–11.
Tivey, Bev (1969), 'But for the Acting . . .', *Bulletin*, 91: 4664, 2 August, 44–5.
Tobias, Mel (1975), '*The Man from Hong Kong*', *Variety*, 11 June, 19.
'Trouble in Kelly Country' (1969), *Canberra Times*, 20 June, 10.
Tube (1960), '*The Sundowners*', *Variety*, 2 November, 6.
Turnour, Quentin (1998), 'Lost in Space', *Metro/CTEQ Annotations on Film*, 117, 68.
'20th-Fox Team Stirs Adelaide' (1950), *Film Weekly*, 7 December, 5.
'US Films May Be Made Here' (1950), *Sunday Herald (Sydney)*, 26 November, 7.
Verevis, Constantine (2004), 'Through the Past Darkly: Noir Remakes of the 1980s', in Alain Silver and James Ursini (eds), *Film Noir Reader 4: The Crucial Films and Themes*, New York: Limelight, pp. 307–22.
Verhoeven, Deb (2006), *Sheep and the Australian Cinema*. Melbourne: Melbourne University Press.
'Vice-Regal Guests at Film Premiere' (1952), *Age (Melbourne)*, 5 June, 5.
Wake in Fright (1971), United Artists Press Sheet, AFI Research Collection at RMIT University.
Watt, Harry (1949), 'You Start from Scratch in Australia', in Roger Manvell (ed.), *The Penguin Film Review 9*, London: Penguin Books, pp. 10–16.
Watt, Harry (1958), 'Films in Australia', in William Whitebait (ed.), *International Film Annual No. 2*, London: John Calder, pp. 105–8, 113.
Watt, Harry (1974), *Don't Look at the Camera*, London: Elek.
Webby, Elizabeth (2004), 'Ealing Studios' Australian Adventure', *Arts: The Journal of the Sydney University Arts Association*, 26, 51–67.
Weir, Tom (1958), 'No Daydreams of Our Own', *Nation*, November 22, 14–16.
White, David (1984), *Australian Movies to the World: The International Success of Australian Films Since 1970*, Sydney and Melbourne: Fontana Australia and Cinema Papers.
White, Matt (1975), 'Aussie Kung Fu Rates a New Look', *Daily Mirror*, 4 November, n.p.
'Wild West – By Japanese' (1968), *Sydney Morning Herald*, 21 April, 3.
Williams, Deane (2007), '*The Overlanders*: Between Nations', *Studies in Australasian Cinema*, 1: 1, 79–89.
Wilson, Jake (2019), 'Borrowed Time', *Age (Melbourne)*, 19 January, Spectrum, 6–7.
'Worth Reporting' (1945), *Australian Women's Weekly*, 30 June, 15.
Yomota, Inuhiko (2019), *What is Japanese Cinema? A History*, trans. Phil Kaffen, New York: Columbia University Press.
Zinnemann, Fred (1992), *Fred Zinnemann: An Autobiography*, London: Bloomsbury.

INDEX

Adams, Brian, 54, 79
Adam's Woman (1970), 9, 142, 148
Adventures of Barry McKenzie, The (1972), 98
Adventures of Long John Silver, The (1955), 10
Adventures of the Terrible Ten, The (1959–60), 11
Against the Wind (1948), 20
Age of Consent (book), 99–100, 103–7, 109
Age of Consent (1969), 9, 12, 80, 95–111, 124, 142, 148
Agutter, Jenny, 146, 149–51
Albright, Sydney, 38, 44
All Quiet on the Western Front (1930), 34
Alvin Purple (1973), 98, 189
Anderson, Donna, 54, 58, 60
Anderson, Joseph L., 81
Another Shore (1949), 20
Armand and Michaela Denis on the Barrier Reef (1955), 16
Armand and Michaela Denis Under the Southern Cross (1954), 16
Astaire, Fred, 10, 50, 52, 54, 57–8
Atkinson, Michael, 174–5

Australia (2008), 26
Australian Walkabout (1958), 8

Babe: Pig in the City (1998), 5
Baby Doll (1956), 65
Back of Beyond, The (1954), 7–8, 41, 155, 159n14
Baker, Reginald, 24
Balcon, Michael, 15–17, 22, 24, 29
Barr, Charles, 14–16, 18
Barry, John, 153
Bassler, Robert, 33–4, 36–7
Baxter, John, 104
Bazin, André, 46
Beach of the War Gods (1973), 179
Behold a Pale Horse (1964), 65
Bello onesto emigrato Australia sposerebbe compaesana illibata (1971); see *A Girl in Australia* (1971)
Bennett, Colin, 55–6, 62, 99, 147
Big Boss, The (1971), 179
Big Sleep, The (1946), 121
Birtles, Dora, 26, 46
Bitter Springs (1950), 4, 7–8, 16, 20–1, 27–8, 32, 35, 39, 78, 167
Black Narcissus (1947), 74

Blazing Continent (1968), 11, 81, 83–6, 92–3, 117, 148, 182
'Blind Faith' (recording), 165
Blood Money (1980), 114
Body Double (1984), 123
Bogarde, Dirk, 161
Boldrewood, Rolf, 10
Bond, Edward, 151–2
Bond, Gary, 161
Bonjour Balwyn (1971), 149, 161
Bonjour Tristesse (1958), 74
Bonython, Kym, 111n9
Boone, Richard, 36–7
Borradaile, Osmond, 26
Boyd, Arthur, 146
Boyle, Anthony, 152
Brand, Henry, 47n2
Braun, Eric, 189
Bridges, Beau, 9, 149
Broderick, Mick, 53
Bronson, Charles, 180
Brooks, Dallas, 55
Brown, Max, 46–7
Buckley, Anthony, 100–2, 110, 174
Bungala Boys (1961), 10
Burstall, Tim, 3
Bush Christmas (1947), 8, 10, 19
Bye, Susan, 2

Campbell, Daphne, 22
Canterbury Tale, A (1944), 106
Captain Starlight, or Gentleman of the Road (1911), 32
Captain Thunderbolt (1953), 4, 8, 46
Cardinale, Claudia, 149
Carr-Glyn, Neva, 102, 107
Cars That Ate Paris, The (1974), 175, 189
Cat on a Hot Tin Roof (1958), 65
Chan, Jackie, 188, 190
Chant of Jimmie Blacksmith, The (1978), 175
Charge of the Light Brigade, The (1968), 128
Chauvel, Charles, 4, 8, 21, 24
Chiari, Walter, 52–3, 97, 106, 161
Children, The (book), 149, 152–3, 159n4
Chinatown (1974), 113
Chinese Boxer, The (1970), 179
Chow, Raymond, 177
Christie, Ian, 99

Clarke, Charles G., 35–6, 39–40
Cleary, Jon, 29, 31n3, 66, 70, 73, 75, 79n1, 93n2
Cleopatra Jones and the Casino of Gold (1975), 178
Coburn, John, 108
Collateral (2004), 115
Collins, Bill, 93n4
Collins, Felicity, 2, 155
Color Me Dead (1970), 10, 112–26, 148, 182
Cook, Kenneth, 11, 160–3
Cooney, Kevin, 87, 90
Cooper, Gary, 26, 67
Cooper, Ross, 2–3, 125, 191n3
Corfield, Justin, 128
Craydon, Letty, 35
Crocodile Dundee (1986), 1, 175
Crowther, Bosley, 62
Cunningham, Stuart, 7, 13n3
Currie, Finlay, 36–7

Dad and Dave Come to Town (1938), 187
Danks, Adrian, 2, 12n1
Dark City (1998), 5, 125
Davey, Philip R., 58
Davis, Eddie, 10, 112, 116, 121
Davis, Therese, 155
Deathcheaters (1976), 179
Defiant Ones, The (1958), 51
Delprat, Paul, 108
Dermody, Susan, 2
Desser, David, 178
Detective, The (1968), 112
Devereaux, Ed, 154
Division 4 (1969–75), 114, 126n4
D.O.A. (1949), 112, 114–20, 124–5
D.O.A. (1988), 112–13, 125n2
Don't Look Now (1973), 158
Dragnet (1951–9), 112, 115
Dragon Flies, The (1975), 187–8; see also *Man from Hong Kong, The* (1975)
Drewe, Robert, 142
Drifting Avenger, The (1968), 4, 9, 11, 63, 80–94, 148, 176, 190
Drysdale, Russell, 68, 146
DuBose, Martha, 147, 170
Duguid, Mark, 15
Dunkirk (1958), 28
Dust in the Sun (1958), 4

Eastwood, Clint, 180
Eliot, T. S., 54, 57
Eliza Fraser (1976), 178
Ellis, John, 18
Entertainer, The (1960), 128
Enter the Dragon (1973), 177–9
Eureka Stockade (1949), 1, 7–8, 16, 20–1, 24, 26–7, 32, 97, 167

Faithfull, Marianne, 129–32, 136
Fatal Friendship: Ned Kelly, Aaron Sherritt and Joe Byrne, The (book), 129
Fear and Loathing in Las Vegas (book), 160
Fegan, John, 35
55 Days at Peking (1963), 184, 191n2
Finch, Peter, 29
Finney, Albert, 128
Fires Were Started (1943), 24
First Strike (1996), 190
Fistful of Dollars, A (1964), 89
Fist of Fury (aka *The Chinese Connection*, 1972), 177, 179
Flynn, Errol, 36, 67, 130
Foley, Gary, 154, 159n10
Fort Apache (1948), 46
For the Term of His Natural Life (1927), 5
Fraser, John, 177, 186
Friendly Persuasion (1956), 76
From Here to Eternity (1953), 74, 76
Front Page, The (1931), 34
Fugitive, The (1963–7), 112, 121
Funny Things Happen Down Under (1965), 11

Gardner, Ava, 10, 50–4, 56–8, 60
Gaunson, Stephen, 2, 128
Georgy Girl (1966), 105
Get Smart (1965–70), 116
Ghost in the Shell (1995), 87
Gibson, Mark, 93n1
Gilling, Rebecca, 186
Girl Happy (1965), 117
Girl in Australia, A (1971), 11–12, 117, 148
Glenrowan Affair, The (1951), 143
Golden Swallow (1968), 179
Goldsmith, Ben, 3, 49
Goldsworthy, Reginald, 10, 112
Goodbye Paradise (1983), 114

Goodlet, Ken, 83, 87, 136
Grace, Helen, 53
Grant, Bruce, 46–7
Grass is Greener, The (1960), 74
Greene, Clarence, 114, 116, 121
Greenham, Alfred, 40–1
Grierson, John, 7
Guinness, Daphne, 99
Gulpilil, David, 145, 150–1, 153–5, 157–8, 158n2
Gulpilil: One Red Blood (2003), 159n9
Gunn, Jeannie, 26

Haigh, Gideon, 49
Hall, Ken G., 21, 24–5, 70, 86, 186–7
Hall, Sandra, 172
Hanlon, Jr., Tommy, 108
Harper (1966), 112
Harper, Sue, 15–16
Harris, Max, 52
Harris, Mike, 188
Hartley, Mark, 189
Hartley, Neil, 133
Hasluck, Paul, 134
Hawaiian Eye (1959–63), 119
Hawkins, Jack, 15
Heaven Knows, Mr. Allison (1957), 74
Herbert, Jocelyn, 132–4
Herzog Blaubarts Burg (aka *Bluebeard's Castle*, 1963), 96
Heyer, John, 7, 22, 159n14
Higham, Charles, 100
Hildyard, Jack, 69
Holmes, Cecil, 4, 8, 46
Holt, Seth, 29
Holten, 'Mac', 130
Homesdale (1971), 149
Homicide (1964–77), 114, 126n4
Hoorn, Jeanette, 106, 108–9
Horton, Robert, 71
Hoskin, Dave, 169
Houston, Penelope, 54, 70
Hue and Cry (1947), 15
Hung, Sammo, 178
Hunter (1967–9), 121, 126n4
Hunt, Leon, 188

I am Legend (book), 57
Intruders, The (1969), 80, 93n2, 149
Irving, Freda, 53
It Takes All Kinds (1969), 10, 112

Jacka, Elizabeth, 2
Jack and Jill: A Postscript (1970), 149
Jagger, Mick, 129–34, 138–9, 141–3, 149, 160
James Bond (films), 116, 178–80, 185, 188
James, Sid, 25
Jason, Rick, 114, 117, 125n3
Jedda (1955), 4, 70
Jennings, Grahame, 144–6
Jennings, Karen, 169–70
Jennings, Waylon, 135
Jewison, Norman, 52
Johns, Glynis, 67, 76
Jones, Carolyn, 114, 116, 125n3
Jones, Evan, 161
Jones, Ian, 129, 131, 133–4
Journey Out of Darkness (1967), 154

Kael, Pauline, 52, 166, 173–4
Kangaroo (1952), 7–10, 21, 32–47, 63, 67, 76, 132, 190
Kangaroo Kid, The (1950), 9
Kamahl, 154
Katsaros, Andonia, 107
Kaufman, Joseph, 66
Keavney, Kay, 99
Keays-Byrne, Hugh, 186
Kehr, Dave, 103
Kelly, Ned, 127–43, 160
Kemp, Philip, 18
Kendall, Suzy, 118, 126n4
Kerr, Deborah, 10, 67, 69, 72, 74, 76–8, 79n4, 109
Khoo, Olivia, 2, 12n1, 84, 88, 92, 177
Kind Hearts and Coronets (1949), 15
King Boxer (aka *Five Fingers of Death*, 1972), 179
King of the Coral Sea (1954), 8
Kirk, Mark-Lee, 34–5
Kitamura, Hiroshi, 88–9
Kobayashi, Akira, 89
Korda, Alexander, 19
Korman, Stanley, 117
Kotcheff, Ted, 2, 11, 98, 144–6, 160–5, 172–4
Koya no toseinin (1968); see *Drifting Avenger, The* (1968)
Kramer, Stanley, 1, 8–9, 50–4, 57, 61–2, 67
Kung Fu (1972), 178
Kung Fu Killers (1974), 177

Kunze, Peter C., 2
Kurahara, Koreyoshi, 89
Kurosawa, Akira, 89

Lady in Cement (1968), 112
Ladykillers, The (1955), 14
Landman, Jane, 2
Last Outlaw, The (1980), 127
Lavender Hill Mob, The (1951), 15
Lawford, Peter, 10, 36–7, 40
Lawler, Ray, 10, 64
Lawson, Sylvia, 12, 69–70, 77, 97, 100, 142
Lazenby, George, 179, 181, 186
Lee, Bruce, 177, 179–80
Legend of the 7 Golden Vampires, The (1974), 178
Leitch, Thomas, 120
Lennart, Isobel, 73, 79n1
Leone, Sergio, 89
Limb, Bobby, 161
Limbrick, Peter, 9, 18, 32–3
Lindsay, Norman, 95, 97–100, 103–9
Litchfield, Roland, 91
Little Jungle Boy (1970), 11
Lolita (1962), 105
Loneliness of the Long Distance Runner, The (1962), 128
Long Goodbye, The (1973), 113
Long John Silver (1954), 10, 66
Look Back in Anger (1959), 128
Losey, Joseph, 161
Lovers and Luggers (1937), 25, 187
Lowe, Barry, 160
Luhrmann, Baz, 189

McCallum, John, 96
MacDonald, Dougal, 141
MacGowran, Jack, 106–7
McMahon, William, 172
McWilliam, Kelly, 3
Madden, E. S., 51
Mad Max (1979), 1, 179, 186
Mad Max: Beyond Thunderdome (1985), 179
Mad Max 2 (aka *The Road Warrior*, 1981), 179
Magic Pudding, The (book), 95, 104
Magnificent Seven, The (1960), 89
Making of 'The Man from Hong Kong', The (1975), 187
Maltese Falcon, The (1941), 122

Man For All Seasons, A (1966), 65
Man from Hong Kong, The (1975), 3–4, 11, 176–91
Man from Snowy River, The (1982), 1
Man from U.N.C.L.E., The (1964–8), 116
Man in the White Suit, The (1951), 15
'Man is a Man is a Man, A' (song), 185
Man Who Fell to Earth, The (1976), 158
Man with the Golden Gun, The (1974), 179, 188
Manzie, Keith, 44
Marshall, James Vance, 149, 152–3, 158
Marty (1955), 65
Mason, James, 98–107, 109, 149
Maté, Rudolph, 114
Matheson, Richard, 57
Matrix, The (1999), 5
Matsubara, Chieko, 84
Matter of Life and Death, A (1946), 97
Meillon, John, 66–7, 145
Mexico Wanderer (1962), 89
Midnight Cowboy (1969), 188
Milestone, Lewis, 1, 8–9, 33–5, 37–9, 46–7, 67
Miller, George, 189
Mills, Jane, 97
Mirren, Helen, 98–9, 105–8, 110n1
Mission: Impossible (1966–73), 116
Mission: Impossible II (2000), 5
Mr. Nice Guy (1997), 190
Mitchum, Robert, 10, 69, 72, 74–6, 79n4, 109
Moeru tairiku (1968); see *Blazing Continent* (1968)
Molloy, Bruce, 12n2, 18, 78
Money Movers (1978), 114
Moran, Albert, 2
Morgan, Stephen, 18
Morris, Meaghan, 88, 179–81
Morrison, Peter, 43
Murphy, Jim, 188
Murray, Scott, 161
Musgrove, Nan, 86, 125n1
Myers, Stanley, 107

Naked Bunyip, The (1970), 103, 111n7
Naked City (1958–63), 112
Naked Spur, The (1953), 87
Naremore, James, 113–14
Nature's Half Acre (1951), 42
Neary, Jack, 161

Ned (2003), 127
Ned Kelly (1970), 9, 64, 127–43, 161, 163
Ned Kelly (2003), 142–3
Ned Kelly: A Short Life (book), 129
Ned Kelly: Australian Paintings by Sidney Nolan (1960), 143
Nickel Queen (1971), 117
Night of the Hunter, The (1955), 157–8
Niland, D'Arcy, 29
Nine Men (1942), 23
Nolan, Sidney, 108, 128, 140, 146, 157, 159n14
Norrie, Willoughby, 43
North, Loretta, 43–4
Nothing Like Experience (1970), 149
Not Quite Hollywood: The Wild, Untold Story of Ozploitation! (2008), 189
Nowhere to Go (1958), 20, 29
Nowra, Louis, 150, 152
Nun's Story, The (1959), 65, 67, 71, 76
Nyu jirando no wakadaisho (1969); see *Young Guy on Mt. Cook* (1969)

O'Brien, Gabrielle 164, 169
Of Mice and Men (1939), 34
O'Grady, John, 96–7
O'Hara, Maureen, 10, 36–7, 40–2
Oklahoma! (1955), 67
One-Armed Boxer (1972), 179
One-Armed Swordsman (1967), 179
On Her Majesty's Secret Service (1969), 116, 179
On the Beach (book), 9, 49–52, 54, 58–9, 61, 63, 66
On the Beach (1959), 4, 7–10, 29, 33, 42, 48–64, 66, 69, 78, 190
O'Regan, Tom, 2, 7–8, 23, 32, 49
Osborne, John, 128
O'Shea, Tessie, 25
Our Sunshine (book), 142
Outback (1971); see *Wake in Fright* (1971)
Out of the Past (1947), 115
Overlanders, The (book), 29
Overlanders, The (1946), 4, 7–9, 14–32, 46, 63, 68, 72, 78–9, 97, 167, 176

Page, Grant, 177, 186
Palmer, R. Barton, 114–15, 119
Passi, Federico, 56
Passport to Pimlico (1949), 20

Pate, Michael, 101, 104
Patrick (1978), 189
Payne, Donald Gordon, 152
Peck, Gregory, 10, 50–1, 54, 56–7, 59, 62
Peeping Tom (1960), 96, 106
Performance (1970), 149, 151, 159n6
Perkin, Graham, 57
Perkins, Anthony, 52, 54
Perry, George, 18–19
Petulia (1968), 149
Phantom Stockman, The (1953), 8
Picnic at Hanging Rock (book), 95
Picnic at Hanging Rock (1975), 70, 95, 155, 189
Pierce, Peter, 155
Pike, Andrew, 2–3, 82, 92, 100, 125, 191n3
Playford, Tom, 35–6, 38, 41
Play Misty For Me (1971), 185
Pleasence, Donald, 161
Police Story series (1985–2013), 188
Pomerance, Murray, 61
Porter, Vincent, 15–16
Powell, Michael, 2, 9, 52, 64, 67, 74, 95–101, 103–7, 109–10
Pressburger, Emeric, 97, 99

Queen's Guards, The (1961), 96

Rafferty, Chips, 7–8, 26–7, 35, 67, 104, 130, 167
Rank, J. Arthur, 19
Rattigan, Neil, 145–6
Ray, Aldo, 29
Redes (1936), 71
Red Shoes, The (1948), 97, 100, 106
Reisz, Karel, 128
Restless and the Damned, The (1959), 7
Reunion at Fairborough (1985), 74
Richardson, Tony, 2, 9, 128–34, 137, 139, 141–3, 161–3, 169
Riches, Lindsay, 35
Richie, Donald, 81
Ride Lonesome (1958), 87
Road to Bali, The (1952), 48
Robbery Under Arms (book), 10
Robbery Under Arms (1907), 32
Robbery Under Arms (1957), 8, 10, 19, 96
Roberts, Judith, 83
Robinson, Lee, 7–8

Roeg, Nicolas, 2, 9, 98, 144–53, 156, 158, 161
Romeo and Juliet (1968), 102
Rotunno, Giuseppe, 51, 56–7
Rouse, Russell, 114, 116, 121
Routt, William D., 32, 143
Ryan, Mark David, 3

Saltzman, Harry, 128
Salwolke, Scott, 98
San Demetrio London (1943), 24
Sanders, Andrew, 134
Saraband for Dead Lovers (1948), 17
Sarris, Andrew, 70
Sato, Junya, 2, 90–1
Saved (play), 151
Sawai, Shinji, 90
Schwartzman, Jack, 149
Scorsese, Martin, 99
Scott of the Antarctic (1948), 17
Sculthorpe, Peter, 100, 107
Season of Passion (1959); see *Summer of the Seventeenth Doll* (1959)
Seidler, Harry, 117
Server, Lee, 74
Set, The (1970), 103, 111n, 124, 149
Seven Samurai (1954), 89
Seventh Cross, The (1943), 71
Seventh Veil, The (1945), 105
77 Sunset Strip (1958–64), 119
Shadow of the Boomerang (1960), 9
Shane (1953), 88
Shatter (1974), 178
'She Moved Thru' the Fair' (song), 136
Sherwood, John, 83
Shiralee, The (1957), 8, 16, 18, 21, 25, 28–9, 32, 57, 67–8, 72
Shirley, Graham, 54, 79
Shropshire Lad, A (poems), 155
Shute, Nevil, 9, 49–52, 54–5, 58–9, 61, 63, 66
Siege of Pinchgut, The (1959), 1, 8–9, 16, 18, 20, 28–30, 32, 48, 64, 79n1, 96, 115
Silverstein, Shel, 135
Sirens (1994), 104
Skippy the Bush Kangaroo (1968–70), 80
'Sky High' (song), 181–2, 187
Smaill, Belinda, 2, 12n1, 177
Smart, Ralph, 7, 10
Smiley (1956), 10, 29, 167
Smiley Gets a Gun (1958), 10

Smithy (1946), 187
Smyth, J. E., 71
Snody, Robert, 34–6
Solomon, Eric, 42
Sons of Matthew (1949), 4, 70
Sordi, Alberto, 149
Squatter's Daughter, The (1933), 86
Squeeze a Flower (1970), 11, 124, 148, 161
Stagecoach (1939), 88–9
Stone (1974), 179
Stone in the Bush, A (1970), 143
Storey, David, 128
Stork (1971), 3, 98, 149, 161, 175
Story of the Kelly Gang, The (1906), 32, 127
Stowaway, The (1958), 7
Strange, Dorothy, 149
Strange Holiday (1970), 11
Stratton, David, 145, 154
Streetcar Named Desire, A (1951), 65
Stringybark Massacre (1967), 143
Stuart-Codde, H., 38
Stuntmen, The (1973), 177
Stunt Rock (1978), 179
Summer of the Seventeenth Doll (play), 10, 64, 66
Summer of the Seventeenth Doll (1959), 7–8, 10, 48, 64, 66–7, 132
Sunday Too Far Away (1975), 68, 72, 189
Sundowners, The (book), 66, 70, 73–4, 79n2
Sundowners, The (1960), 4, 7–10, 33, 46, 57, 64–79, 109, 149, 167, 173, 176, 190
Surfside Six (1960–2), 119
Suzuki, Seijun, 84

Tait, Frank, 96
Takakura, Ken, 86, 90, 149
Tales of Hoffmann, The (1951), 106
Target for Tonight (1941), 24
Taste of Honey, A (1961), 128
Taxi Driver (1976), 113, 115
Taylor, Rod, 66
Tennant, Kylie, 104
Teo, Stephen, 88, 178, 185
They Found a Cave (1962), 10–11
They're a Weird Mob (1966), 9, 11–12, 52, 64, 78, 95–100, 102, 106–7, 100, 167

Thompson, Hunter S., 160
Thoms, Albie, 142
Thornhill, Michael, 145
Three in One (1956), 4, 8
Three to Go (1970), 161
Thring, Frank, 108, 138, 184
Thunderbolt (1910), 32
Tiger Boy (1966), 179
Timms, Peter, 162, 165
Tingwell, Charles 'Bud', 35
Tinker, Les, 161
Tiomkin, Dimitri, 71
Tivey, Bev, 99, 110n3
Treasure Island (1950), 10
Trenchard-Smith, Brian, 176–80, 184–7, 189
Tokyo Drifter (1966), 84, 93n6
Tomasetti, Glen, 136
Tom Jones (1963), 128
Too Late the Hero (1970), 90
Touch and Go (1955), 14–17, 30–1
Town Like Alice, A (1956), 29
True History of the Kelly Gang (2019), 127
Tryon, Tom, 114, 116, 125n3
Turkey Shoot (1982), 179
Turnour, Quentin, 68
Two Thousand Weeks (1969), 110n6, 149

Ustinov, Peter, 67, 76

Verevis, Constantine, 12n1
Verhoeven, Deb, 18

Wake in Fright (book), 161–3, 170–1
Wake in Fright (1971), 11, 70, 78, 98, 144–5, 147, 159n3, 160–75
Walkabout (book); see *Children, The* (book)
Walkabout (1971), 9, 70, 98, 132, 142, 144–59, 161, 173, 175–6, 190
Walk into Paradise (1956), 7–8
'Waltzing Matilda' (song), 16, 55, 59, 86
Wang Yu, Jimmy, 179–81, 183, 189
Ward, Susan, 49
Ward, Tony, 121
Warner, Jack, 65
Watari, Tetsuya, 84
Watt, Harry, 1, 7, 18, 20–4, 26–7, 29, 67, 97
Way of the Dragon, The (1972), 179

Webby, Elizabeth, 18
We of the Never Never (book), 26
West, Morris, 161
West of Zanzibar (1954), 18
When Worlds Collide (1951), 61
Where No Vultures Fly (1951), 18
Whisky Galore! (1949), 20, 24
White, Thomas, 40–1
Wicked Lady, The (1945), 105
'Wild Colonial Boy, The' (song), 137, 140
Wild Turkey (book), 46–7
Williams, Deane, 22
Williams, Tennessee, 65
Willoughby, George, 162

Woodham, Bob, 177
World of Kung Fu, The (1973), 177

Yabe, Hisashi, 90
Yojimbo (1961), 89
Yomota, Inuhiko, 83
You Can't See 'Round Corners (1969), 80, 93n2, 149
Young Guy on Mt. Cook (1969), 11, 82
Yue, Audrey, 2, 12n1, 177

Zanuck, Darryl F., 34, 38–9
Zinnemann, Fred, 1, 9, 31n3, 65–71, 74–6, 78–9, 149